The
TORAH

The TORAH

AN INTRODUCTION FOR CHRISTIANS AND JEWS

David J. Zucker

Paulist Press
New York/Mahwah, N.J.

Excerpts from *The Jewish Publication Society Torah Commentary* volumes on Genesis, Exodus, Leviticus, Numbers, and Deuteronomy by authors Sarna, Levine, Milgrom, and Tigay are used with kind permission of the Jewish Publication Society.

Unless otherwise noted, the scripture quotations outlined herein are from the New Revised Standard Version Bible, copyright © 1989 by the Division of Christian Education of the National Council of Churches of Christ in the U.S.A. Used by permission.

Cover design by Graphical Jazz
Book design by Lynn Else
Study Questions and index prepared by Michael Kerrigan, CSP
Copyright © 2005 by David J. Zucker

Library of Congress Cataloging-in-Publication Data

Zucker, David J., 1942–
    The Torah : an introduction for Christians and Jews / David J. Zucker.
       p. cm.
    Includes bibliographical references and index.
    ISBN 0-8091-4349-6 (alk. paper)
    1. Bible. O.T. Pentateuch—Criticism, interpretation, etc. I. Title.
    BS1225.52.Z83 2005
    222′.1061—dc22

2005013497

Published by Paulist Press
997 Macarthur Boulevard
Mahwah, New Jersey 07430

www.paulistpress.com

Printed and bound in the
United States of America

Contents

Contents

Contents

Contents

Contents

Contents

To my students across the years,
who have raised wonderful questions
and shared their insights
in our study of Torah together

Foreword

The bedrock of scripture for Jews and Christians is the Torah. The word *Torah,* however, sometimes referred to as *Chumash* (the "Five,") or *Pentateuch,* often conjures up to the uninitiated some kind of outdated, enigmatic religious literature. For individuals who have little experience with Torah, the word may connote that which is inaccessible except to experts in the Hebrew language. Consequently, this foundation piece of the Bible remains largely unknown or unexplored by vast numbers of people—even by some who consider themselves knowledgeable in the origins of "Judeo-Christian" religion.

Rabbi David Zucker is a scholar–teacher of the Jewish tradition. He has done his readers a real service in writing this book in that he unpacks and demystifies the meaning of Torah. One of his aims in writing this introduction to Torah is to open up the subject in language lay and professional students of scripture can understand. In this task he succeeds brilliantly. He puts the "cookies" on a shelf where the hungry can grab them and also readily digest them.

Are there not, however, some challenging—if not seemingly indigestible—parts of Torah? Indeed there are, and Rabbi Zucker is very much aware of these places. An advantage of his approach in this book, however, is that he never bogs down in any of the more obscure and incomprehensible tidbits of Torah. Rabbi Zucker refuses to atomize the Torah, chopping it into the tiniest of morsels. His specialty is the main course, not exotic side dishes. In this regard, the author's goal is very effectively accomplished. Rabbi Zucker clarifies the main message of the Torah and also allows his readers to savor and to acquire a strong taste for Torah's remarkable influence on Jewish and Christian thought.

The first five books of the Bible pose a whole host of questions for modern readers. Who wrote the Torah? Is it relevant? Why should one study it? Why all those strange regulations? If the Torah is Jewish literature, what is its message for Christians? How did later writers build on the Torah in drawing out its meaning? David Zucker's introduction to the Torah provides answers to these and many other questions.

As a Christian, for many years my perspective on the Bible has been deeply enriched through Jewish scholarship. Although not always fully aware of the fact, we must recognize that Jews and Christians tend to read the biblical text differently, through a different set of spectacles. This is one important reason why I believe this book ought to have an important niche on bookshelves dealing with biblical literature and its interpretation. Sensitive to the above issue, David Zucker writes for Jews and Christians. I must say it is rather unusual to find an introductory work on the Torah written specifically for an interfaith readership.

I have had the joy of knowing Rabbi Zucker since the mid-1980s. During this time I have learned much from his warm friendship, his open spirit of dialogue, and his fine written contributions to the field of biblical studies and Christian-Jewish relations. In this introduction to the Torah, one will quickly discover that Rabbi Zucker is one who cares deeply how Jews perceive Christians and how Christians perceive Jews.

Why is the above question how we perceive the other of such importance? Jews and Christians often pass like ships in the night. As a result, we simply do not readily grasp the nuances of the other's faith. In addition, each community has tended to define itself over against the other. Definition by negation—that is, by attempting to state merely who we are not or to state what we do not believe—has led to ignorance, half-truths, and often contributed to the rather troublesome relationship we have had with the other over the centuries. From my Christian perspective, there are many myths, half-truths, and stereotypes that Christians have concerning Jews and Judaism. Many of these derive from faulty understandings of Torah.

A considerable number of these misunderstandings can begin to be eliminated if Christians understand they share a book with their Jewish friends. The first 5,845 verses of that book are the Torah.

It is to be acknowledged that Jews read the Torah through the eyes of the sages and rabbis of Israel. Christians, on the other hand,

Foreword

read the same scriptures through their interpretive lenses of the New Testament authors and later Christian thinkers. Despite this fact, there is much both communities hold in common. Here Rabbi Zucker has provided an important aid to the encounter between Christians and Jews. He explores the common roots, but he also instructs how Christians and Jews may understand Torah differently. For example, he points out how each community today has its own interpretive understanding of father Abraham, levitical sacrifices, and the Passover celebration. Accordingly, I celebrate the significance and substance of this book. I believe when we become better informed with a knowledge of the other's religious traditions, the wall of unfamiliarity will begin to become transformed into a bridge for building respectful conversations around these and other common scriptures.

Martin R. Wilson
Professor of Biblical & Theological Studies
Gordon College
Wenham, MA

Introducing the Torah

1. INTRODUCTION

A Word of Torah

The Hebrew word *Torah* has many meanings. The most common definition refers to "the" Torah, the first five books of the Bible* (Genesis, Exodus, Leviticus, Numbers, Deuteronomy). Yet the word *Torah** has a significantly larger usage. It can also mean "a teaching" or, by extension, Jewish learning in general.[1] The word *torah* in Hebrew* is directly connected to the word for instruction or teaching (*morah* = female teacher; *moreh* = male teacher).

In Hebrew, *torah* has several nuances. It could mean law; doctrine, system, theory; instruction; or teaching.[2] Someone who says that she or he is "studying Torah" means that the person is involved in some aspect of Jewish studies, and not necessarily biblical studies.

In this book, however, unless specified otherwise, Torah will always mean "the" Torah, the first five books of the Bible.

The Bible was written in Hebrew, and later was translated into other languages.[3]

English-speaking readers are familiar with the names of the five books of the Torah: Genesis, Exodus, Leviticus, Numbers, and Deuteronomy. These titles reflect the Greek terms used to translate the Torah around 2,250 years ago, in the translation known as the Septuagint.*

Genesis begins with the creation of the world, and then soon focuses on the family of Abraham and Sarah and their descendants.

Exodus commences with the Israelites* enslaved in Egypt, and then describes their departure from Egypt, as well as the encounter at Mt. Sinai.

1

Leviticus deals with matters of the Levites, the priests. It is largely formulaic writing, instructions *for* the priests on how to live a sacred life, and instructions *by* the priests to the Israelites on how to live a sanctified life.

Numbers, the fourth biblical book, contains various censuses and also historical material and legislation.

Deuteronomy features primarily Moses' recapitulation of the last forty years in the desert and a reiteration of some of the key legislation found in Exodus, Leviticus, and Numbers.

The Overall Structure of This Book

This book is an introduction to the Torah (i.e., the Pentateuch,° the first five books of the Hebrew Bible°). A major chapter is devoted to each of those books.

These chapters contain several sections:

1. An introductory overview
2. Highlights of the particular book—a chapter-by-chapter description
3. Representative quotations of that book within the Christian scriptures
4. Representative examples of the book in rabbinic literature (see section on midrash, below)
5. A section of text study with suggested readings[4]

Throughout the book, certain words are followed by an asterisk (°). This indicates that the word appears in the glossary at the close of this work.

Translations used for this book (unless specifically otherwise noted) come from *The New Revised Standard Version (NRSV*°): The New Oxford Annotated Bible with the Apocryphal/ Deuterocanonical Books.*[5] This Bible was chosen because it presents both a modern translation and inclusive, gender-neutral language. Reference will be made to differences in verse numbering as reflected in the Masoretic (traditional Jewish) edition of the Hebrew Bible. The NRSV translation will be followed by the

Hebrew tradition in brackets and marked with an "H" for Hebrew (e.g., Exod 20:17 [20:14 H]).

Whenever possible, gender-neutral language is utilized. God is above and beyond sexuality. The Hebrew language, like Romance languages (French, Spanish, and so on), does not have a neutral case. Unlike English and German there is no "it." Nouns are either masculine or feminine. While God is described with masculine pronouns, feminine imagery is also used in the Bible. Isaiah explains that God says, "As a mother comforts her child, so I will comfort you" (Isa 66:13; cf. Isa 42:14; 49:15; 66:9). Since the word *Lord* has masculine overtones unless quoting directly from a text, the neutral term *God* is used.

The historical purview of the biblical period covers the time from creation to about 200/150 Before the Common Era. This phrase, *Before the Common Era* (BCE*), and its counterpart, *Common Era* (CE*), are terms that refer to the same time periods as BC and AD. BC (Before Christ) and AD (*Anno Domini*) technically are Christian descriptions. *Christ* is the English form of the Greek *Christos;* it is a synonym for *Messiah. Anno Domini* is Latin for the "year of our Lord." Those both are Christian faith terms, though for many years they had wide usage. In the contemporary world, BCE and CE have become standard usage among both the scholarly community and the laity.

Defining Midrash

Around the same time that the early Christian writers were setting down the traditions of the Christian scriptures,* often quoting from the Jewish scriptures* (also termed the Hebrew scriptures,* the Hebrew Bible, or Jewish Bible*), the rabbis were developing their own religious literature. They too often based their teachings on the Jewish scriptures. Indeed, these rabbinic writings both precede the time of the Christian scriptures and continue for several centuries thereafter. The rabbis develop a whole code of laws and commentaries on the Jewish scriptures. Broadly speaking, rabbinic literature is composed of the Talmud* and various collections of midrash.*

Whenever the Bible was not explicit or specific, the early interpreters of the Jewish postbiblical world (i.e., the rabbinic period, and their successors as well) sought to provide new insights as to what might be meant in a given context. Consequently there developed alongside the Bible a supplement, an additional way to understand what God desired of humans. The generic term for this exegesis or interpretation is *midrash* (plural, *midrashim**). The Hebrew for sermon, *derasha,* is based on the word *midrash*.

Midrash allowed the rabbis to develop new interpretations. They could fill in the gaps and offer new insights. By way of midrash, scripture provided additional instruction. "The sacred words became an inexhaustible mine...of religious and ethical teaching."[6] As a talmudic tradition teaches, "one biblical statement may carry many meanings."[7]

Midrash involves many genres: tales and allegories, ethical reflections, epigrams, and legends.[8]

Midrash develops out of the biblical text.[9] The midrashic literature was written by rabbis. At times the rabbis disagree among themselves. Stating that something is *a* rabbinic view or even *the* rabbinic view does not mean that all rabbis support that position or that interpretation.

2. THE HEBREW BIBLE

A Source of Inspiration

The Bible is the most beloved book for Jews and Christians. A source of inspiration and guidance for millions of people, it is the foundation stone of their respective faiths. The earliest Christians were Jews, and their Bible was the Hebrew Bible. When the author of 2 Timothy 3:16 says "All scripture is inspired by God and is useful for teaching," the writer was referring to the *Hebrew* scriptures.[10] In addition the Bible had an enormous influence on the Qur'an, the sacred scriptures of Islam. The Bible remains one of the world's most influential documents. It has shaped religions, and it has served as the blueprint for governance in ages past. Recognizing its inexhaustible richness, a first-century rabbi, with the intriguing name ben Bag Bag, said: "turn it over, turn it over again, for everything is contained within it."[11]

The Bible is a vast library. It contains narrative and poetry, history and ritual legislation, riddles and prophecy, wise sayings and love songs. The Bible contains material that is both eternal and time-centered. The narratives of Genesis and early Exodus, as well as the historical sections of Joshua, Judges, Samuel, Kings, Chronicles, Ezra, and Nehemiah, tell the story of ancient Israel. These narratives depict the formation of a people, called by God, bound by a covenant at Mt. Sinai, and then their subsequent settlement of the land of Israel through times of triumph and tribulation. The earliest chapters of Genesis, from creation to the time of Abraham, address some of the great questions: how was the world created, who were the first people, where did they live, and why are people scattered all over the world? Genesis 12–36 addresses the origins of the Israelite people and relates the adventures and misadventures of the matriarchs and patriarchs.

Ritual and Prayer, the Synagogue

The ritual legislation found in parts of Exodus, Leviticus, and Numbers relating to the ancient priesthood presents a picture of religious life at that time. As explained in the chapter on Leviticus, the sacrificial system of ancient Israel, animal and grain offerings, clearly reflects the norm of that day and age. The rites and rituals described in those chapters form the background for the priesthood in Jerusalem at the period of the Temple. The Jerusalem Temple, built by Solomon, stood for about four hundred years. It was destroyed by the Babylonians in the sixth century BCE. A second Temple, built in the late sixth century, stood for well over five hundred years. The Romans destroyed it in 70 CE.

While the Temple stood, animal and grain sacrifices were the normal way to communicate with God. The priesthood was that society's accepted "infrastructure" that mediated between humans and the deity. That elaborate animal- and grain-centered ritual ended abruptly for the Jewish community when two thousand years ago the Romans razed the Temple. Judaism's central shrine and sanctuary no longer existed. Psychologically this was a devastating moment. It was the defeat of the nation centered in Judea.

Though the Second Temple was destroyed, Judaism* continued to flourish. Even as the Temple stood, Judaism had developed a parallel structure, which allowed Jewish religious life to continue in a post-Temple world. For several centuries, Jews had gathered together to socialize, to worship, and to transmit their traditions no matter where they lived. The locus of this gathering was called, in Greek, the *synagogue*, the place of assembly. We do not know a lot about the early synagogues. Some suggest that the references in the book of the prophet Ezekiel to the elders coming before him (8:1; 14:1; 20:1) may refer to an early form of the synagogue. Likewise, Ezekiel's reference to the little "sanctuary" (11:16) that exists in the exile suggests a pre-synagogue. The Talmud credits Ezra's successors, the leaders of the Great Synagogue, as the authors of the earliest prayers.[12]

By the first century CE, the synagogue was a well-established institution. Both Josephus and Philo, important Jewish writers of the first century CE, make reference to synagogues both in and outside of the land of Israel. Though people traveled to Jerusalem to the Temple, in the meantime the Diaspora communities formed local places to congregate and to worship. The Talmud states that there were nearly four hundred synagogues in Jerusalem at the time of the Temple.[13] There were synagogues throughout the country-side of Judea and in the many countries where Jews dwelled. One proof of this comes from the Christian scriptures. Throughout the Book of Acts Paul writes of visiting synagogues in Asia Minor (e.g., 13:14; 14:1). In the Gospels* Jesus clearly visits synagogues in the Galilee even though the Temple is the central shrine in Jerusalem (Matt 13:54; Luke 4:15, 31–33).

> With the destruction of the Temple [in the year 70 CE], however, and the consequent automatic cessation of the sacrificial service, the synagogue remained without a rival as the focus and center of Jewish religious life. Many of the customs and rituals of the Temple were deliberately and consciously transferred to the synagogue, and on the other hand, some of these rituals [specifically animal and grain sacrifices] were forbidden just for the reason that they belonged to Temple and the

Temple only. Prayer was regarded as the substitute for sacrifice, and it was no accident that the word *avodah*, referring to the sacrificial system, was now applied to prayer which was the 'Avodah [Service] *of the heart'* [*Sifre Deuteronomy* 41].[14]

For two thousand years in Jewish life, prayer—the service of the heart—has replaced animal and grain sacrifices. As this is true of Judaism, so prayer is central for Judaism's daughter religions, Christianity and Islam.

The "Old" Testament

When most Christians refer to "the Bible," they think of the volume that contains, to use Christian terminology, both the Old Testament* and the New Testament.* When Jews use the phrase "the Bible," they refer to the work that Christians call the Old Testament. Jews do *not* call it the Old Testament; they refer to it as the Jewish Bible, the Jewish scriptures, the Hebrew scriptures, or the Hebrew Bible. The phrase *Old Testament* suggests that there is a new, improved version. Jews believe that the *original* covenant/contract/testament with God remains in force. For Jews, there is no need for an updated version; God's covenant with the Jewish people is eternal. For Jews, Judaism is not a prototype—or merely the roots—of another religion that has now been "improved." For Jews, Judaism is very complete in itself, and it continues to have a full life of its own. For Jews, the Torah—one of the most hallowed and revered objects in Judaism—is not the "Old Testament" that has been replaced by a newer version. It is THE irreplaceable Testament.[15]

The Christian scriptures, known also as the *New* Testament, is a sacred document for *Christians*. It records *their* understanding of their special relationship with God. The Christian scriptures are sacred to and for Christians, and Christians revere them. They are respected by Jews as being the holy writings of Christians, just as the Qur'an is the holy scripture of Muslims, and the Buddhist scriptures are holy to and for Buddhists. The New Testament, as the story of early Christianity, however, is not sacred scripture for Jews, any more than it is sacred scripture for Muslims or Buddhists.

Many of the Bible's central ideas influenced Western civilization through the growth of Christianity and Islam. Among these notions is the concept of monotheism itself, that there is but one God ruling humankind (Deut 6:4; Ps 9:7–8 [9:8–9 H]; 47). Another biblical teaching says that there is but one moral standard, whether people are privileged or impoverished. The revolutionary concept that all humans need a day of rest each week—a Sabbath—is first mentioned in the Bible (Exod 20:8ff.). The Bible instructs that this day of rest needs to be sanctified. The concept that humans have a moral obligation to protect the poor, the widow, the orphan, and the stranger is first found in the Torah (Lev 19). That the Jewish people were chosen to spread God's word was such a powerful idea that first Christianity, and then later Islam, incorporated this notion into their teachings, seeing themselves respectively as the final word of God. Christianity speaks of the old covenant passing on to the new Israel, the church, and Islam regards Muhammad as the final prophet.

That both Christianity and Islam, daughters of Judaism, have important messages is evident. Each of these religions has a special connection with God, but their relationship does not replace the ongoing covenant between God and the Jewish people, which is eternal.

TaNaK: Torah, Neviim, Ketuvim

As mentioned, Jews refer to the Bible as the Hebrew Bible or the Jewish Bible. Alternate designations are the Hebrew scriptures, the Jewish scriptures, or sometimes the term *TaNaK** or *Tanakh.** *TaNaK/Tanak/Tanakh* is not a real word, but rather it is an acronym for the titles of the three divisions of the Hebrew Bible: **T**orah—Teaching; **N**eviim*—Prophets; and **K**etuvim*—Writings. Indeed, the newest standard Jewish translation of the Bible is called *TANAKH: The Holy Scriptures* [also the New Jewish Publication Society translation—NJPS*].[16]

TaNaK [TaNaKH]

Torah—Teaching

Neviim—Prophets

Ketuvim—Writings

The full Jewish Bible is truly a library. It contains many books, with a variety of different subjects: narrative, history, poetry, song, prophecy, wise sayings, romance, and drama.

Torah/Teaching

The first section, the *Torah*, features five books (Genesis, Exodus, Leviticus, Numbers, Deuteronomy), which are sometimes called the Five Books of Moses because traditionally their authorship is ascribed to Moses. In Hebrew the Torah is sometimes known as the *Humash** (the "five"), and scholars often will refer to the Torah as the Pentateuch (from the Greek, *penta* = five; *teuch* = books). The Torah contains the foundational stories of Judaism. The first book, Genesis, begins with the primeval history of the creation of the world and the early human settlers. This is followed by the narratives of the matriarchs and the patriarchs: Abraham and Sarah, Isaac and Rebekah, Jacob, Leah, and Rachel. Genesis tells the story of the family's development, and its trials and tribulations, as well as its triumphs. Exodus, Leviticus, Numbers, and Deuteronomy begin several hundred years later, with the family, now divided into twelve tribal clans, living initially in Egypt. In the Bible's second book, Exodus, we learn about Moses, Miriam, and Aaron, the Exodus from Egypt, and then the revelation at Mt. Sinai, and Moses receiving the Ten Commandments from God. Exodus then continues with the revelation of many laws for daily life in biblical times. The next three books (Leviticus, Numbers, and Deuteronomy), which complete the Torah, contain some narrative sections, but they are largely the listing of legislation for daily living, revealed to Moses by God. The end of the book of Deuteronomy features the transfer of leadership to Joshua, the death of Moses, and the Israelites poised to conquer Canaan,* the proverbial promised land of Israel.

Neviim/Prophets

The second section of the Hebrew Bible is *Neviim* or Prophets. It contains both the continuing history of Israel from Joshua to the end of the biblical period and the teachings of those people known as the literary prophets. This section is further divided into two parts. The initial part is made up of a historical section, where one first meets those people termed the Former Prophets (also known as the early, or preliterary prophets, such as Samuel and Nathan). Then the second part contains the books of the Latter Prophets (or the later, or literary prophets, Isaiah, Jeremiah, Ezekiel, and the "Twelve").

Six books comprise the section of the Former Prophets (Joshua; Judges; 1–2 Samuel; 1–2 Kings.) It starts with the leadership of Joshua, circa 1200 BCE, followed by the period of the judges, and continues with the history of the kings and queens of Israel. It closes with the destruction of the Temple in Jerusalem circa 586 BCE. The latter section of *Neviim* features the words of the fifteen literary prophets (whose names are associated with specific books). The books of the three most prolific prophets, Isaiah, Jeremiah, and Ezekiel, are followed by the books of the twelve minor prophets, who include Amos, Micah, Jonah, and so forth. Prophets (*neviim;* singular, *navi*) were spokespersons for God. While most of the prophets were male, the Bible also features female prophets, for example, Huldah (2 Kgs 22:14) and Noadiah (Neh 6:14).

Ketuvim/Writings

Finally, the *Ketuvim* or Writings contains some history, a part of which (Chronicles) overlaps material in *Neviim*/Prophets, but then other books (Esther, Daniel) are set in the early Persian period, circa 400–150 BCE. In addition in *Ketuvim*/Writings, many of the books are devoted to what is termed wisdom literature, such as Psalms, Proverbs, and the book of Job.

The books of the Jewish Bible are those that Christians term the Old Testament. Yet, there are several major differences. The order of the books, while essentially the same, is not exactly alike, and there are differences between the Roman Catholic and Protestant canons[17] of the Bible. Occasionally the numbering of verses will differ between a Jewish Bible and some Christian editions of the Bible. In the course of canonization (the process by which the books of the Bible were "officially" recognized as genuine and sacred), different criteria were used. This becomes evident when considering the chart below (The Books of the Hebrew Bible

[TaNaK]). In the Jewish Bible there are twenty-four books; forty-six in the Roman Catholic canon (forty-five in the Eastern Orthodox canon); and thirty-nine in the Protestant traditional canon. The differences in the count between the number of books in the Jewish and Protestant canons is simple to explain. The books of the twelve minor prophets (Hosea through Malachi) are counted as one book in the Judaic tradition. Likewise, the sets of 1 and 2 Samuel, 1 and 2 Kings, 1 and 2 Chronicles, and Ezra and Nehemiah, are considered one book each (see the chart below).

"The Christian enumeration follows the pattern of the Septuagint," explains biblical scholar James King West. The early church's Bible patterned itself on that Greek translation of the Hebrew Bible that was produced in Egypt somewhere around 250 BCE. "Thus, the books of the Jewish and Protestant Old Testaments are identical, differing only in their titles and arrangements within the collection....

"The different arrangements of the books in the Jewish and Christian canons is also associated with the early Church's use of the Septuagint. Whereas the Jewish canon's division into Law ['Teaching'], Prophets, and Writings corresponds to the three stages of Hebrew canonical development, the Septuagint (and hence Christian) order resulted from a combination of factors." These factors included a concern for chronology, subject matter, and likewise reputed authorship. In both the Jewish and Christian traditions practical considerations, such as size of a book, were sometimes determinative of the sequence.[18]

For example, in terms of subject matter, in Christian Bibles the last book in the canon is the prophet Malachi. In Malachi 3:1 there is a reference to God's messenger who is to clear the way for God. Then, in the closing words of the book, it identifies that name with Elijah: "I will send you the prophet Elijah before the great and terrible day of the LORD comes" (Mal 4:5 [3:23 H]). In Matthew 11:10 Jesus quotes Malachi 3:1 and then says that John the Baptist (who earlier on had baptized Jesus [Matt 3:13ff.]) is none other than Elijah himself. The religious message for Christians is clear. As the Jewish Bible had ended with the prediction of Elijah's return to clear the way for God, so would this be fulfilled in the person of John the Baptist, who then baptized Jesus.

Not subject matter as such but rather chronological sense dictated the placing of the Book of Ruth. In the Christian canon, the Book of Ruth follows Judges and precedes 1 Samuel. This makes chronological sense in that Ruth is the great-grandmother of David, whose story is first mentioned in the books of Samuel. The Book of Ruth, however, only was accepted into the Hebrew canon at a later date as part of the Writings, after the order of the Prophets (where the books of Samuel appear) had been set.

In Christian Bibles the historical books of Samuel-Kings-Chronicles and Ezra-Nehemiah are placed together, followed by the books of the prophets. In the Hebrew canon, as noted above, the second section, *Neviim* (Prophets), is made up of some historical books (Joshua, Judges, Samuel, Kings) as well as the literary prophets. The Hebrew canon's third section, *Ketuvim* (Writings), begins with Psalms and Proverbs and ends with Chronicles.

The Books of the Hebrew Bible *(TaNaK)*

Torah (Pentateuch) Teaching (sometimes translated as the Law)

1. Genesis	(*Bereshit**) "When [God] began to [create]"/"In the beginning"
2. Exodus	(*Sh'mot**) "[These are] the names"
3. Leviticus	(*Vayikra**) "[The LORD] called"
4. Numbers	(*Bemidbar**) "…in the wilderness [of Sinai]"
5. Deuteronomy	(*Devarim**) "[These are] the words"

Neviim (Prophets)

The Former Prophets
6. Joshua
7. Judges
8. 1, 2 Samuel   (8, 9)
9. 1, 2 Kings   (10, 11)

The Latter Prophets
10. Isaiah   (12)

11. Jeremiah   (13)
12. Ezekiel   (14)
13. The Twelve
    Hosea   (15)
    Joel   (16)
    Amos   (17)
    Obadiah   (18)
    Jonah   (19)
    Micah   (20)
    Nahum   (21)
    Habakkuk   (22)
    Zephaniah   (23)
    Haggai   (24)
    Zechariah   (25)
    Malachi   (26)

Ketuvim (Writings)
14. Psalms   (27)
15. Proverbs   (28)
16. Job   (29)
17. Song of Solomon
    [Song of Songs] (30)
18. Ruth   (31)
19. Lamentations   (32)
20. Ecclesiastes   (33)
21. Esther   (34)
22. Daniel   (35)
23. Ezra-Nehemiah (36, 37)
24. 1, 2 Chronicles (38, 39)

The Books of the Christian Canon

Protestant Canon	**Roman Catholic and Orthodox Canon**
Pentateuch	*Pentateuch*
1. Genesis	1. Genesis
2. Exodus	2. Exodus

The Torah

3. Leviticus	3. Leviticus
4. Numbers	4. Numbers
5. Deuteronomy	5. Deuteronomy

Historical Books

6. Joshua	6. Joshua
7. Judges	7. Judges
8. Ruth	8. Ruth
9–10. 1, 2 Samuel	9–10. 1, 2 Samuel
11–12. 1, 2 Kings	11–12. 1, 2 Kings
13–14. 1, 2 Chronicles	13–14. 1, 2 Chronicles
15. Ezra	15. Ezra
16. Nehemiah	16. Nehemiah
	17. Tobit**
	18. Judith**
17. Esther	19. Esther***
	20–21. 1, 2 Maccabees**

Poetical and Wisdom Books

18. Job	22. Job
19. Psalms	23. Psalms
20. Proverbs	24. Proverbs
21. Ecclesiastes	25. Ecclesiastes
22. Song of Solomon	26. Song of Songs (Song of Solomon)
	27. Wisdom of Solomon**
	28. Ecclesiasticus (Wisdom of Ben Sirach)**

Prophetic Books

23. Isaiah	29. Isaiah
24. Jeremiah	30. Jeremiah
25. Lamentations	31. Lamentations
	32. Baruch#
26. Ezekiel	33. Ezekiel
27. Daniel	34. Daniel***
28. Hosea	35. Hosea
29. Joel	36. Joel

30. Amos	37. Amos
31. Obadiah	38. Obadiah
32. Jonah	39. Jonah
33. Micah	40. Micah
34. Nahum	41. Nahum
35. Habakkuk	42. Habakkuk
36. Zephaniah	43. Zephaniah
37. Haggai	44. Haggai
38. Zechariah	45. Zechariah
39. Malachi	46. Malachi

** Deuterocanonical (apocryphal) book; canonical in Roman Catholic and Orthodox canons.

*** Book includes materials in the Roman Catholic and Orthodox canons that are featured in the Protestant Apocrypha as additions to Esther and additions to Daniel (the Prayer of Azariah, the Song of the Three Jews, the story of Bel and the Dragon, and the story of Susanna).

Canonical book (deuterocanon) in Roman Catholic canon only.

In the Roman Catholic canon, Ezra and Nehemiah are sometimes labeled as 1, 2 Esdras.

The Prayer of Manasseh, a book found in the Apocrypha, is not included in the Roman Catholic canon but is considered deuterocanonical by the Eastern Orthodox community.

3. A BRIEF HISTORICAL OVERVIEW OF THE BIBLICAL PERIOD

Biblical history can be divided into five sections: (1) the primordial history; (2) the patriarchal/matriarchal period; (3) the period of the wilderness and the conquest/settlement of Canaan; (4) the monarchy; and finally, (5) the exilic/postexilic section.

The Torah

The Book of Genesis features the Bible's first two sections: primordial times and the days of the patriarchs and matriarchs. Beginning with the days of creation, it moves through the time in Eden and the expulsion of Adam and Eve; Noah and the great flood; and then by chapter 12 introduces the founders of the faith, Abraham and Sarah. The narrative continues with the stories of Isaac and Rebekah, and Jacob, Leah, and Rachel, and their respective histories. It relates the fact that Jacob gains an additional name, Israel. The Book of Genesis concludes with initially Joseph, and then the full Jacob/Israel clan settling in Egypt. Scholars differ as to this dating, but in broad figures the Book of Genesis concludes about 1500 BCE, some 3,500 years ago.

The third section is that of the wilderness and the conquest/settlement of Canaan. Exodus, Leviticus, Numbers, and Deuteronomy address the time of the wilderness. Exodus opens with a mention of the settlement of Jacob/Israel's clan (circa 1500 BCE) but then concentrates on the latter days of Egyptian slavery, circa 1250 BCE. Moses is introduced, and the early chapters of Exodus feature Moses' confrontation with Pharaoh* and the ten plagues. By the period of the Exodus, the clans have grown into twelve tribes. The book continues with the actual escape from Egypt, the miracle at the Reed Sea,* and the early days in the desert wilderness, including the revelation at Mt. Sinai, and Moses' accepting God's gift of the Ten Commandments. Leviticus, Numbers, and Deuteronomy continue the period in the desert and conclude with the death of Moses and the tribes about to enter Canaan.

Joshua and Judges tell the history of the conquest and settlement of Canaan. The time frame of these books is about 1200 to 1050 BCE.

The fourth period, that of the Israelite monarchy, commences about 1050 BCE. Saul is the first king of Israel, but he is unable to establish a dynastic rule. This feat will be achieved by David, who captures Jerusalem and establishes it as his capital. David is followed by his son Solomon, who builds the Temple in Jerusalem. Solomon's son (David's grandson) is Rehoboam. Rehoboam is not up to the task of successfully dealing with the demands of governance. The ten northern tribes secede, setting up their own rule, which they call the Kingdom of Israel. The northern kingdom experiences a series of dynasties, for no one family is able to maintain power for more than a few generations. The northern kingdom ends with the destruction of its capital by the Assyrians in 721 BCE. The southern two tribes, Judah and Benjamin, form the Kingdom of Judah. The Davidic family will rule continuously for over four hundred years, until the Babylonians close out its rule with the destruction of Jerusalem (and the razing of the Temple in Jerusalem) in 586 BCE.

The major literary prophets flourish during the period of the divided monarchy: Amos, Hosea, (First) Isaiah, Micah, Jeremiah, and Ezekiel.

The fifth and final section in biblical history begins with the Babylonian Exile (the exilic period) in 586 BCE. Technically the exile ends about fifty years later, when Cyrus the Persian allows those who wish to do so to return to Jerusalem and Judah. Many Jews choose to remain in Babylonia, though a remnant return, and by about 516 BCE they succeed in rebuilding the (second) Jerusalem Temple. The prophets Haggai and Zechariah live in this latter period, as do the leaders Ezra and Nehemiah. The political background of the exilic/postexilic period moves from the Babylonian empire through that of the Persians, and includes the early years of the Greek empire. The books of Esther and Daniel come from this section in biblical history. The biblical period concludes about 200/150 BCE, approximately fifteen hundred years or so after the time of Abraham and Sarah.

Women in the Biblical Period

Clearly, half of biblical Israel were women. Their voices are not as audible as those of men; nor are their persons as visible. Women, however, were a very important part of biblical society. It was an agrarian world, and the economic role of women in supporting the family was powerful. Carol L. Meyers points out that most households

> survived by growing grains (mostly wheat but also some barley), olives (as a foodstuff and for oil) and grapes (as fruit and for wine) in varying proportions. A number of other orchard and garden crops—figs, dates, nuts, seeds, legumes, vegetables, and leeks—supplemented the basic diet.

In addition, specialty crops such as flax were produced in a few locations. Each family also kept a small number of animals—sheep, goats, probably cows and oxen. These animals were a source of dairy products, and they served to supplement the diet occasionally (perhaps mainly on feast days) with animal protein....However, the work load of Israelite women, in their intensive agricultural system, went far beyond the crop production process...foodstuffs had to be converted into forms that could be stored for use in the months following the harvest....Women were responsible for many, if not most, of these food preservation tasks.

Women also had very important roles in terms of procreation and parenting in biblical society. Infant mortality was high, and there probably were multiple pregnancies. Meyers suggests that the estimated life span for biblical women was about thirty years (and about a decade more for men who did not have to face the rigors of childbearing). Childless women were disadvantaged (Gen 16:1ff.; 25:21; 1 Sam 1:5ff.; Ruth 1:11ff.). Women were involved in socializing children (Prov 4:1–9; 6:20; 8:1–36). "Females were mothers, daughters, sisters, wives; and they were also bakers, cooks, weavers, managers, teachers, worshipers and so on. All of these roles involved some combination of social, economic, and biological functions." They had important roles within the household (Prov 31:10–31).[19]

4. "A KIND OF HISTORY"; WHO WROTE THE BIBLE?

This book considers the Bible a text inspired by God and written by human beings, women and men searching for an understanding of their relationship with the divine. As Everett Fox has noted, historical reporting in the commonly understood sense of history is not the central goal of the text.

Although the first large part of its text, Genesis through Kings, *does* recount a kind of history of the Israelite people, from its

> origins down to the sixth century B.C.E., it is history with a purpose: an account of the dealings of Israel with its God....In the end, the Bible is primarily concerned with who Israel is and what its obligations are. Some history *can* be gleaned from the text, but the historian must do his/her work with great care.

Fox also accurately points out that the Bible reflects the world of ancient Judaism, and ancient Jewish beliefs. Judaism has its roots in the Bible, but it has evolved, changed, and developed over the years. "Therefore, anyone wanting to learn Judaism through reading the Bible will be disappointed. As a way of life and thought, Judaism is better grasped through the study of post-biblical materials such as Talmud and Midrash."[20]

For example, in Genesis, at times the text "seems to speak with many voices. For a book whose basic arrangement is chronological, tracing the history of a single family, it exhibits a good deal of discontinuity on the surface. Here time flows uniformly, there it takes startling jumps."[21]

A critical analysis of the Torah suggests that there were a number of sources that comprise various traditions which, in time, were edited into the inherited Torah text. These are referred to as documentary sources or textual archives and represent different interests or schools. The most common explanations refer to five major sources: J, E, P, and D, plus R. **J** stands for the writer (or school) that referred to God by the name *Jehovah*. In fact, this is a mistaken reading of the Hebrew word generally translated as LORD and spelled (with the Hebrew letters) *Yud-Hey-Vav-Hey*, roughly YHVH, sometimes spelled in English as *Yahveh* or *Yahweh* (i.e., Jehovah). In Jewish tradition, this term is called the tetragrammaton, the four-lettered word. By custom, one does not attempt to pronounce it because it is God's sacred name.

The second source or school referred to the deity by the name **Elohim**. This is termed the **E** source. A further explanation of these schools and their differences appears in the chapter on Genesis. The third source or school is the **P**, which refers to the **P**riestly tradition. P is found in Genesis, Exodus, Leviticus, and Numbers. P generally is credited with the total book of Leviticus. **D** refers to the **D**euteronomic source or school and generally is credited with the whole Book of Deuteronomy. **R**, the **R**edactor(s) or editor(s), perhaps in the sixth century BCE took the various traditions and wove them together as one book.

5. THE DEVELOPMENT OF JEWISH LAW: FROM BIBLICAL TIMES TO MODERNITY

The Jewish biblical period closed about 200/150 BCE. Society in that era was vastly different from both the period of Moses (c. 1200 BCE) and that of the major changes that took place during the century before the Babylonian Exile. During the two centuries before the Common Era, the community of Israel spread far and wide: from the lands of the Tigris-Euphrates, through Judah, all the way to Alexandria in Egypt. Likewise, there were communities throughout the Mediterranean basin. It was a more urbanized life. The institution of the synagogue had come into being. Sometime during this period, the rabbinate develops.

The term *rabbi* is derived from the Hebrew noun *rav*. It does not occur in the Jewish Bible as a word that refers to a teacher or communal leader; the rabbinate is, for Judaism, a postbiblical institution. The term *rabbi* means literally "my master," and it initially referred to sages who were ordained in the land of Israel. The Babylonian sages of the Talmud bore the title *rav* as opposed to *rabbi*. The sages of the Talmud, whether located in the land of Israel or in Babylon were great scholars, teachers in the sense that they interpreted and expounded Jewish law, but they were not communal leaders as we would understand them today. Many of the rabbis probably were associated with the Pharisees. The origins of the Pharisees are unknown, but they may well have been a professional class that actively preserved, interpreted, and then applied the vast oral tradition that was developing alongside and supplementing the written biblical tradition.

After the destruction of the Temple by the Romans in 70 CE, the Pharisees became the teachers and interpreters of Jewish law and tradition. If not before, by that period the Pharisees and the rabbinate are indistinguishable institutions.

> The Rabbis believed not only that the Torah given at Mount Sinai anticipated all that would happen in the course of history, but that all new interpretations are an implicit part of the original text. They taught that whatever students will teach in future generations...was already given to Moses on Mount Sinai....Therefore, the written text [of the Bible] and its interpretation [by the rabbis] are not viewed as totally distinct entities. On the contrary, they were thought to be part of the same revelation. What is deduced from the biblical text is not separate from it, but rather a latent part of it. It is the text within the text.[22]

In the words of the rabbis, "Scripture, Mishnah, *Halakhot,* Talmud, *Tosefta, Haggadot* [and Midrash], even that which a faithful disciple would in the future say in the presence of his master, were all communicated to Moses at Sinai; for it says, 'Is there a thing of which it is said: See, this is new?' (Ecclesiastes 1:10). The other part of the [Ecclesiastes] verse provides the answer to this: 'It occurred long since, in ages that came before us.'"[23]

The initial document that the rabbis produced was the six-volume Mishnah,* compiled 200 CE, and after that, the *Gemara,** which together form the Talmud. There are two Talmuds, the Jerusalem or Palestinian Talmud and the more authoritative Babylonian Talmud, which was codified in 500 CE. Over the next thousand years, as Judaism developed and new conditions arose, Jewish law expanded. New conditions required new interpretations, based on the past traditions. Various codes were developed, and there is a whole literature of *responsa*—questions to and responses from the greatest sages of each age. In the sixteenth century, Rabbi Joseph Karo of Safed in Palestine compiled what still remains as the standard legal code of Judaism, the *Shulkhan Arukh.* His code was supplemented by his contemporary, Rabbi Moses Isserlis of Poland.

Orthodox Jews today continue to be guided by *Halakhah,** Jewish traditional legislation. Orthodoxy believes that the Torah is the revealed word of God, given at Mt. Sinai well over three thousand years ago. To be a "Torah-true" Jew, Orthodoxy maintains that every word and every law, indeed every commandment that is found in the Bible as explained and developed by the rabbis over the intervening years, is binding on a loyal Jew. Orthodox Judaism states that each and every one of the traditional 613 laws is of equal importance. The Bible is God's word. Having said this, within Orthodoxy there are varying approaches and honest disagreements about how God's law is to be interpreted in the modern age. Conservative, Reform, and Reconstructionist Jews, while respectful of this tradition, approach Torah in a different way. Some suggest that God's revelation was a one-time historical event, while others speak of an ongoing process. Most Conservative Jews take the position that God did not actually speak each word to Moses at Mt. Sinai. "Conservative Judaism…views the Torah as the product of generations of inspired prophets, priests, and teachers, beginning with the time of Moses but not reaching its present form until the postexilic age, in the 6th or 5th century B.C.E. The Torah is…'God's first word, not God's last.'"[24] W. Gunther Plaut in the introduction to the Torah commentary produced by the Reform movement expresses similar ideas.[25] No matter where they stand on the spectrum of Jewish religious tradition, rabbis agree that Jewish law is evolving. Orthodox rabbis would support the ancient rabbinic notion that these interpretations were all previously revealed to Moses on Mt. Sinai, and those in the non-Orthodox group broadly lean toward a concept of progressive revelation.

6. THE BIBLE IN JEWISH LIFE; THE BIBLE IN CHRISTIAN LIFE

The Bible in Jewish Life

The Torah is the most sacred book in all of Judaism. Some Jews regard the Torah as literally divine writ, the word of God, dictated to Moses on Mt. Sinai more than three thousand years ago. For them, the Torah is immutable, unchanging, fixed, and free from error. Other Jews regard the Torah, and indeed the whole Bible, as *inspired* by God but reflecting human authorship. Nonetheless, whether seen as literally or figuratively God's words, for Jews the Torah historically remains the most sacred and revered work within Judaism. As the Bible explains, it "is a tree of life to those who lay hold of [it]; those who hold [it] fast are called happy" (Prov 3:18).[26]

Oftentimes Christians explain that they regularly spend part of each day (or they set aside part of their week) reading the Bible. Some Christians read through the Bible word for word, and have done this several times. Though there may be Jews who could make a similar claim, most Jews do not turn to the Bible for daily reading. The most commonly read books, even by religious Jews, are the Torah, the Psalms, and the Five Scrolls (Song of Songs, Ruth, Lamentations, Ecclesiastes, and Esther). Of these, Esther is by far the best known.

Each week in the synagogue a set section of the Torah (Pentateuch) and certain sections from the Prophets are read as part of the regular Shabbat* (Sabbath) services. Likewise on the High Holy Days of Rosh Hashanah* and Yom Kippur,* and on the three pilgrimage festivals (Passover/*Pesach;** Weeks/*Shavuot** [Pentecost]; and Booths/*Succot**), there are set readings in the Torah and Prophets. The Five Scrolls are read respectively at the Sabbath during Passover/*Pesach* (Song of Songs); on Weeks/ *Shavuot*/Pentecost (Ruth); on the Ninth of Av/*Tisha b'Av* (Lamentations); the Sabbath during Booths/*Succot* (Ecclesiastes); and on *Purim** (Esther).

In Judaism, the Torah itself is divided into fifty-four sections, and a preset section is read or chanted each week. Beginning with Genesis and then over a year's time, the whole Torah will be completed.[27]

The reading of set biblical selections in the regular Sabbath services—known as a lectionary* of readings—is a tradition that reaches back well over two thousand years. It was the custom of the early synagogues. This tradition was taken up by Christianity. In several Christian churches, among others the Roman Catholic, Eastern Orthodox, Lutheran, and Presbyterian traditions, there will be regular readings from the Bible. In these Christian traditions the readings will be from the Gospels, the Epistles, and often from the Jewish Bible as well. Within Judaism, only selections from the Jewish Bible are recited.

Sections of the Bible also are found within the prayerbooks of Judaism. For example, on a daily basis Jews affirm God's unity, reading the *Sh'ma*° (*Shema*°), the words from Deuteronomy 6:4, "Hear, O Israel: the LORD is our God, the LORD alone." This is followed by the continuing words in Deuteronomy, "You shall love the LORD your God, with all your heart, and with all your soul, with all your might." Quotations from all three sections of the Jewish Bible are found in the prayerbook. For example, in the evening and morning liturgies, there are quotations from the Torah: Exodus 15, the Song of the Sea. In the morning liturgy a section from the Prophets is read: "Holy, holy, holy is the LORD of hosts, the whole earth is full of his glory" (Isa 6). The morning and afternoon services feature numerous psalms from the Writings.

Other parts of the Bible are woven into the liturgy. Quotations from Jeremiah form components of the wedding service; quotations from Job, Deuteronomy, and Psalms form parts of the funeral service; quotations from Numbers and Psalms are part of the service surrounding the reading of the Torah.

The Bible is taught in Jewish religious schools, and it is a regular subject at adult education classes.

The standard Jewish translation of the Bible in English, as mentioned above, is the Jewish Publication Society's *TANAKH: The Holy Scriptures* (Philadelphia: Jewish Publication Society, 1985 [NJPS]). There are a number of popular Jewish commentaries on the Torah.[28]

For Judaism, the books and beliefs of the TaNaK are God's word in its entirety; there will not be further *torah* coming from God by way of direct revelation. As will be explained in the section Deuteronomy in Rabbinic Literature, the rabbis stated that there would not be a new Moses to come along and teach a new Torah. The rabbinic interpretation of Deuteronomy 30:12, "It is not in heaven," meant, "no part of it has remained in heaven."[29]

The Bible in Christian Life

By way of contrast, for the Christian church, the books of the Jewish Bible are important, but more than that, they contain promises for the future. The words of the Jewish Bible were not God's words in its completeness, but as the word of his promise: their significance lay not in themselves, but in a fulfillment, which was beyond them. Hence the Christian reader of these books, which he calls the "Old Testament," notices within them signs of longing for the future and predictions of things to come: the kingdom of God; the day of Yahweh, a new covenant, a new temple, an outpouring of spirit, a re-creation of the world....In these ways he reads these scriptures as God's word of promise, and looks to Jesus Christ and the apostles for the exposition of their fulfillment.

Christianity, in the form of the early Christian church, eagerly took in the books and beliefs of the Tanakh, the Old Testament. "The Church of the apostolic age accepted the books of the Old Testament as sacred scriptures, and every New Testament writer cites them or alludes to them as having divine authority. Their inspiration is explicitly defined in 2 Tim. 3:16, 2 Pet. 1:20–1."[30]

The early church took that Jewish Bible and adopted images, reframing them as Christian teachings.

Many Old Testament institutions and themes are radically reinterpreted in the New Testament, often in ways...that the majority in New Testament times were unable to discern.... Jesus subordinated many of the central symbols of Judaism to himself, and the New Testament writers continued that subordination. Thus, Jesus became the Temple (John 2:19–21) and the atoning sacrifice ("the Lamb of God, who takes away the sin of the world"—John 1:29).

In early Christianity, matters such as the Sabbath, the Temple, and the Law (Torah) are "christologically reinterpreted."[31] The redemption of the Exodus became the deliverance offered by Jesus as Christ (1 Cor 10:1–10; 1 Pet 1:2). Similarly the manna from heaven, part of the desert experience, was understood to be Jesus as the living bread from heaven (John 6:32–40).

The Gospel of John states that Jesus-as-Christ was there with God "in the beginning," that the word and the person were one (John 1:1; 1 John 1:1; Rev 19:13). Jesus was "the utterance of God's grace and truth in the world...the word and the person were utterly one." The life of Jesus, in the eyes of the church, both fulfilled past scripture and brought to fruition "a series of historical events in whose sequence the mighty hand of God had been at work." In fact, the "use of the scriptures within the Church was thus wide and varied." Ramsey notes that "the apostolic writers used the scriptures for proving and illustrating of points in theological or moral arguments. Sometimes methods of exegesis were used *akin to those of the Rabbis* [italics in original]."[32]

A thoughtful contemporary writer of popular Christian books, Philip Yancey, writes, "When we [Christians] read the Old Testament, we read the Bible Jesus read and used. These are the prayers Jesus prayed, the poems he memorized, the songs he sang…the prophecies he pondered. He revered every 'jot and tittle' of the Hebrew Scriptures. The more we comprehend the Old Testament, the more we comprehend Jesus." Reflecting the Christian understanding that the Hebrew Scriptures are fulfilled in the life of Jesus, Yancey goes on to write that Jesus "traced in its passages every important fact about himself and his mission. He quoted from it to settle controversies with opponents such as the Pharisees, Sadducees, and Satan himself. The images—Lamb of God, shepherd, sign of Jonah, stone which the builders rejected— that Jesus used to define himself came straight from the pages of the Old Testament."[33]

7. WHAT DOES THE BIBLE SAY ABOUT LIFE TODAY?

What does the Bible say about life today? How does one find personal meaning in the biblical text? It is paradoxical, but the Bible is at the same moment timeless, and time-centered. Biblical characters and institutions, Abraham and Sarah, Isaac and Rebekah, Jacob and his wives, Leah, Rachel, Bilhah, and Zilpah, Moses, Miriam, and Aaron, Deborah, the priests, the prophets, Ruth, and Esther, the monarchs, all existed at a particular point in time. Moses spoke to a specific community. The prophets addressed real women and men in real time. Their concerns were specific, not broadly abstract. Yet other parts of the Bible, such as the wisdom of the Proverbs or the teaching of Ecclesiastes (Qohelet), have a timeless quality to them simply because they address the human condition. "For everything there is a season, and a time for every matter under heaven: a time to be born, and a time to die; a time to plant, and a time to pluck up what is planted; a time to kill, and a time to heal; a time to break down, and a time to build up; a time to weep, and a time to laugh; a time to mourn, and a time to dance" (Eccl 3:1–4). Likewise, the statement that God is one and that we are to love God with all our heart, soul, and might (Deut 6:4f.) has guided Jews and Judaism since it was first expressed thousands of years ago.

The narratives of the Bible contain truths that are timeless in their observation of the human condition. The Bible, and especially the Torah, is a crown, a treasure of life experiences, and contains wisdom and insights that have spoken to the generations past and will speak to the generations to come. The Bible, which speaks so often in a human voice, addresses the existential issues that confront the changing human society in which people live. The Bible mixes stories, poetry, laws, history, and wise sayings. It is a library, an anthology, a guide book to living, and at the same time contains materials that are of interest largely to scholars of the ancient past.

The Bible is at the same time cosmic and personal in its approach. It is the sacred literature of Jews and of Christians. It is sacred to Muslims. The Bible speaks to all people who would hear its message.

Notes

1. When Jews offer "a word of Torah" this could mean some kind of pithy teaching or possibly a short ethical homily. Some people refer to the whole Jewish Bible as the Torah, though technically the Torah is (as shall be explained below) the first of the three sections that make up that sacred document.

2. The "word 'torah' means primarily 'teaching,' it...has the sense of *binding* teaching or legal demand....Clearly, law is a primary element of the Pentateuch, taking up many parts of the Book of Exodus, all of Leviticus, Numbers 1–10 and 27–30, and Deuteronomy 1–30" (Lawrence Boadt, *Reading the Old Testament: An Introduction* [New York and Mahwah, NJ:

Paulist, 1984], 184). A. M. Ramsey addresses this issue. "The word *Torah*, rendered 'law' in the English versions of the Old Testament, properly means 'direction' or 'teaching'. Moses had given decisions on particular matters...and also general precepts forming a code of conduct for the community, known comprehensively as 'the law of Yahweh' and 'the law of Moses'" ("The Authority of the Bible," in *Peake's Commentary on the Bible,* ed. Matthew Black [London: Nelson, 1962], 1).

3. Many people in the English-speaking world are most familiar with the so-called King James Version (KJV) of the Bible. They often assume that the Bible was written in English, and that the KJV is the actual original text. It is not. The KJV is an English translation of the Hebrew text. It is a familiar and poetic rendering of the Hebrew, but it was neither the first nor the latest English translation.

4. This book follows a similar format to a previously published volume, David J. Zucker, *The Prophets: An Introduction for Christians and Jews* (New York/Mahwah, NJ: Paulist, 1994).

5. *The New Revised Standard Version (NRSV): The New Oxford Annotated Bible with the Apocryphal/Deuterocanonical Books* (New York: Oxford University Press, 1991).

6. A. Cohen, *Everyman's Talmud* (London: Dent; New York: Dutton, 1949), xviii.

7. Babylonian Talmud *Sanhedrin* 34a.

8. For this book *midrash* is understood as a generic term for *midrash/aggadah*. For a detailed description of midrash and its relationship to *aggadah,* consult the article by Joseph Heinemann in the bibliography.

9. "Midrash is 'a type of literature, oral or written, which has its starting point in a fixed, canonical text, considered the revealed word of God by the Midrashist and his audience, and in which this original verse is explicitly cited or clearly alluded to.'...For something to be considered Midrash it must have a clear relationship to the accepted canonical text of Revelation. Midrash is a term given to a Jewish activity which finds its locus in the religious life of the Jewish community. While others exegete their revelatory canons and while Jews exegete other texts, only Jews who explicitly tie their comments to the Bible engage in Midrash" (Jacob Neusner, *The Way of Torah: An Introduction to Judaism,* 5th ed. [Belmont, CA: Wadsworth, 1993], 55), quoting Gary G. Porton, "Midrash: The Palestinian Jews and the Hebrew Bible in the Greco-Roman Period," *Aufstieg und Niedergang der romischen Welt,* ed. Hildegard Temporini and Wolfgang Haase [Berlin and New York, 1979], II 19.2, 104).

10. "The first disciples and Christian writers...searched the Old Testament for passages that would throw light on the events of Jesus' life,

death and resurrection. Matthew's Gospel is a case in point. It is filled with quotations from the Old Testament to explain each major step in Jesus' life....Even Paul and the Church Fathers...cited the Old Testament far more often than they did the Gospels" (Boadt, *Reading the Old Testament*, 537–38).

As Bruce Metzger explains, "The gospels, like the other New Testament books...are the literary productions of a believing community....They are written with the aim of changing the reader or of building up the community's faith." In the Fourth Gospel, John says clearly, these things are "written so that you may come to believe that Jesus is the Messiah, the Son of God, and that through believing you may have life in his name" (John 20:31) (Bruce M. Metzger, "The Narrative Books—Gospels and Acts," NRSV, NT, ix).

11. *Mishnah Avot* 5.25.

12. Louis Isaac Rabinowitz, "Synagogue" ["Origins and History"] in *Encyclopedia Judaica* (Jerusalem: Keter, 1972), 15:580; Babylonian Talmud *Berachot* 33a; *Megilla* 29a.

13. Babylonian Talmud *Ketubot* 105a.

14. Rabinowitz, "Synagogue," 15:583. See also relevant sections dealing with prayer and ritual in the chapters devoted to Leviticus and Deuteronomy.

15. Cf. Boadt, *Reading the Old Testament*, 19.

16. *TANAKH: The Holy Scriptures* (Philadelphia: Jewish Publication Society, 1985).

17. The word *canon* is a Greek word, which was borrowed from a Semitic root. It means a reed or stalk, something that could be used to measure. In time the word came to signify a norm, a rule, or a list of books.

18. James King West, *Introduction to the Old Testament*, 2nd ed. (New York: Macmillan, 1981), 5.

19. Carol L. Meyers, "Everyday Life—Women in the Period of the Hebrew Bible," in *The Women's Bible Commentary*, ed. Carol A. Newsom and Sharon H. Ringe (London: SPCK; Louisville, KY: Westminster John Knox, 1992), 246–50.

20. Everett Fox, "The Bible and Its World," in *The Schocken Guide to Jewish Books*, ed. Barry W. Holtz (New York: Schocken, 1992) 29–30.

21. Everett Fox, *The Schocken Bible, Volume I, The Five Books of Moses*, trans. Everett Fox (New York: Schocken, 1995), 3.

22. Norman J. Cohen, *The Way into Torah* (Woodstock, VT: Jewish Lights, 2000), 54–55.

23. *Midrash Leviticus Rabbah* 22.1; cf. *Midrash Exodus Rabbah* 28.6; Babylonian Talmud *Megilla* 19b; Babylonian Talmud *Berachot* 5a, and elsewhere.

24. David L. Lieber, "Introduction," in *Etz Hayim: Torah and Commentary*, ed. David L. Lieber (New York: The Rabbinical Assembly, The United Synagogue of Conservative Judaism, 2001), xxi.

25. *The Torah: A Modern Commentary*, ed. W. Gunther Plaut (New York: Union of American Hebrew Congregations, 1981), xviii–xxi.

26. Technically Prov 3:1 begins by extolling Torah ("my teaching, *torati*") and then goes on to celebrate "wisdom," the reference point of Prov 3:18. In Jewish tradition, however, this phrase from Proverbs, "It is a tree of life," clearly is taken to mean the Torah and is part of the regular liturgy of the Torah service in the synagogue.

27. These sections vary in their length. The Book of Genesis is divided into twelve sections, each several chapters long. Exodus has eleven sections, again each comprising several chapters. The same pattern holds for Leviticus, Numbers, and Deuteronomy, though in Deuteronomy at a couple points the weekly Torah section is but one chapter in length.

28. In recent decades the Reform, Conservative, and Orthodox movements have published commentaries on the Torah. The Reform commentary is *The Torah: A Modern Commentary* (1981), W. Gunther Plaut, editor. The Conservative commentary is *Etz Hayim: Torah and Commentary* (2001), David L. Lieber, senior editor. The Orthodox commentary is *The Tanach: The Stone Edition* (1996), Nosson Scherman, editor (New York: ArtScroll, Mesorah Publications). For many years before that, *The Pentateuch and Haftorahs* (1936), Joseph H. Hertz, editor, was regarded as the premier commentary on the Torah. Other notable new English translations have appeared, including a very literal/literary translation, trying to be faithful to the Hebrew syntax, *The Schocken Bible, Volume I, The Five Books of Moses* (1995), translation by Everett Fox, and the recent offering by Richard Elliot Friedman, *Commentary on the Torah* (New York: HarperSanFrancisco, 2001).

29. *Midrash Deuteronomy Rabbah* 8.6.

30. Ramsey, "The Authority of the Bible," see endnote 2, 2–3. See also Samuel Sandmel, *The Hebrew Scriptures: An Introduction to Their Literature and Religious Ideas* (New York: Knopf, 1963), 537–46.

31. Marvin R. Wilson, *Our Father Abraham: Jewish Roots of the Christian Faith* (Grand Rapids, MI: Eerdman's; Dayton, OH: Center for Judaic-Christian Studies, 1989), 55.

32. Ramsey, "Authority of the Bible," 4, 3.

33. Philip Yancey, "The Bible Jesus Read" (Grand Rapids, MI: Zondervan, 1999), 25, 24.

Genesis

1. INTRODUCTION

The first book of the Bible, Genesis, earns its name from the Latin used in the Vulgate translation, which in turn derives from the Greek word *genesis*. In Hebrew, the common term for Genesis is *Bereshit,* which generally is translated as "In the beginning" (NRSV); but it likewise can be rendered, "When [God] began [to create]" (NJPS.)[1] Genesis literally and figuratively is about origins. It describes the origin of the cosmos; the origin of humans; and the origin of the Abraham–Sarah clan. In addition, it explains the origin of the special relationship between God and that clan's descendants, the people of Israel.

What Genesis does not explore is the origin of God. God is there from before the beginning. God is beyond and above nature; God is not subject to nature. In the beginning, God is.

Some fifty chapters long, Genesis literally covers thousands of years, unlike any other book in the Bible. Taking the genealogies of the biblical period and counting backward, the Book of Genesis covers a time span of just over 2,300 years. This period includes the creation of the world to the death of Joseph in Egypt. The first eleven chapters (creation through the birth of Abraham) constitute just less than two thousand years. From Abraham through Joseph's death, some 361 years, form the bulk of the book.

Unlike the rest of the Torah, Genesis is primarily narrative. Migrations are a continuing theme. The patriarchal/matriarchal stories take that family into the Promised Land and out again, but with the assurance that they will return.

As with the Book of Exodus, Genesis contains images and stories that are so interwoven into Western culture that it is nearly impossible

31

to imagine what life would be like without their familiar ring. There is creation itself, and the well-known words, "In the beginning."

Other familiar phrases and figures include the following: "and there was light" (Gen 1:3); Adam and Eve; "You are dust, and to dust you shall return" (Gen 3:19); Cain and Abel; "Am I my brother's keeper?" (Gen 4:9); Noah; the ark and the flood; the tower of Babel; Sodom and Gomorrah; Abraham's two sons, Ishmael and Isaac; Abraham's (near) sacrifice of Isaac on the mountain; Jacob's vision of the stairway to heaven; Jacob wrestling with the angel; Joseph and the special coat; as well as Joseph and his ability to interpret dreams. The women of Genesis are strong personalities in their own right. Seven women are particularly significant: Eve, Sarah, Rebekah, Leah, Rachel, Tamar, and Ms. Potiphar. These are people with whom to be reckoned.

"The women of Genesis are markers and creators of transition and transformation....The women succeed in behind-the-scenes ways...and their power is in the private rather than the public realm."[2]

Seven is an important number in Genesis: seven days in the week; the Sabbath as the seventh day; seven pairs of clean animals in the ark; seven sheep at Abraham's covenant with Abimelech (Gen 21:28ff.); Jacob supplicating before Esau seven times (Gen 33:3), to name but a few examples. The number seven figures further in Israel's religious life: the seven-branched lampstand (Hebrew: *menorah** [Exod 25:31–37]); the induction of the priesthood (Exod 29:35ff.); cleansing from leprosy (Lev 14); the festivals (Lev 23) and many other examples throughout the Bible.[3]

There are seven major themes in Genesis:

1. *Origins:* Of the world, of humanity, of the people of Israel.
2. *Order/Meaning in History:* By means of stylized or patterned chronology—reliance on certain round numbers such as 3, 7, and 40—it is suggested that human events are not random but somehow planned.
3. *Blessing:* From creation onward God bestows divine blessings on creatures in general and on the fathers and mothers of Israel in particular.
4. *Covenant:* God concludes agreements with human beings.

5. *God Punishes Evildoing:* God is provoked to anger, not because God is capricious, but by human failure to uphold justice and morality.

6. *Sibling Conflict, with the Younger Usually Emerging the Victor:* The order of nature (primacy of the firstborn) is overturned, demonstrating that God, not nature, is the ruling principle in human affairs.

7. *Testing:* God tests those who are to carry forth the divine mission; the result is the development of moral character.[4]

In terms of the sources of Genesis, the **J** (Yahweh), **E** (Elohim), and **P** (Priestly) traditions are well represented. Scholars differ as to the details of these sources, and it is common to speak of an **R** (Redactor) source that wove together the various strands. A schematic source analysis of Genesis is found in the *Encyclopedia Judaica*,[5] and E. A. Speiser's presentation in the Anchor Bible also sets out the various source divisions.

2. GENESIS CENTERS ON INDIVIDUALS

Genesis is a book very distinct from the rest of the Torah. It centers on individuals, not on the biography of the nation. Genesis is rich in stories and presents foundational narratives, which influenced Western civilization. It is a book filled with tensions. Individual survival and family survival are recurring themes. Fertility and barrenness; brothers threatening the lives of brothers; bitter interfamilial struggles; jealousy; competition between wives for the attention of their common husband; the threat of starvation; incest, rape, and murder; threatened and real annihilation; love and exile—all are found in the Book of Genesis. With all these varied themes, how much more amazing is it that for all its diversity there also are clear patterns of storytelling in Genesis.

Everett Fox demonstrates that there is an overall design discernible in the four sections—primeval history; and then, respectively, the Abraham cycle; (Isaac and) Jacob cycle; and Joseph cycle.

1. *Primeval History* (Gen 1–11)
   Chosen figure (Noah)
   Sibling hatred (Cain–Abel), with sympathy for the youngest
   Family continuity threatened (Abel murdered)
   Ends with death (Haran, Terah; Sarai barren)
   Humanity threatened (Flood)
   Ends away from Land of Israel ("in Harran")
2. *Abraham Cycle* (Gen 12:1—25:18)
   Chosen figure (Abraham)
   Sibling hatred (Ishmael–Isaac) implied, with sympathy for the youngest
   Family continuity threatened (Sarai barren; Isaac almost sacrificed)
   Ends with death (Sarah, Abraham)
   Rivalry between wives (Hagar–Sarah)
   Barren wife (Sarai)
   Wife–sister story (chaps. 12 and 20)
   Ends with genealogy of noncovenant line (Ishmael)
3. *[Isaac and] Jacob Cycle* (Gen 25:19—36:43)
   Chosen figure (Jacob)
   Sibling hatred (Esau–Jacob), with sympathy for the youngest
   Family continuity threatened (Jacob almost killed)
   Ends with death (Deborah, Rachel, Isaac)
   Rivalry between wives (Leah–Rachel)
   Barren wife (Rachel)
   Wife–sister story (chap. 26)
   Ends with genealogy of noncovenant line (Esau)
4. *Joseph Cycle* (Gen 37–50)
   Chosen figure (Joseph)
   Sibling hatred (brothers–Joseph), with sympathy for the youngest
   Family continuity threatened (Judah's sons die; Joseph almost killed; family almost dies in famine)
   Ends with death (Jacob, Joseph)

Humanity threatened (famine)
Ends away from Land of Israel ("in Egypt")[6]

3. PRIMEVAL HISTORY: GENESIS 1–11

Genesis opens with a quick overview of the epic of creation. Genesis 1:1—2:4 reflects a symmetrical artistry, a stark simplicity that links the first group of created days, days one-two-three, and the second group, days four-five-six. "The light of the first day is given the form of luminaries on the fourth day; the seas and sky (second day) provide the domains for fish and fowl (fifth day); and earth and plants (third day) sustain man and beast (sixth day)."[7]

In chapter 2 of Genesis, a second creation epic begins right here on earth. The focus is the creation of humans. How are they going to make their way in the world? What challenges will they face? All kinds of questions are answered by the second creation story, which commences with Genesis 2:4. (See Text Study at the end of the chapter, "The Creation of Humans," for a discussion of the differences between the first and the second creation epics.) This second creation narrative answers a variety of important questions in the less than fifty verses that comprise Genesis 2:4—3:24. It provides explanations for such issues as why women and men are mutually attracted; why people do not live in paradise; and why people have to work hard for a living. It also answers why the earth only reluctantly yields its produce and why people wear clothes. It offers a theory why there is tension between women and snakes and why snakes, lacking legs, crawl on the earth.

Chapter 4 deals with human reproduction, and then suggests that God prefers animal sacrifice to that of vegetation. It explains that humans can be violent and capable of murder. The first city on earth appears here (vs. 17), and the chapter concludes with the information that "At that time people began to invoke the name of the LORD" (vs. 26).

The chapters in this first section are uniform in length, between twenty-two and thirty-two verses each. Chapter 5 is devoted to a long list of genealogies. We learn that there are ten generations between Adam and Noah and also that there will be ten generations between Noah and Abraham.

Chapters 6–9 deal with the life of Noah (though, technically, he is born at the end of the previous chapter [Gen 5:28, the son of Lamech]). Though Noah is "blameless in his generation…[and] walked with God," the earth "was corrupt in God's sight, and the earth was filled with violence" (Gen 6:9, 11). God decides to make a total end to human life, though the deity is willing to spare Noah, his family, and a full set of representatives of the animal world.[8]

The Noah story demonstrates the multiple-source theory quite well. There are elements of both the J and the P documents.[9]

Chapter 10 returns to the list of genealogies, and then chapter 11:1–9 brings the reader to the wonderful story of Babel. The earth has but one language and the same words. Humans gather in the land of Shinar (probably ancient Sumer in the Tigris-Euphrates basin). They want to build a city, with a high tower, "otherwise we shall be scattered abroad upon the face of the whole earth" (Gen 11:4). Whether or not this tower was based on the idea of the ancient ziggurats is a matter of debate. Nahum Sarna favors the idea, but Speiser thinks not.[10] The story echoes parts of the ancient Babylonian epic, the *Enuma Elish*. The story is divided almost evenly; the first four verses are devoted to the humans, the final five to God. God descends to check out what the people are doing. Their trespass is not that they want to reach up to heaven, for God is not threatened by mere humans. No, their offending act is that they want to thwart God's command to "be fruitful and multiply, and fill the earth and subdue it" (Gen 1:28). The people at Shinar are clear in their intent; they do not want to be scattered all over the earth, but that is exactly what happens to them (Gen 11:9).

This narrative is a J source. The rest of chapter 11 continues with genealogies, moving through the generations, until finally the tenth is reached, that of Abraham (Gen 11:27, though at this point he goes by the name Abram). In a seemingly throwaway remark, Genesis 11:29–30 mentions that Abram (Abraham) married Sarai (Sarah) and that Sarai is barren; she had no child. Like a good mystery story, important clues are embedded in the text. Their importance will come out later.

4. PATRIARCHS AND MATRIARCHS: GENESIS 12–50

Abraham Cycle (Gen 12:1—25:18)

Abraham was born in the ancient city-state of Ur, located near the northern coastline of the Persian Gulf in southern Iraq. It was part of ancient Mesopotamia.

Without any introductory remarks, chapter 12 begins abruptly with the words "Now the LORD said to Abram, 'Go from your country and your kindred and your father's house to the land that I will show you. I will make of you a great nation, and I will bless you, and make your name great'" (Gen 12:1–2). The divine voice had been absent for ten generations, for not since the days of Noah had God spoken to humans. Not only does God promise Abram fame and multiple descendants, but also through him all the world will know blessing. "(I will bless you, and make your name great) so that you will be a blessing. I will bless those who bless you, and the one who curses you I will curse; and in you all the families of the earth shall be blessed" (Gen 12:2–3).

Abram, accompanied by his wife Sarai, his nephew Lot, and the persons that they had acquired in Haran, set out on this divinely commanded journey. There is no discussion, no questioning, and no debate. They just leave, without a stated destiny. They do not seem to be in a particular rush. Verse 9 specifically states that they "journeyed on by stages" until they reached the Negeb. When they came to Canaan, they paused at Shechem, in the middle of the country. Shechem often is mentioned in the Bible. It is there that God promises to give this specific land to Abram's progeny. In the hill country, with Bethel on the east and Ai toward the west, Abram built an altar and invoked God's name. He then continued on to the Negeb, the southland. The journey takes them through the rolling hill country; they seem to avoid cities and populated areas; they follow a pastoral route, which allows them to pasture their flocks. We still have to hear Abram's first words and see him interact with others. That moment is swiftly coming.

The rest of chapter 12 is devoted to Abram and Sarai in Egypt. There is a famine, and they find it necessary to travel to Egypt. They had essentially two choices: return to Mesopotamia or head southwest to Egypt. Those were the only areas that had abundant water sources in the Tigris-Euphrates and the Nile rivers respectively. God had promised Abram that he would prosper; this did not mean that there would not be difficulties along the route. This Egyptian episode is referred to as the "first wife–sister motif" and will be repeated again with Abraham, and then again in Isaac's life (Gen 12:10–20; 20; 26:6–16).

As Abram and Sarai approach Egypt he says, please pretend you are my sister. You are good looking, and if they think you are my wife, they will kill me. We do not have Sarai's reply, but presumably, she agrees. The Egyptians do admire her and place her in the quarters of the pharaoh. Abram prospers on her account and increases his wealth. God, however, plagues Pharaoh and his household "because of Sarai, Abram's wife." The pharaoh then figures out that he has been duped and says, with some righteous indignation, Why did you not tell me that she is your wife? Why did you say she was your sister? In short measure Abram, Sarai, and all their possessions are unceremoniously escorted out of the land.[11]

Chapter 13 finds Abram, Sarai, and Lot traveling back to the Negeb. There is tension between the herdsmen of uncle and nephew concerning grazing rights; this results in a decision to split forces. Lot opts to move to the Jordan rift valley and settles in the area of Sodom and Gomorrah. The small details mentioned there (vss. 10, 13) that the area is "well watered everywhere like the garden of the LORD," but that the inhabitants "were wicked, great sinners against the LORD" is not without significance. The denouement will come in chapter 18. God again promises this area to Abram and his descendants. Abram returns northward, settles near Hebron, and once there he offers a sacrifice to God.

Chapter 14 features a skirmish between some local tribal units. A group of four allied tribes attacks a second alliance of five and defeats them. They end up taking hostages, which include Abram's nephew Lot. Abram learns of this; he organizes his own household, gives chase, and rescues those kidnapped. He returns them and is thanked for his efforts.

Chapter 15 recounts Abram and God reiterating their special relationship and their establishing a covenantal contract. As at the end of chapter 15, God promises that the land will be given to Abram's descendants.

Chapter 16 marks a major turning point in Abram's life. Heretofore he had been promised descendants; he was told that God would make of him a great nation, but as verse 1 indicates, "Sarai, Abram's wife bore him no children." What to do? In that time and culture, if a wife, especially of the upper classes, was unable to bear children, she could designate what in today's world is termed a surrogate mother. This woman bears the husband's child, and that child becomes the official heir.[12] Given the importance of having an heir of quality, the surrogate mother would likely be someone of a good family, though impoverished.

Sarai "had an Egyptian slave-girl whose name was Hagar." Sarai designates Hagar "that I shall obtain children by her," and so she gave Hagar "to her husband Abram as a wife" (Gen 16:1–3).[13] The Torah is silent about Abram's and Hagar's personal reactions to this request. Hagar is clearly a younger woman, but it is presumptuous to think that she was—or was not—attractive to Abram. The concern here is not romantic love but a business/property/inheritance decision. Hagar conceives, but then "she looked with contempt on her mistress" for she was able to achieve what Sarai could not. Sarai is beside herself and angrily turns to Abram and blames him (!). Abram, in fairness, is in an awkward position, perhaps an intolerable one. He could say, "Sarai this was *your* idea in the first place!" Alternatively, he could say, "I just did what you asked me to do," or he could reprimand Hagar, who might then turn to him and say, "This is the gratitude I get for bearing your child?" No matter what he did, he would have been in the wrong in someone's mind. Abram decides not to triangulate (to use modern terminology), but turns to Sarai and says, she is your property, "do to her as you please." Sarai deals harshly with Hagar, and Hagar runs away into the desert.

There Hagar is met by an "angel of the LORD" (!) who speaks to her, telling her that she is to return to her mistress and submit to her. God, however, will remember her, and see to it that she will be the mother of a great people. Hagar acquiesces, returns, and gives birth to Ishmael, Abram's firstborn child (Gen 16:7–15). There is something daring here in that the text has God's angel, and, in Hagar's eyes, actually God, speaking directly to her ("Have I really seen God and remained alive after seeing him?" [vs. 13]). Hagar is an alien, an "other." Her very name, Hagar, hints of the alien/stranger. (In Hebrew, the word *ha-ger* literally means "the alien/stranger.") Yet she is accorded this phenomenal honor of having God address her directly, an honor not yet accorded to Sarai.

Chapter 17 brings the assurance of major changes in the lives of the first patriarch and matriarch. Thirteen years have passed. Once again God speaks to Abram, promising plenteous progeny, but, in addition, there is a change of name, which is a pun reflecting his new status. He is no longer Abram, but Abraham, "ancestor of a multitude"; Sarai will now be known as Sarah, and she shall bear a son, Isaac. In addition, as a mark of the special bond between God and Abraham, the patriarch is to circumcise himself and all his household. Further, all future male children are to be circumcised on the eighth day, as a sign of the covenant. Abraham is somewhat incredulous, but agrees and circumcises himself and all his household (see Text Study below, "Abraham Incredulous").

Chapter 18 is one of the dramatic moments of Genesis. Several things happen. The chapter divides into two sections, nearly equal in length. Verses 1–15 describe a group of (angelic?) visitors to Abraham's encampment; verses 16–33 explain what they intend to do when they come to Sodom and Gomorrah. Abraham is resting by his tent, presumably recovering from the ordeal of his circumcision. It is midday. Suddenly he notices three men standing near him. He runs (!) to greet them, and offers them food and refreshment. They agree and he attends to them. They ask about Sarah, and Abraham indicates that she is in the tent. One of them says to Abraham, "I will surely return to you in due season, and your wife Sarah shall have a son" (vs. 10). The text, then, in an aside, indicates that Sarah is postmenopausal, "Now Abraham and Sarah were old, advanced in age; it had ceased to be with Sarah after the manner of women." This is hardly surprising; she is, according to the text, eighty-nine and he is ninety-nine. Not without a touch of incredulity and wide-eyed wonder, Sarah exclaims, laughing to herself, "After I have grown old, and my husband is old, shall I have pleasure?" (vs. 12). Often, when one halves the ages of people found in Genesis, the narrative makes greater sense. Yet, this means that she was a mere forty-five and not nearly ninety as the Bible states. This answer, however, does not explain how, with her being "after the manner of women," that is, postmenopausal, she suddenly finds herself fertile.[14] God then turns to Abraham and asks, "Why did Sarah laugh?...Is anything too wonderful for the LORD?" Sarah, embarrassed and frightened, denies laughing, but God then turns and, addressing her directly, says, "Oh yes, you did laugh." At the opening line of the chapter it states God "appeared to Abraham" as he was sitting by his tent. Then, suddenly the patriarch saw "three men" standing near him. At no point during this episode are the visitors described as angels, much less that one of them is God. Yet, it is God who addresses both Abraham and Sarah in verses 13–15. As in chapter 17 (see Text Study at the end of the chapter, "Abraham Incredulous"), God is not offended when humans question divine power, even when indeed they laugh at promises of divine providence. God is not angry, merely bemused.

In the second half of the chapter, the (divine) visitors head off to Sodom. God then decides to share with Abraham the purpose of that mission: the destruction of Sodom and Gomorrah, because of the gravity of the sin found in those cities. The next verses (Gen 18:23–32) are unparalleled in biblical thought and certainly unmatched in world literature. Abraham, respectfully, even fearfully, starts to argue with God. Abraham is courageous. He questions God's judgment; he debates divine decisions. He does this on behalf of what are indisputably evil, violent people. Abraham dares to challenge God, despite having just been promised that he will soon have his long-awaited, long-desired child with his beloved Sarah. Initially, the deity agrees that should there be fifty righteous people found in the cities, God would not destroy Sodom and Gomorrah. Then, bit by bit, Abraham makes his case. Abraham bargains with God—there really is not a more accurate term—so that the minimum number of righteous people needed to save the cities is less than a dozen, a mere ten people. As detailed in chapter 19, the cities lack even this minimal number.[15]

Chapter 19 details the encounter at Sodom and its aftermath. The visitors are sometimes termed angels (vss. 1,15) and sometimes merely men (vss. 5, 10, 12). In any case, when they arrive at Sodom, Lot, Abraham's nephew, invites them to stay overnight with him, and the visitors accept this offer. The men of Sodom come to Lot's home and demand access to the visitors, explaining that they wish to "know" (i.e., have homosexual relations with) them (Gen 19:5). Lot tries to dissuade the locals, even offering his own daughters in place of the visitors! The angels cause the Sodomites to be blinded and urge Lot to leave the next day with his family, for the cities are doomed. Lot pleads with his family to leave, but in the end, only his two virgin daughters and his wife accompany him from the city. Though told not to look back, Lot's wife does so and is turned to a pillar of salt (vs. 26). Unable to understand the wider picture, Lot and his daughters assume that they are the last people remaining on the earth. His daughters then make a terribly difficult existential choice: if they are the sole remnant of civilization, are they not required to repopulate the earth, despite the taboo of incest? They decide in the affirmative, and so, according to biblical tradition, become the progenitors of the tribes of Moab and Ammon (Gen 19:30–38).

Chapter 20 is a close reprise of the wife–sister motif found in chapter 12 (see above), but the ruler this time is Abimelech of Gerar.

Chapter 21 celebrates the birth of Isaac, but also returns to the tensions between Sarah and Hagar, detailed in chapter 16. The chapter has three distinct sections: verses 1–7 are devoted to Isaac's birth and repeat puns on Isaac's name, in Hebrew, *Yitzhag*, which is connected to the Hebrew word for laughter *(tzahag)*. Abraham had laughed when first informed about Isaac's predicted birth (Gen 17:17) as did Sarah (Gen 18:12ff.); and now Sarah again refers to laughter (Gen 21:6). A second section, verses 8–21, deals with the shameful expulsion of Hagar and Ishmael (see Text Study at the end of the chapter, "Family Tensions"); finally, the rest of the chapter, verses 22–34, tells of the relationship with Abraham and Abimelech, including a covenant concluded at Beer-sheba.

Chapter 22 is arguably the best-known chapter in Genesis after chapter 1 (the first creation narrative). It tells the story of the binding (and near sacrifice) of Isaac. It is part of the lectionary reading for Rosh Hashanah, the Jewish New Year, and surely one of the most debated episodes in the Bible. It has served as the basis for innumerable sermons and articles, and is echoed in the Christian scriptures in the passion of Jesus. God, without warning, tests Abraham. "Take your son Isaac and offer him as a burnt-offering sacrifice on a mountain that I will show you." Abraham does not argue; he simply takes Isaac, and they proceed to the appointed place. At the final moment, God relents. Abraham has passed the test. Alternatively, is it God who passed the test? Again, Abraham is told that he will have numerous descendants.[16]

Chapter 23 finds Abraham negotiating for a burial plot with the local Hittites, for Sarah has died.

Chapter 24, the longest in Genesis, details how Abraham sends his senior servant to the land of his kin to find a wife for Isaac. What is plainly stated is that under no circumstances is Isaac to return to that area (vs. 8). The servant makes his way to Aram-naharaim and, following a long discussion with Abraham's nephew Bethuel, brings Rebekah back to Canaan, and Isaac marries her.

Genesis 25 is divided into two sections. The first eighteen verses detail the closing days of Abraham, including his taking on another wife and siring six more sons; included here are some genealogical matters and information about the twelve princes who are descendants of Ishmael. In this section we learn that Abraham's sons Isaac and Ishmael, far from being estranged, come together to bury their father following his death at a goodly age (vs. 9).

(Isaac) Jacob Cycle (Gen 25:19—36:43)

Though Isaac is less of a forceful personality than his father, Abraham, and sons, Esau and Jacob, he is not without his moments. That Isaac could go on and function in any significant way following the encounter in Genesis 22 is testimony to the triumph of his personal will. It also is testimony to his yet unspecified relationship with God. Through Abraham, God had promised Isaac a lineage of honor, and in saving him (even at the last moment), God kept faith with Isaac and his place in God's divine plan. In his late fifties, Isaac actively seeks God's help in relieving him and Rebekah of the burden of being barren, so he can fulfill the covenant. God hears, intervenes, and Esau and Jacob are born.

Isaac continues to mature and develop as a personality. Following Abraham's death, God addresses Isaac directly and maintains an open connection with him, promising that he will prosper (Gen 25:11; see also 26:2ff.). Moreover, he does.

In Genesis 26 God instructs Isaac that (unlike Abraham and Jacob) he is to remain directly connected to the land of future promise: he is not to go to Egypt (vs. 2). Isaac moves to Gerar, and he dwells there a long time. There is a repetition of the wife–sister motif, with Isaac and Rebekah as the protagonists. The second patriarch sows and reaps; he builds up large flocks and herds, and a retinue of servants. Enterprisingly, he reclaims wells sunk by his father. These are clear signs of material success. The Hebrew text is emphatic about Isaac's prosperity. Three times in Genesis 26:13 it stresses his success. This is illustrated in the Schocken Bible translation by Everett Fox: "The man became great, and went on, went on becoming greater, until he was exceedingly great." God continues to speak to Isaac and reassure him of future blessings. Later in the chapter, Isaac is approached by Abimelech of Gerar, who seeks an alliance. Though he is not keen about it, Isaac shrewdly accedes to the request. This is a man who has grown in wisdom through his life experiences. He has grown past the traumatic memory of Genesis 22, at least outwardly.

Genesis 27 is one of the most intriguing chapters in the book. Modern scholars have characterized the episode in disparaging terms. Descriptions include: "Jacob's moral lapse in his treatment of his brother and father,"[17] alternately, Jacob "practices outrageous deceit on a helpless father and a guileless brother";[18] and the episode is termed "The Cunning Acquisition of the Blessing."[19]

On the surface, Jacob and Rebekah successfully conspire to steal the blessing of the firstborn, purportedly deceiving near-blind Isaac. Yet, another explanation is possible, one that suggests that Isaac certainly was *not* the object of a deception. Indeed, to the contrary, it is "Jacob the deceiver" who actually is the one deceived. (See Text Study below, "Deception in the Dark.")

Chapter 28 has Jacob escaping for his life. Esau has threatened to kill him (Gen 27:41), and so, at his parents' advice, he travels to Haran to spend some time with his mother's brother, Laban. In vs. 12 he dreams of a ladder (alternately, stairway, ramp) reaching up to heaven. God is standing beside Jacob and promises to take care of him, seeing that he will return in safety. The narrative continues in chapter 29, and soon Jacob is in Haran. At a sheep watering well he meets his first cousin, Rachel, and, in short order, her family. Laban welcomes his nephew, and after a month, Jacob agrees to work for his uncle for seven years in consideration of his marrying Rachel. Laban agrees, but in the event deceives Jacob. The morning following the wedding Jacob finds out that he has married Leah, Rachel's older sister (Gen 29:21–30). The chapter concludes with the notice that Rachel is barren but Leah has delivered four sons by Jacob: Reuben, Simeon, Levi, and Judah.

Chapter 30 finds Rachel bereft. She gives to Jacob her maid Bilhah, who conceives twice, resulting in Dan and Naphtali. Leah follows suit and offers her maid Zilpah, who in turn produces two more sons, Gad and Asher. Next Leah sleeps with Jacob, and gives birth to Issachar, Zebulun, and then a daughter, Dinah. Finally, barren Rachel conceives, and Joseph is born. Jacob is keen to return to his own country, but Laban places obstacles in his path. Nonetheless, Jacob manages to outwit his father-in-law, and though he is unable to leave, he does prosper and becomes a rich man.

Chapter 31. It is now time for Jacob to return. God approaches him and says, "Return to the land of your ancestors and your kindred, and I will be with you." Jacob approaches his wives and shares that information with them. They are both resentful of the way their father has treated the family, and so they say, "Now then, do whatever God has said to you" (vs. 16). Jacob makes preparations and leaves with all his possessions while Laban is off shearing his own flocks. Without telling Jacob, Rachel steals her father's household gods. It is unclear if these were proof of legal title[20] or if they were used for divining purposes.[21] Laban gets wind of their escape and catches up with the family as they are traveling toward Gilead. He complains that he should have been told, but it is clear that his concern is much more the loss of his household gods than the welfare of his daughters and grandchildren. Laban goes searching for his stolen property but is outwitted by Rachel, who placed them underneath the camel's saddle and sat upon them. She claims she cannot rise before her father, because "the way of women is upon me," that is to say, she is in the midst of her menstrual cycle (Gen 31:32–35). It is a well-written, humorous scene, and the "narrator cannot have intended it to be heard without provoking laughter."[22] The chapter ends with the families parting ways. Note that in the Hebrew Bible, verse 1 is counted as part of the prior chapter (vs. 55) in NRSV and most other Christian Bibles.

Chapters 32–33 relate what happens when Jacob meets up with Esau. There are four divisions: first, Jacob's preparations for meeting Esau, sending him gifts, and Jacob dividing his camp (32:3–21 [32:4–22 H]); second, the "night encounter," and more of this below (32:22–32 [32:23–33 H]); third, the actual rendezvous with Esau (33:1–17); and fourth, Jacob settles close to the city of Shechem, in the land of Canaan (33:18–20).

Following a twenty-year forced exile, Jacob is about to meet his brother, a man who, the last time they were together, had vowed to kill Jacob (Gen 27:41). Understandably, Jacob is nervous. He rightfully fears for his life. Having sent his family ahead, Jacob beds down by the river Jabok. That night he has an encounter with—a man? an angel? God? his own conscience? The text says, "Jacob was left alone; and a man wrestled with him until daybreak." The two are evenly matched. They struggle throughout the night, and neither can best the other. Finally, at dawn Jacob's adversary asks the patriarch his name and is told that it is Jacob. The man then blesses Jacob with a new name, Israel. He says, "You shall no longer be called Jacob, but Israel, for you have striven with God and with humans, and have prevailed" (vs. 28 [29 H]). Jacob's new name, Israel, is a pun on the word *strive* or *wrestle*—hence, the name Israel could be translated as *God-wrestler*, or *one who strives with God*. While Jacob asks his wrestling opponent about *his* name, the man deflects the question, and then takes his leave. Finally, we learn that following this eerie encounter, Jacob limps, and may have limped for the rest of his life. The next morning Jacob reflects on this strange event. He calls the place Peniel (literally, Face of God), and says, "I have seen God face to face, and yet my life is preserved." Jacob's opponent is not given a name; he seems to be able to speak for God; he refuses to be seen during daylight hours; and Jacob believes he has seen God "face to face," albeit in the dark. Was this a man? An angel? God? His own conscience? Whatever the answer, Jacob's life is changed. Hereafter, physically he literally limps; and the post-Peniel Jacob is a much more subdued and cautious person.

Chapter 34 is devoted to a short episode in the life of Dinah, Jacob's one daughter. Dinah is at the center of the narrative, yet ironically we never hear her voice. She is spoken about; she never speaks. It is a violent tale, brutal and uncompromising, echoing what is sometimes called frontier justice. One day while visiting the women of the region, Dinah is seized and raped by Shechem, the son of the local chieftain, Hamor. Despite his outrageous behavior, Shechem is drawn to Dinah and wants to marry her. He asks his father to approach the family and make arrangements. Dinah's older brothers Simeon and Levi (they all share a common mother in Leah) carefully plan their revenge. They tell Hamor and Shechem that they will consent to the marriage on one condition. All the men in their city need to be circumcised. Hamor and Shechem convince their compatriots. Their argument is simple: we outnumber them, and in time they will intermarry with us, and we will assimilate them. "Will not their livestock, their property, and all their animals be ours?" (Gen 34:23). On the third day, when the men of the city are still in pain, Simeon and Levi enter the city, kill all the men including Shechem and Hamor, and rescue Dinah. They take as booty the wealth of the city, the women and children, and their flocks and herds. Jacob objects to his sons' actions, telling them that they have bought trouble and made Jacob's name odious in the land. The chapter closes with their reply: "Should our sister be treated like a whore?"

Chapter 35 finds Jacob and his family returning to the area of Bethel, which is associated with his stairway-to-heaven dream so many years ago (Gen 28:19). There, as before, God appears to Jacob and affirms his change of name from Jacob to Israel (vss. 9ff.). In this chapter Rachel dies giving birth to Jacob's twelfth son, Benjamin. Jacob is reunited with Isaac, and together with Esau, they bury the second patriarch (vss. 27–29).

Chapter 36 closes out the (Isaac) Jacob cycle. It is filled with genealogical information pertaining to the descendants of Esau.

Joseph Cycle (Gen 37–50)

Chapter 37 begins the long Joseph cycle, which fills the final quarter of the book of Genesis. Joseph is seventeen years old, his father's favorite, and he relishes his special place of honor. On two occasions he dreams dreams and then relates to his family that they will be in an inferior position to him (vss. 5–11). His brothers can barely speak a civil word to him. Jacob cannot be oblivious to this tension, but nonetheless one day he sends Joseph out alone to check on how his older brothers are faring with the flocks. When he finally meets up with them, they vent their anger and frustration by first placing Joseph in an empty pit. Then they sell him to a group of caravan traders, who in turn take him to Egypt and sell him into slavery. The brothers take a goat and slaughter it, placing blood on Joseph's tunic. They then claim they found the cloak. Jacob surmises that Joseph has been killed and is disconsolate.

The Joseph story abruptly pauses at the end of chapter 37. When last we hear of Joseph, he is in Egypt, sold to Potiphar, one of the pharaoh's officials. The reader wants to know what will happen to him, but that will have to wait. Chapter 38 is a separate story in its own right. It tells the story of an enterprising woman, Tamar, the daughter-in-law of Joseph's older brother Judah. Tamar is married to Er, the oldest of Judah's three sons. For some unspecified reason, Er displeases God and dies. Following the tradition of levirate marriage (see Deut 25:5–10 in the chapter on Deuteronomy), the next oldest son, Onan, is expected to marry Tamar and produce progeny. The biblical text is clear, "Since Onan knew that the offspring would not be his, he spilled his semen on the ground whenever he went in to his brother's wife, so that he would not give offspring to his brother" (Gen 38:9). In short, he withdrew before ejaculating. That, too, was evil in God's sight, so Onan died. Judah is nonplused. On one hand, he knows the local custom, and he should ask his third son, Shelah, to impregnate Tamar. On the other hand, two sons have already died after associating with this woman. The omniscient reader knows what Judah cannot: it is his sons who were at fault. Tamar herself is innocent in the matter. Nonetheless, he asks his daughter-in-law to return to her father's house. Time passes. Tamar notices that Shelah has grown up, but Judah has not required him to impregnate her. Resourceful woman that she is, she puts on a disguise, and through an unsuspecting Judah, she accomplishes her mission. Like a carefully crafted mystery, the narrative is so well told that if one is not familiar with the story it is worthwhile to read this thirty-verse chapter in its entirety. Coincidentally, one of Tamar's eventual children will be the ancestor of King David, and hence, traditionally, an ancestor of the Messiah (see Ruth 4:18–22).

Chapter 39 takes the reader straight back to Egypt, as it continues the focus on Joseph. Chapter 38 portrayed an innocent but venturesome woman (Tamar) who pushed the limits of societal propriety to achieve a righteous result. Chapter 39 features an innocent (Joseph) who chooses to stay well within the limits of societal propriety to avoid breaching his master Potiphar's trust. Potiphar's wife lusts for Joseph. When he refuses to lie with her, she accuses him of attempted rape. Potiphar seems to have limited options: he is publicly infuriated and has Joseph incarcerated. The chapter, however, ends on an optimistic note: God favors Joseph in prison, and the chief jailer promotes him to a position of power.

In chapter 40 Joseph remains imprisoned, but he has the opportunity to interpret two more dreams, in this case the dreams of two fellow prisoners, both of whom had served recently in the pharaoh's household. In the case of the chief baker, he has a limited future, but the chief cupbearer is told that within a short time he will return to favor. Joseph implores the cupbearer to remember him when he earns his predicted freedom. In contrast to the previous chapter, this one ends on a note of seeming despair. The pharaoh "restored the cupbearer to his cupbearing, and he placed the cup in Pharaoh's hand....Yet the chief cupbearer did not remember Joseph, but forgot him" (Gen 40:21, 23).

Chapter 41 opens far from Joseph in prison; it begins with the pharaoh himself. Two years have passed. One night the pharaoh dreams two (note again, two) dreams. They cause him great upset, but none of his magicians or wise men can provide a clear interpretation (vs. 8). The cupbearer comes forward and, apologizing, recalls that when he was imprisoned, he met a "young Hebrew" who was "a servant of the captain of the guard." The young man was able to interpret dreams correctly. In short order, Joseph is brought before the pharaoh. Little details make the story credible. The pharaoh sends for Joseph. Hurriedly brought out of the dungeon, he has himself shaved and puts on new clothes. Pharaoh says to him, I had a dream, which no one can interpret, but I heard that when you hear dreams, you are able to do so.

Joseph's answer carries just the right amount of assurance and humility. He does not claim to be a professional interpreter of dreams; rather the credit goes directly to God: "It is not I; God will give Pharaoh a favorable answer" (Gen 41:16). A deeper purpose is intimated here. "It is God, the author assures us through Joseph, who causes dreams to serve as guideposts to the future."[23] The pharaoh relates both of his strange dreams, and then Joseph explains that the two are really manifestations of the same phenomenon. Seven years of bumper crops will be followed by seven years of blight. Famine will stalk the land. "It will be very grievous. And the doubling of Pharaoh's dream means that the thing is fixed by God, and God will shortly bring it about. Now therefore let Pharaoh select a man who is discerning and wise, and set him over the land of Egypt" (Gen 41:31–33). Joseph even comes up with a plan to deal with the predicted shortages, a plan that will increase Pharaoh's power. It is hardly surprising then that Pharaoh selects Joseph for this position.

Joseph is immediately invested with power. He is now thirty years old; he has been in Egypt for thirteen years. He entered as chattel, and now he is second in power in the land. Events transpire as he had said. He is married to Asenath, daughter of Potiphera, priest of On, and soon he is the father of two sons, Manasseh and Ephraim. The Bible explains that Joseph chooses these names as a play on words on two statements. These are: "God has made me forget all my hardship and all my father's house," and "For God has made me fruitful in the land of my misfortunes" (vss. 51–52). As far as Joseph believes, he has put his difficult past behind him, including connections to his family of origin. The chapter concludes with the famine in full force and "all the world" coming to Joseph to buy grain, for the shortage of food is widespread.

Chapter 42 redirects the action to Jacob, who is living in Canaan. The famine is strongly felt there. In short order, ten of Joseph's brothers are headed to Egypt. Jacob refuses to send Benjamin, for he feared harm could come to him. The brothers arrive in Egypt and meet Joseph, who is in charge of food distribution. He recognizes them, but they are unaware of who he is. He treats them like strangers and speaks harshly to them, accusing them of coming to spy out the land of Egypt. They protest their innocence, but he is adamant. They explain that they are of a family of twelve sons and the youngest remains with his father in Canaan. Joseph refuses to accept their account and demands that they bring the youngest to Egypt. The youngest son, Benjamin, is Joseph's blood brother; they shared Rachel as a mother. The omniscient reader (and of course, Joseph) knows this; the brothers are very much in the dark. To create a bit more terror in their minds, Joseph has the brothers imprisoned for three days. On the third day he frees them and gives them the dual stipulation that first they must return with their youngest brother and second that they need to leave a hostage.

Keeping Simeon imprisoned in Egypt, Joseph then sends them off but surreptitiously returns their money to their grain sacks. On the way back home they find their money and, trembling, say to each other, "What is this that God has done to us?" (Gen 42:28). What indeed?

They return to Jacob and relate their strange adventures. As the chapter closes, Jacob says, I am a bereaved parent. Joseph is no more, now Simeon is no more, I shall certainly not send Benjamin to Egypt.

In chapter 43 the famine continues. Jacob wants his sons to return to Egypt, but they refuse to go unless they can take Benjamin with them. It will be a futile trip without him. Jacob finally relents but urges them to take "choice fruits of the land…a little balm and a little honey, gum, resin, pistachio nuts, and almonds." Also, they are to take back the money and double it. Try to bribe this governor of Egypt. Then Jacob says, maybe God Almighty will yet allow me to see Benjamin and his other brother (Simeon).

When the brothers arrive, Joseph has them invited to his private house for a meal. They present their gifts, and Joseph sees

Benjamin for the first time in more than twenty years. He is so overcome with emotion that he retires to another part of his house, lest he weep before them.

Chapter 44 finds an increase in drama. Joseph arranges that his brothers leave Egypt with full grain sacks, and their money on top of the grain. In Benjamin's sack, however, he secrets his silver divining cup. He lets them leave the city and then sends his steward in hot pursuit. "Why have you returned evil for good?" he asks (vs. 4). The brothers protest their innocence. This makes sense; they *are* innocent! They explain not only did they not take the cup, but if it were to be found, let the person who took it die, and the rest will become slaves. When the cup that Joseph had hidden in Benjamin's sack is found, they are devastated.

Mortified, in disgrace and embarrassment they return to Joseph, who receives them haughtily. The brothers prostrate themselves before Joseph, and in a gesture of seeming magnanimity Joseph says, let the guilty one remain as a slave; the rest of you can go free (vs. 17).

Judah then stands, and at some great length (vss. 18–34) recounts their family history, including the fact that the youngest son (Benjamin) once had an older brother (Joseph), who his father believes to be dead. If we return to Canaan without the youngest, Judah correctly claims, Jacob will die. Consequently, Judah argues, let me stay in his place. "Now therefore, please let your servant remain as a slave to my lord in place of the boy; and let the boy go back with his brothers. For how can I go back to my father if the boy is not with me? I fear to see the suffering that would come upon my father" (Gen 44:33–34).

Chapter 45 brings the drama to its high point. Joseph confesses who he is. He tells his brothers, "God sent me before you to preserve life" (vs. 5). There are still many more years of famine ahead. Go back to Canaan, tell father Jacob I am alive, and bring him and the family to Egypt. You shall settle in the land of Goshen (in the Nile Delta) and you shall prosper there. The brothers weep and reconcile. Shortly thereafter, they return to Canaan, inform Jacob, and the chapter concludes with Jacob saying, "My son Joseph is still alive. I must go and see him before I die" (Gen 45:28).

Chapter 46 begins with Jacob and all his household heading south to Egypt. When they reach Beer-sheba, Jacob offers a sacrifice to God, and God speaks to him in a vision in the night. God reassures Jacob that Joseph will be there when the patriarch dies. The rest of the chapter lists the children of Jacob by his various wives, as well as grandchildren. His direct male descendants are numbered sixty-six (vs. 26), to which are added Joseph and Joseph's two sons already in Egypt, plus Jacob, resulting in a total of seventy persons. When Jacob meets Joseph he says he is ready to die, but that will not come for another seventeen years.

Chapter 47 begins with Joseph first rehearsing with his brothers and father what they are to say when they meet Pharaoh, and then continues with the family in Pharaoh's court. Through Joseph, the pharaoh had invited them to come to Egypt (Gen 45:17ff.), but had not specifically designated the area of Goshen. This is now confirmed as the place of their settlement. When Jacob meets Pharaoh he claims that his life has been long and difficult. Jacob adds that his ancestors lived even longer than he did (vs. 9). The chapter also includes data on how Joseph organized the famine relief in Egypt. Said simply, he forced people to sell their land to Pharaoh in return for food, and the people were reduced to servitude (vss. 20–21); and on top of that, when they harvested their crops, a fifth was ceded to Pharaoh. The only exception to this rule was the land of the priests (vs. 26). The chapter closes with an announcement of the pending death of Jacob at age 147.

Joseph brings his sons Manasseh and Ephraim to meet with his father in chapter 48. Jacob adopts them as his own, and then he blesses them but gives the firstborn blessing to Ephraim, Joseph's second son. Joseph thinks that his father is confused and tries to correct him. Jacob makes it clear that this is his intent. Once again, the pattern of blessing the firstborn male is put aside, as it was in the case of Isaac and Jacob. As Everett Fox notes, often in Genesis the "order of nature (primacy of the firstborn) is overturned, demonstrating that God, not nature, is the ruling principle in human affairs."[24]

Chapter 49 is a long blessing of Jacob's twelve sons. It describes them with images that in time become their pictorial depiction, such as the lion for Judah, the doe for Naphtali, and a fruitful bough (a wild ass, NJPS) for Joseph. The chapter closes with the death of the patriarch Jacob.

Chapter 50 begins with Jacob being embalmed, and then Joseph seeking Pharaoh's permission to return his father to the land of his birth, to the family burial site. A large contingent of chariots and charioteers go with the family. Jacob is buried at Machpelah.

Back in Egypt the brothers come to Joseph, fearful that with Jacob dead Joseph will wreak revenge. They tell him that before he died, Jacob had said to them that they should go to Joseph and that he should forgive the brothers. There is no indication of such a conversation in Genesis, but in any case, Joseph says, "Do not be afraid....Even though you intended to do harm to me, God intended to do good...have no fear" (Gen 50:19–21). Some time later, Joseph sends word to his brothers that he is dying, and says, when the time comes that you will return, take my bones with you. In the Book of Exodus, mention is made that Joseph's bones indeed were taken with the Israelites when they left Egypt (Exod 13:19). The chapter ends with Joseph's death and his being placed in a coffin in Egypt.

5. GENESIS IN THE CHRISTIAN SCRIPTURES

The writers of the Christian scriptures certainly know the Jewish Bible and quote from it extensively. In the Book of Genesis, the figure of Abraham is featured prominently. Abraham is the man of faith; he is the father of the Jewish people and, by extension, of Christians (Rom 4:16; Gal 3:29). For that reason alone he is revered. Abraham is also the father of Isaac, and Isaac becomes the paradigm for Jesus, the beloved son who then becomes the sacrifice chosen by God.

References from Genesis actually begin with the creation narrative. Often the quotes are structured in such a way as to promote the Christian message. For example, God's statement in Genesis 1:3, "let there be light," is utilized this way: "For it is the God who said 'Let light shine out of darkness' who has shone in our hearts to give the light of the knowledge of the glory of God in the face of Jesus Christ" (2 Cor 4:6).

As with rabbinic midrash, the author of 1 Timothy refers to scripture, and then builds on the text, teaching a certain value. "For everything created by God is good [basing himself on Gen 1:31] and nothing is to be rejected, provided it is received with thanksgiving; for it is sanctified by God's word and by prayer" (1 Tim 4:5).

In Romans, Paul teaches the concept of original sin, suggesting that Adam brought sin and death into the world, but life is through Jesus as the Christ. For "just as sin came into the world through one man, and death came through sin, and so death spread to all because all have sinned…just as sin exercised dominion in death, so grace might exercise dominion though justification leading to eternal life through Jesus Christ our Lord" (Rom 5:12, 21).

The waters at the time of Noah prefigured the waters of baptism (1 Pet 3:20–21). Luke explains that the day of the Son of God will come unexpectedly, just as the flood came at Noah's time (Luke 17:26–27).

Noah, like Abraham, was a man of faith, explains the author of Hebrews (Heb 11:7–8), "By faith Noah, warned about events as yet unseen…built an ark to save his household.…By faith Abraham obeyed when he was called to set out for a place that he was to receive as an inheritance."

In the Acts of the Apostles, Stephen addresses the Sanhedrin and recounts biblical history from the time of Abraham, mentioning specifically the call from Mesopotamia, the land of the Chaldeans, Haran, the covenant of circumcision, Isaac, Jacob, Joseph, the sojourn in Egypt, Moses, the Exodus, and so on. He displays familiarity with Genesis, Exodus, and the prophets (Acts 7). As mentioned in an earlier chapter, the early church "accepted the books of the Old Testament as sacred scriptures, and every New Testament writer cites them, or alludes to them as having divine authority."[25]

As stated above, in terms of Genesis, it is Abraham as the man of faith who gets rich play in the Christian scriptures.

The Gospels were announced to Abraham, says the writer of Galatians. "The scripture, foreseeing that God would justify the Gentiles by faith, declared the gospel beforehand to Abraham, saying 'All the Gentiles shall be blessed in you' [Gen 12:2–3; 18:18; 22:18]. For this reason, those who believe are blessed with Abraham who believed" (Gal 3:8–9).

Abraham is justified by faith, explains Paul in Romans 4. Referring to Genesis 15:6, Paul says, "Abraham believed God, and it was credited to him as righteousness" (Rom 4:3). Paul goes on to point out that God first visits and makes promises to Abraham before the patriarch is circumcised, so Abraham is the father of all who are uncircumcised but have faith (vs. 9ff.). Abraham is also the man of hope, because "Hoping against hope, he believed that he would become 'the father of many nations'" (vs. 18).

The writer of Galatians refers to the story of Abraham, Sarah, Hagar, Ishmael, and Isaac to support his theology. The epistle writer is quite clear in his intent; he says specifically that the narrative of Abraham and his two sons "is an allegory" ("may be taken figuratively," NIV) (Gal 4:24). He goes on to posit that Hagar stands for Mt. Sinai and corresponds to the present city of Jerusalem. Hagar's children are slaves. There is, however, a heavenly Jerusalem. "But the other woman [Sarah] corresponds to the Jerusalem above; she is free, and she is our mother" (Gal 4:26). You are Sarah's children, the writer of Galatians explains, and are therefore children of promise. Paraphrasing Sarah's demand to Abraham to exile that slave woman and her son (Gen 21:10) so that the son of the free woman (Sarah) would inherit, Galatians states, "So then, friends, we [who are believers in Jesus] are children, not of the slave, but of the free woman" (Gal 4:31).

Sodom and Gomorrah are featured in the Christian scriptures as symbols of evil (Matt 10:15; Jude 7), as earlier they were in the Jewish Bible (Isa 1:9–10; Jer 23:14).

A specific reference to the binding of Isaac (Gen 22) appears in Hebrews 11:17ff.

6. GENESIS IN RABBINIC LITERATURE

There are several midrashic collections accessible in English. Among them are *Midrash Genesis Rabbah* and the *Midrash Tanhuma on Genesis,* both of which comment on specific verses. The *Pirke de Rabbi Eliezer* takes a more narrative approach to such topics as creation and the lives of the matriarchs and patriarchs.

It Was Very Good

God's statement in Genesis 1:31 that the world was "very good" prompts the rabbis to ask, did this include the "Evil Inclination," the drive toward impulsive action. Yes, the rabbis say, for without the *Yetzer haRa* (Evil Inclination) a person would not marry, build a house, or start a business.[26]

God's Attributes of Both Mercy and Justice

In Genesis 2:4 the deity is titled *LORD God,* but in Genesis 1 it was consistently *God. LORD God,* the rabbis explain, reflects two of the deity's major attributes, mercy and justice. God first created a world ruled by strict justice, and human life was impossible, for no one can meet that standard. Then God created a world where mercy was the accepted norm, and people took advantage of that, and so again, civilized life was impossible. What did God do? The rabbis offer an analogy. It is as when someone fills a thin glass beaker with ice-cold water, the beaker will crack. Likewise, when someone fills such a beaker with boiling water, it will crack. Therefore, the deity, taking the form *LORD God* (mercy and justice) blended the divine attributes, mercy with justice, and the world stood.[27]

Gain for Loss

In Genesis 2:21 the LORD God takes one of the man's ribs and forms a woman. This is likened to a thief who stole a silver cup and left in its place a gold one.[28]

Sin Is Present, But It Can Be Controlled

Cain is told, "sin is lurking at the door; its desire is for you, but you must master it" (Gen 4:7; "yet you can be its master" [NJPS translation]). Sin is present, but if a person chooses to overcome that power, it is possible to do so.[29] The rabbis explain, "When people occupy themselves with Torah [Jewish studies]; the Evil Inclination has no power over them."[30]

Seven Basic Laws for Civilized Society

Though the Torah was initially given to Israel, there were seven basic laws for civilized society that the rabbis extrapolated from God's instructions to Noah and his family following the flood (Gen 9:4–7). These fundamental laws were (1) establishing courts of justice; (2) prohibition of blasphemy; (3) prohibition of idolatry; (4) prohibition of sexual sins; (5) prohibition of bloodshed; (6) prohibition of robbery; and finally, (7) not eating the flesh of a living animal. There are some variations on these laws. These are known as the Noahide (or Noahic) laws.[31]

Nothing without Its Purpose

God gathered the waters (Gen 1:9) during creation and then used them during the flood.[32]

Perhaps They Will Learn

Why did God not simply take Noah and his family to a secure place and then suddenly unleash the flood? God hoped the people would repent. Noah took fifty-two years to build the ark in the hope that the people might see what is coming and then change their ways.[31] According to another midrash, Noah was at this work for 120 years, and the people paid no attention to him when he told them that God was going to bring a flood.[34]

A Holy Place

According to the rabbis, the place where Noah brought his sacrifices following the flood was the exact spot where ten generations later Abraham was to bring Isaac as a (near-) sacrifice, and this would be the same locale as the Temple in Jerusalem.[35]

Abraham's Ten Trials

The (near-) sacrifice of Isaac was the final, the tenth of Abraham's trials. Twice he was asked to move from his home (Gen 12:1f.; 12:10); two of the trials deal with his sons, Ishmael and Isaac (Gen 21:10; 22:1ff.); two deal with his wives (Gen 12:11ff.; 21:10); one is the war with the kings (Gen 14:13ff.); another is the covenant of the pieces (Gen 15); one trial was at Ur of the Chaldeans (Gen 15:7); and one was at the covenant of circumcision (Gen 17:9ff.; 23f.)[36]

Investigative Reporting

In Genesis 18:21 God says, "I must go down and see whether they [the inhabitants of Sodom and Gomorrah] have done altogether according to the outcry that has come to me; and if not, I will know." This sparks a rabbinic explanation that God personally takes the time to investigate what is happening with humankind. God does not credit rumors but seeks direct involvement. The implication is that we humans should also discount rumors and take the time to check out reports for ourselves.[37]

God's Ten Descents to Earth

The rabbis also explain that God has made and will make ten descents to earth. These are the following: (1) the Garden of Eden (Gen 3:8); (2) the Tower of Babel (Gen 11:1ff.); (3) Sodom (Gen 18:21); (4) the thornbush (Exod 3:8); (5) once in Egypt (Gen 46:4); (6) once at Sinai (Exod 19:20); (7) once at the cleft of the rock (Exod 34:5); (8) and (9) the tent of meeting (Num 11:16ff. with the seventy elders; and Num 12:5 with Aaron and Miriam); and (10) once in the future (based on Zech 14:4).[38]

Angels with Specific Roles

Angels have specific roles; one angel does not perform two tasks, and two angels do not perform one task. Three angels came to Abraham and two went on to Sodom. Michael announced that in a year's time Sarah would give birth; Gabriel was sent to overturn Sodom, and Raphael was sent to rescue Lot.[39]

Further, when Jacob saw angels ascending and descending (Gen 28:12), this meant that angels have specific roles: there were those who accompanied him in the Land of Israel, and another set who are with him outside of the Land.[40]

Jacob's Ladder Stood on the Temple Site

The base of Jacob's ladder was the Temple site.[41]

The Last Words of the Books of the Torah

"The last words in each of the five books of the Torah, 'Egypt, journeys, Sinai, Jericho, Israel,' are a virtual summary of the Torah's narrative about the people Israel, from slavery to Sinai, to the Promised Land."[42]

7. TEXT STUDY

A. Genesis 2:4–25. The Creation of Humans

The second creation story (Gen 2:4b—3:24), which focuses on humans, begins with a subtle clue. Genesis 2:4 reads: "These are the generations of the heavens and the earth when they were created. In the day that the LORD God made the earth and the heavens." It is easy to read this verse as a complete thought in its own right. In English, these are two sentences; in the Hebrew, they constitute one verse. Sentences in the Hebrew Bible generally have a pause point (something like a comma) about halfway through the verse. Scholars differentiate the first part of these sentences with pause points as the "a" section of the verse and the second part as the "b" section. Hence, "These are the generations of the heavens and the earth when they were created" is Genesis 2:4a.

"In the day that the LORD God made the earth and the heavens" is designated Genesis 2:4b. Notice how in Genesis 2:4a the heavens precede mention of the earth. That is because the first creation epic, beginning in Genesis 1:1, has as its focus the view from the heavens. It is the cosmic, the macrocosm view. Only on the sixth day does God get around to creating humans, and then it is "male and female" together (Gen 1:27). This is the P document, which is concerned with an orderly, detailed, day-by-day approach to creation. All things in their time. First light and darkness; then sea and sky; and finally dry land and vegetation. So the first three days. Then come the luminaries; fowl and fish; and finally animals and humans, on days four, five, and six respectively.

The second creation epic, which focuses on humans, starts with the "b" section of Genesis 2:4. It says clearly, "In the day that the LORD God made the earth and the heavens." Earth precedes heavens, because the author is concerned about earthly matters, what is happening right here on earth. The author of the second creation epic wants to tell the story of humanity's creation. Here the first human will be created from the dust of the earth. This is a J document. J loves puns. The man, who will be designated as Adam, is created from the earth (Hebrew, *adamah*). His very name, *Adam*, is a pun, a play on words in the Hebrew. *Adam* (earthling) is created from *adamah* (earth).

Adam is created, but creation is not yet complete. Unlike the first creation epic, which has male and female created at the same time (Gen 1:27), this story lacks a female. Adam, the man, lacks a true partner. God brings the animals to the man, "but for the man there was not found a helper as his partner" (vs. 20). God decides to resolve the dilemma. God causes a deep sleep to fall upon the man, and then, while he is in this coma, without seeking his opinion, much less the man's assistance, God creates a woman. The man "is neither participant nor spectator nor consultant at her birth. Like man, woman owes her life solely to God."[43] Now creation is complete, and with a typical J pun, the man says, "this one shall be called Woman, for out of Man this one was taken" (vs. 23). The pun is more evident in Hebrew, for "this one shall be called Woman [Hebrew, *isha*], for out of Man [Hebrew, *ish*] this one was taken."

B. Genesis 17:1–22. Abraham Incredulous

Speiser credits this whole chapter to the P tradition. He points out the concern about chronological detail in verse 1, the overriding feature of circumcision, and a formal pronouncement by God. "P's approach, in short, is ritualistic and impersonal."[44]

Yet it could be argued that this is a P document with strong hints of the J source. The J source loves to tell stories. Speiser describes J as "the most gifted biblical writer....J's style is clear and direct....The leading actors on J's stage are realized in depth...his earth is peopled with actors so natural and candid that even their relations with Yahweh are reduced to human scale, so that God himself becomes anthropomorphic."[45] For sixteen long and detailed, even ponderous verses, God addresses the newly named Abraham. This is probably God's longest speech to Abraham. At first, in awe and submission, the patriarch had thrown himself on his face (vs. 3). After hearing God's explanation, again promising him direct progeny with Sarah, Abraham is perfectly incredulous. This is not the picture of a passive personality, a cardboard figure, bowing and scraping before God, giving thanks for this additional promise. Quite the contrary. In verse 17, Abraham is doubled over with laughter. He cannot believe what he is hearing. In colloquial English he is saying, "God, you are kidding me. You are putting me on. You are making fun of me." The Torah text says it clearly: "Then Abraham fell on his face and laughed, and said to himself, 'Can a child be born to a man who is a hundred years old? Can Sarah, who is ninety years old, bear a child?'" This kind of audacious writing, where Abraham challenges the promise that God has just made to him, is reminiscent of the J source *(his earth is peopled with actors so natural and candid that even their relations with Yahweh are reduced to human scale, so that God himself becomes anthropomorphic)*. God's response to Abraham is patient; it is kind, as if God were addressing a student who does not quite seem to understand the problem at hand. God is not insulted or upset, much less is he furious with Abraham for challenging the divine decree. God simply says, "No, but your wife Sarah shall bear you a son, and you shall name him Isaac." In chapter 18, when Sarah is equally incredulous and amused and filled with laughter, God again is very understanding, even bemused at the ways of humans (see Gen 18:11–15). God also explains that Ishmael will become the ancestor of twelve princes, and he too will become a great nation. Yet, the real covenant between God and Abraham will be established through the yet-to-be-born Isaac.

C. Genesis 21:8–21. Family Tensions

When Isaac is two or three years old, he is weaned. Abraham arranges a feast to acknowledge his son's reaching this important moment. Either then, or sometime later, Sarah *sees* Ishmael, now fifteen or sixteen, laughing (or playing, the words are the same in Hebrew, *metzaheq*). Sarah takes instant umbrage. She confronts Abraham, saying, "Cast out this slave woman with her son; for the son of this slave woman shall not inherit along with my son Isaac" (Gen 21:10).

Just what does Sarah see? What occasions her reaction? What turns Sarah's laughter to such bitterness? Was Ishmael amusing or abusing his younger brother? Was he laughing at Isaac's expense? Traditional rabbinic sources such as the midrash are very ready to point out that Sarah *saw* or sensed that Ishmael was to become a thorough scoundrel. That Ishmael, Abraham's firstborn, should be such a disappointment, such a cruel person, is identified by the rabbis as the source of the ninth of Abraham's ten trials.[46] In the midrash, basing their interpretations on the word *playing* ("Sarah saw the son of Hagar the Egyptian, whom she had born to Abraham, playing"), the rabbis conjure up a host of possible villainous acts. They locate other instances of the same verb, *metzaheq* [*mem-tzadeh-het-quf,* or variations of its verbal form, or a near-homonym, such as *mesaheq—mem-sin-het-quf*], and suggest that Ishmael was constantly bent on doing evil deeds. He is accused of rape and seduction (the verb *letzaheq* is used by the wife of Potiphar in her denunciation of Joseph [Gen 39:17]). Ishmael is accused of idolatry (the verb *letzaheq* is used to describe the idolatrous revel at the time of the Golden Calf [Exod 32:6]). He is called a "killer" (based on a verse in 2 Sam 2:14 with reference to the near-homonym *yisahaqu*). It is also said that Ishmael used to take Isaac into the fields and then, pretending to play, he shot arrows at Isaac. This is in reference to the near-homonym *mesaheq* in Proverbs 26:18–19, where it says, "Like a madman shooting…deadly arrows…who deceives his neighbor and says, 'I was only joking'" (NIV). Finally, the rabbis suggest that Ishmael was deriding the weaning feast for Isaac, saying with mocking laughter: I am Abraham's firstborn, and it is I who shall be the chief inheritor.[47]

In the biblical world (and subsequently in the view of later rabbinic Judaism) all non-Israelite people are understood to be the "Other," and are portrayed in a negative light. These facts, naturally do not preclude biblical leaders from making military or political alliances with former enemies, when it is in their perceived self-interest to do so. This *demonizing* of "Others" was standard fare for all nations and peoples, it was the norm in terms of pre-modern thought in the West and Middle East, and much of the East as well.

Sarah considers Ishmael to be an Egyptian; he is, after all, the son of Hagar the Egyptian. Sarah has very bitter memories of Egypt (see chapter 12).

Hagar herself is an ongoing and constant reminder of what Sarah had to suffer, the pain she felt as a "failure" to be a complete woman, a mother, a child bearer.

Alternately, a literal explanation is correct: the two boys *are* only playing together. Isaac is thirteen or fourteen years younger than Ishmael. Ishmael, who later will earn renown as an archer, is simply helping Isaac shoot a bow and arrow, demonstrating his own expertise before his younger brother. In its context the Isaac–Ishmael episode in 21:9 could well be understood as Ishmael amusing [babysitting?] his younger brother.

Sarah understands too well that Isaac idolizes his older sibling. That is what frightens her so much. Not that Ishmael is a physical threat to Isaac; quite the contrary, rather he is *too much of an influence* upon her son both psychologically and emotionally. Sarah worries that Isaac will be unduly influenced by Ishmael. She and Abraham are older parents, and Ishmael and Hagar are much younger; they probably will outlive Abraham and Sarah. Sarah agonizes that Isaac will become "Egyptianized." He will reject the cultural norms of his Mesopotamian-oriented parents. He will adopt the polytheistic religious ideas of Hagar and Ishmael, in contrast to the monotheistic ideas of Abraham and Sarah. Sarah's active intervention, which forces Ishmael and Hagar into exile, allows Isaac the opportunity to forge a relationship with Abraham's God.

Sarah's fears concerning the religio/cultural influence of the "Other" is well founded. The Torah, as well as later Israelite history, is replete with examples of how the community repeatedly was seduced by alien cultures. Numbers 25:1ff. recounts the troubles at Shittim, where Phineas took precipitous action to curb foreign practices. Deuteronomy 12:2ff. makes it clear that when the Israelites will enter the Promised Land they are to eradicate idolatry, root and branch. The prophets, repeatedly, inveigh against syncretistic practices among the people.

What Sarah saw, what she really saw—Ishmael (with or without Isaac) laughing/playing/fondling/amusing/abusing—is unclear. What is certain is that God is compelled to support her request to allow her son Isaac to be Abraham's undisputed heir; he shall be raised in a religious environment free from this particular polytheistic influence. God's apparent *necessary* intervention, in support of Sarah's decision, makes it clear that Abraham would have rejected her argument.[48]

D. Genesis 27:1—28:5. Deception in the Dark

In Genesis 27, and in the chapters leading up to it, there are clues, both clear and coded messages that indicate Jacob is to be the designated heir, and further, that Isaac understands this. When Jacob finally acquires the blessing, it is as the culmination of a well-thought-out strategy devised by his parents. It is not Isaac who is "in the dark"; it is Jacob. He is manipulated by his parents to "steal" the blessing.[49]

Jacob needs to break with his settled life; he needs to face serious challenges in order to mature. Forty years old, "a quiet man, living in tents" (Gen 25:27), he is unmarried with no proper prospects in sight. His twin brother Esau has wives, but they are locals and unacceptable in his parents' view (Gen 26:34–35; 27:46). What will motivate Jacob to find a proper wife and continue the challenge of the Abrahamic covenant? He will leave *only if he feels he has no choice; if to remain would put his life in immediate danger.*

Isaac and Rebekah's mutual affection is clear (Gen 24:67; 26:8). Both are aware that, in their society, blessing the firstborn male is the norm, yet (unlike a generation earlier with Sarah's reaction to Hagar and Ishmael) they have no desire to exile Esau. All they require is that he be gone for a few days. Though they know they are correct in their decision, Isaac and Rebekah cannot bear to tell Esau that he is not the right one to pass on the family traditions. It is too painful a task for them to face directly.

The plan is not complex. One day Isaac sends Esau away to hunt game. Rebekah takes Jacob aside and tells him to take two goat kids, which she will prepare for Isaac. Bring them to your father, she says, and then he will give you the blessing before he dies.

Jacob is skeptical and reluctant to participate. Not that he has great moral scruples or serious reservations about tricking his father; rather, he is fearful of being caught and cursed.

The next twelve lines (Gen 27:18–29) are crucial to the narrative. They indicate that Isaac is the coauthor of the ruse, both a willing and a witting participant in the deception.

Six times, Isaac challenges who is *really* standing before him. Why does Isaac keep pressing the issue? He wants to raise the stakes for Jacob. He wants this younger son truly enmeshed in what Jacob is doing.

In verse 18 Jacob merely says, "My father," before Isaac says, "Here I am, who are you, my son?" That Isaac even raises the question is suspicious. From verse 22 below ("The voice is Jacob's voice, but the hands are the hands of Esau"), it is clear that Isaac can distinguish between the voices of his sons. As we follow their conversation, it is evident that Isaac is putting his son through an ordeal, but then in the end he blesses Jacob.

Soon Esau returns and asks Isaac for the promised blessing. It is a strangely poignant moment. When Esau identifies himself, the Torah explains that "Isaac trembled violently" (vs. 33).

Isaac trembles because this has been a difficult burden to carry. He, Isaac, has to act a role, that of a doddering old man. It is an affront to his dignity, though he knows that the ends justify the means. Isaac has "succeeded," but the inner turmoil and tension take its toll on the old man. Isaac trembles a violent trembling, in sadness and in sorrow. Commentators on Genesis 27, Jewish and non-Jewish alike, are troubled by the moral problems posed by the blessing of Jacob. In the rabbinic era, many a midrash is devoted to placing Jacob's dark acts in a brighter light.[50] The Torah text, the received tradition, is less bothered by these incidents. There is a clear line to follow, and the ancestors (patriarchs and matriarchs alike) follow it. For them, it is the correct choice. They understand that children have different strengths and different (directed) destinies. Jacob's destiny was to become the third patriarch, the person who would, in time, become Israel, father of the twelve tribes. Had he remained living among the tents, this would never have come about. Jacob needs to mature, to grow. Only through this painful rite of passage would he make his way in the world. Jacob's growth required a betrayal of faith, deception, and exile. In Genesis 27, Isaac and Rebekah make difficult decisions, but their choices guarantee the continuation of the covenant.

Notes

1. In medieval manuscripts, Genesis is referred to as the *Sefer Beri'at ha-'Olam* (the book of the creation of the world). (Nahum M. Sarna, *The JPS Torah Commentary: Genesis* [Philadelphia: Jewish Publication Society, 1989], xi).

2. Susan Niditch, "Genesis," in *The Women's Bible Commentary*, ed. Carol A. Newsom and Sharon H. Ringe (London: SPCK; Louisville, KY: Westminster John Knox, 1992), 25.

3. Israel Abrahams, "Numbers, Typical and Important," in *Encyclopedia Judaica* (Jerusalem: Keter, 1972), 12:1257.

4. Slightly adapted from Everett Fox, *The Schocken Bible, Volume I. The Five Books of Moses*, trans. Everett Fox (New York: Schocken, 1995), 1:3–4.

5. Nahum M. Sarna, "Genesis, Book of," in *Encyclopedia Judaica*, 7:391–92.

6. Slightly adapted from Fox, *Schocken Bible, Volume I*, 5–6. There are other ways to divide Genesis. E. A. Speiser, *Genesis, Anchor Bible* (Garden City, NY: Doubleday, 1964); Gerhard von Rad, *Genesis: A Commentary*, rev. ed. (Philadelphia: Westminster, 1972); and Lawrence

Boadt (*Reading the Old Testament: An Introduction* [Mahwah, NJ: Paulist, 1984], 110) suggest two major sections: biblical primeval history, chapters 1–11; and biblical patriarchal history, chapters 12–50. William Hallo notes that Genesis can be divided into three parts: (1) primeval history: chapters 1–11, a mythological tradition shared with Mesopotamia; (2) patriarchal [/matriarchal] tales: chapters 12–36; nonhistorical genre-pieces intended to convey the essence of a variety of local traditions associated with shrines and other "sites and sights" of Syria and Palestine; and (3) the story of Joseph: chapters 37–50, an essential link between the patriarchs and the Exodus, an elaborate novella with an ostensible Egyptian setting and background. See William W. Hallo, "Exodus and Ancient Near Eastern Literature," in *The Torah: A Modern Commentary,* ed. W. Gunther Plaut (New York: Union of American Hebrew Congregations, 1981), 367. While Nahum M. Sarna follows the two-part division, he further divides what he terms *Universal History* into two subsections: (1) Creation: from Adam to Noah (Gen 1:1—6:4) and then (2) from Noah to Abraham (Gen 6:5—11:32). See Nahum M. Sarna, "Genesis, Book of," in *Encyclopedia Judaica,* 7:387.

7. James King West, *Introduction to the Old Testament,* 2nd ed. (New York: Macmillan, 1981), 80. For a full explanation, see Umberto Cassuto, *A Commentary on the Book of Genesis, Part One* (Jerusalem: Magnes, 1978), 42.

8. Coincidentally, the rabbis point out that Noah is not labeled "blameless," but merely blameless in relation to his contemporaries. Some argue that in an age with less violence, he would not have stood out. Others argue that if he had the courage to stand out in that generation, how much more he would have been a moral leader in a more beneficent time. See Babylonian Talmud *Sanhedrin* 108a; cf. *Midrash Tanhuma, Genesis,* S. Buber Recension, trans. John T. Townsend (Hoboken, NJ: Ktav, 1989); *Noah* 2.2 Genesis 6:9ff., part II; 2.6 Genesis 6:9ff., part VI.

9. According to many scholars, the J version is found in 6:5–6; 7:1–4, 10, 12; 8:8–12, 20–22. The P version is found in 6:12–13, 14, 20; 7:11, 24; 8:3, 7, 13, 18–19; 9:1–17 (see Plaut, *The Torah: A Modern Commentary,* 62–63). In this scheme, J, who favors the number seven, speaks of seven pairs of clean animals and one pair of unclean animals (7:2ff.). The flood lasts forty days and nights (7:12), and Noah waits seven days between sending out the various birds (8:10ff.). P, on the other hand, always refers to two of each animal (6:20), and the flood lasts for 150 days (7:24; 8:3). The rainbow is a sign from the P source.

10. E. A. Speiser, *Genesis,* Anchor Bible (New York: Doubleday, 1964), 74ff., cf. Sarna, *JPS: Genesis,* 82.

11. In the second rendition of this motif, Abram explains that Sarai is his (half-)sister, "She is indeed my sister, the daughter of my father but not the daughter of my mother" (Gen 20:12).

12. Speiser, *Genesis,* 119ff.; Nahum M. Sarna, *Understanding Genesis* (New York: Schocken, 1970), 127f.

13. The midrash suggests that Hagar is none other than Pharaoh's daughter, a gift from that ruler when Abram and Sarai dwelled in Egypt (*Midrash Genesis Rabbah* 45.1).

14. The rabbis offered the opinion that with her change of name from Sarai to Sarah her barrenness came to an end, but this clearly is a homiletic, not a medical explanation (*Midrash Genesis Rabbah* 47.2).

15. Though unprecedented and unrivaled, Abraham's debate with the divine does set precedent. See Anson Laytner, *Arguing with God: A Jewish Tradition* (Northvale, NJ, and London: Jason Aronson, 1990); for a discussion of this biblical event, see Sarna, *JPS: Genesis,* 132f.

16. See David J. Zucker, "Betrayal (and Growth) in Genesis 22," *CCAR Journal* 46, 1999.

17. Sarna, *Understanding Genesis,* 184.

18. Plaut, *Torah,* 190.

19. Von Rad, *Genesis,* 273.

20. Speiser, *Genesis,* 250.

21. Sarna, *JPS: Genesis,* 216, n. 7.

22. Von Rad, *Genesis,* 309.

23. Speiser, *Genesis,* 315.

24. Fox, *The Schocken Bible,* I, 4.

25. Ramsey, "The Authority of the Bible," 3.

26. *Midrash Genesis Rabbah* 9.7.

27. Ibid., 12.15.

28. Babylonian Talmud *Sanhedrin* 39a.

29. *Midrash Genesis Rabbah* 22.6; *Sifre Deuteronomy, Piska* 45.

30. *The Midrash on Psalms,* ed. William G. Braude (New Haven and London: Yale University, 1987), Ps. 119:64.

31. *Midrash Genesis Rabbah* 34.8; Babylonian Talmud *Sanhedrin* 56a–b; Babylonian Talmud *Hullin* 92a.

32. *Midrash Genesis Rabbah* 28.2.

33. *Pirke de Rabbi Eliezer,* trans. Gerald Friedlander (New York: Sepher-Hermon, 1981), chapter 23.

34. *Midrash Genesis Rabbah* 30.7.

35. *Pesikta Rabbati, Discourses for Feasts, Fasts and Special Sabbaths,* trans. William G. Braude (New Haven and London: Yale University Press, 1968), *Pesikta* 43.2.

36. *Avot de Rabbi Natan: The Fathers According to Rabbi Nathan,* trans. Judah Goldin (New York: Schocken, 1974), chapter 33; with variant explanations in *Pirke de Rabbi Eliezer,* chapters 26–31.

37. *Midrash Genesis Rabbah* 49.6.

38. Ibid.; *Pirke de Rabbi Eliezer,* chapters 14, 39, 40, 41.

39. *Midrash Genesis Rabbah* 50.2.

40. Ibid., 68.12.

41. Ibid., 69.7.

42. *Etz Hayim: Torah and Commentary,* ed. David L. Lieber (New York: Rabbinical Assembly, United Synagogue of Conservative Judaism, 2001), 310.

43. Phyllis Trible, "Depatriarchalizing in Biblical Interpretation," *Journal of the American Academy of Religion* 41 (1973): 37.

44. Speiser, *Genesis,* 126.

45. Ibid., xxvii.

46. *Pirke De Rabbi Eliezer,* chapter 30, beginning.

47. *Midrash Genesis Rabbah* 53.11. See also *Midrash Exodus Rabbah* 1.1; *Tosefta Sotah* 6.6; *Pirke de Rabbi Eliezer,* chapter 30. The Christian scriptures promote the notion that Ishmael persecuted Isaac. See Gal 4:21—5:1, esp. vs. 29. For a different view, that the *metzaheq* issue centers on a religious/idolatry controversy related to circumcision as an Egyptian rite, see Savina J. Teubal, *Sarah the Priestess: The First Matriarch of Genesis* (Athens: Swallow/Ohio University, 1984), 37–41.

48. See David J. Zucker, "Conflicting Conclusions: The Hatred of Isaac and Ishmael," *Judaism* 39 (1990).

49. See David J. Zucker, "Rescuing Rebecca's Reputation: A Midrash on Genesis 27," *CCAR Journal* 48 (2001), and "A Still Stranger Stratagem: Revisiting Genesis 27," *Conservative Judaism* 56 (2004).

50. See the references in David J. Zucker, "Jacob in Darkness (and Light): A Study in Contrasts," *Judaism* 35 (1986).

Exodus

1. INTRODUCTION

The second book of the Torah, Exodus, derives its English title from the Latin version. Earlier, in the Greek translation, it was called *Exodus Aigyptous*. The Hebrew designations were variously *Eleh Sh'mot* ("These are the names," from the opening words of the book itself), or in abbreviated form, *Sh'mot* ("Names").[1]

The essential message of the Book of Exodus is God's redemption of the Israelite[2] people from slavery. God's redemptive act is at the heart of Judaism, and, by extension, at the heart of Christianity and Islam. There are many important lessons in the Book of Exodus; and redemption is not its sole theme, but it is at its center. The Exodus from Egypt arguably is the most crucial event in the Bible. All biblical history resonates with it and the experiences that are associated with the Exodus. The last third of Genesis serves as a prologue that leads to the clans of Jacob moving into Egypt. Early on in the Book of Exodus the Israelites are enslaved. They will serve Pharaoh for many generations until eventually they are liberated by God. The story features Moses as God's human agent. From the Exodus experience flows the covenant with God, the presentation of the Ten Commandments, the journey in the wilderness, and the eventual capture and settlement of the Land of Israel, promised to the patriarchs and the matriarchs.

The Book of Exodus is part narrative, part legislation. Some forty chapters in length, it contains many images and phrases that are woven into the fabric of Western religion and Western civilization itself. There is, of course, the broad image of moving from slavery to freedom, and then specifically the Israelite Exodus from Egyptian servitude. Other images or concepts found or introduced

71

in the Book of Exodus include the following: The Ten Commandments; the Sabbath; the ark of the covenant; and the episode of the golden calf. Further, there is the cry to "let my people go"; the cherubim/angels; the burning bush; manna; the whole image of Moses ascending Mt. Sinai; and the journey toward the Promised Land.

Short of the monarchy itself, which will be introduced in Deuteronomy (17:14ff.), all of the main institutions of biblical Israel are found in the Book of Exodus. God speaks to Israel via prophets and priests; there is a group consecrated to God's service, the Levites; there is a set sanctuary with specific forms of worship, which include daily sacrifices as well as annual rituals; and finally there is God's covenant with Israel.

Themes in Exodus

Exodus features three major themes: biography, history, and legislation.[3]

Biography

The book begins with a section of biography, which focuses on the birth and early days of Moses. This makes perfect sense, for so much of the Book of Genesis, which preceded Exodus, relates the biographies of the patriarchs and matriarchs, concluding with the family of Jacob settling in Egypt. Exodus literally begins with a recapitulation of the family's descent to Egypt.[4] After noting that the family was very fertile, chapter 1 then sets the stage for the family's decline in status: "Now a new king arose over Egypt, who did not know Joseph" (Exod 1:8). This new ruler distrusts the Israelites because they are not of Egyptian stock. He is fearful they might join up with Egypt's enemies; the pharaoh enslaves them, setting ruthless taskmasters over them. Chapter 2 begins with the birth of Moses and his near-miraculous escape from death during his infancy.

History

The Book of Exodus makes a significant shift when Moses takes on the role of God's agent, the leader who will bring about the release of the Israelites from Egyptian bondage.⁵ "When Moses assumes the divinely assigned leadership role, the focus of the narrative shifts from the development of an individual to the birth of a nation or, in literary terms, from the level of biography to that of history."⁶ Using this criterion, the historical section of Exodus begins in chapter 3 and continues through chapter 24. This takes the reader from Moses' commission through his confrontation with Pharaoh; the details of the ten plagues; the crossing of the sea; Moses on Mt. Sinai; the Ten Commandments; and the Covenant Code and its ratification (chapters 20 [or 21]–24).

Legislation

The rest of the Book of Exodus deals primarily with various kinds of legislation, much of which focuses on the ritual and cultic life of ancient Israel. It features the description of the building of various items, including the ark of the covenant, the tent of meeting, the lampstand (menorah), the table, and the altar of burnt offering. Very broadly, these items are referred to as the tabernacle° (chapters 25–40). It also covers the legislation that sets up the priesthood in charge of these ritual items. Specifically Aaron, Moses' older brother, and also Aaron's descendants are to be ordained as the priesthood, and the rest of the tribe of Levi (the Levites) will serve as assistants to these priests. Much of this sacred furniture and the legislation reflect the later Jerusalem Temple and its religious ceremonies. The instructions for building the sacred furniture are found in chapters 24–31. Chapters 35–40 describe the carrying out of these instructions. Chapter 32 centers on the episode of the golden calf, and chapters 33–34 deal with the "replacement" of the Ten Commandments and Moses' direct encounter with God.

God's Roles in the Book of Exodus

Judaism speaks of God's three major aspects or roles in the Bible: God as creator; God as redeemer; and God as revealer. The second and third descriptions are easily demonstrable in Exodus, but, as shall be shown below, a case also can be made for the first aspect/role.

God as Creator

While the opening chapters of Genesis are the standard example of God as creator, the *historical* section of Exodus, explained above, suggests God's strong involvement in the creation of the Israelite nation. God calls upon Moses to go to Egypt to rescue his kin from Egyptian oppression. God explains, "I have observed the misery of *my people* who are in Egypt; I have heard their cry...and I have come down to deliver them from the Egyptians, and to bring them out of that land to a good and broad land, a land flowing with milk and honey....I will send you to Pharaoh to bring *my people,* the Israelites, out of Egypt" (Exod 3:7ff.).

God's claim of Israel as special, as uniquely "my people," or Israel described as "his people" appears throughout the Jewish Bible, in the Torah as well as in the Prophets and the Writings.[7]

God as Redeemer

The theme of God as redeemer pervades the first half of Exodus and will resonate throughout the Bible and subsequent Jewish literature, sacred and secular. Moses' commission states clearly that God fully intends to rescue Israel from the dire straits of Egyptian slavery and degradation. At that initial encounter between Moses and God, the deity makes it clear that God is absolutely committed to the redemption of Israel. While Moses' role is to organize the people and then to entreat the pharaoh to release the Israelites, it is clear from the outset that a mere human's voice is not going to carry the day. God says to Moses, "I know, however, that the king of Egypt will not let you go unless compelled by a mighty hand. So I will stretch out my hand and strike Egypt with all my wonders that I will perform in it; after that he will let you go" (Exod 3:19f.).

God as Revealer

God's revelation of the Torah at Mt. Sinai is the third major theme of the Book of Exodus, and, along with creation and redemption, provides the key images of God in the Bible. God's revelation—and the subsequent contractual relationship with Israel—is the answer to two salient questions: why did God create Israel as a nation, and why did God redeem Israel from slavery?

Following the escape from Egypt's borders, when the people are standing at Mt. Sinai, God elaborates on the unique relationship with Israel. God introduces a new dimension; there is to be a covenant between God and Israel.[8] God has chosen and formed this nation, and they are to have a special purpose. They are forming a contractual connection. God instructs Moses about Israel's destiny. "Thus you shall say to the house of Jacob, and tell the Israelites:...if you obey my voice and keep my covenant, you shall be my treasured possession out of all the peoples. Indeed, the whole earth is mine, but you shall be for me a priestly kingdom and a holy nation" (Exod 19:3–6).

God, who is holiness, expects holiness from Israel. "You shall be holy to me; for I the LORD am holy, and I have separated you from the other peoples to be mine" (Lev 20:26; cf. Lev 11:44–45). Likewise in Deuteronomy, "For you are a people holy to the LORD your God; it is you the LORD has chosen out of all the peoples on earth to be his people, his treasured possession" (Deut 14:2).

The covenantal connection with God is expressed in the Ten Commandments (see Text Study at the end of this chapter, "The Ten Commandments"). Yet, the special connection with God is more than just the gift on Ten Commandments; it is contained within the wider relationship between God and Israel.

Initially God's revelation, this Torah, this Teaching, this instruction given on Mt. Sinai, is for the people of Israel alone. Israel receives God's word and over time Israel will learn what it means to be a priestly kingdom and a holy nation.

The covenant with Israel is eternal and ongoing, but God's teaching has a wider application. Though the understanding of the universality of God's message will not come for several hundred years, eventually it will be articulated, notably by the prophet known as Second Isaiah. It is he who speaks the lines, "It is too light a thing that you should be my servant to raise up the tribes of Jacob and to restore the survivors of Israel; I will give you as a light to the nations, that my salvation may reach to the end of the earth" (Isa 49:6).[9]

It is possible to believe that God's revelation was given to the Jewish people, that God formed the Jewish people to be God's chosen, but that God also has covenants with other peoples.[10]

2. IS EXODUS "REAL" HISTORY?

To date, archaeologists have found no material that independently mentions that a group of slaves, under the leadership of Moses, successfully was able to escape from Egyptian bondage. The actual date for the Exodus is shrouded in the mists of history, but a commonly held view sets it during the decades between 1290 and 1250 BCE. That there is no empirical proof, no irrefutable objective evidence, is not surprising. In all likelihood, this was not newsworthy, as far as the Egyptians were concerned. A small group of slaves had escaped into the desert. In addition, the Egyptians were loath to catalog setbacks on their part, even if this was but a minor event in their long history.

In the absence of archaeological or scientific evidence, can we say that this is history as in the common use of that term? The absence of proof does not mean the proof of absence. Though it is correct that there is no *outside* evidence to *prove irrefutably* that these events took place, for thousands of years they have been accepted as part of the religious tradition of the three major Western faiths. This story has the strong feel of historical events. Yet, even in the absence of documentary or archeological proof, it does not change the fact that the nation was formed at some point and acted on its belief about the incidents portrayed in Exodus. Further, there are compelling arguments in favor of accepting these events as truth.

> Although there is no direct witness in Egyptian records to Israel's presence in Egypt, the Biblical tradition a priori demands belief: it is not the sort of tradition any people would invent! Here is no heroic epic of migration, but the recollection of shameful servitude from which only the power of God brought deliverance. A number of factors lend objective support. Egyptian names prevalent in early Israel, especially in the tribe of Levi, certainly argue for a connection with Egypt. Among these are those of Moses himself, Hophni, Phineas, Merari, and possibly Aaron among others....
>
> Of the exodus itself we have no extra-Biblical evidence. But the Bible's own witness is itself so impressive as to leave little

doubt that some such remarkable deliverance took place. Israel remembered the exodus for all time to come as the constitutive event that called her into being as a people. It stood at the center of her confession of faith from the beginning, as is witnessed by certain ancient poems (Ex. 15:1–18) and credos (Deut. 6:20–25; 26:5–10; Josh. 24:2–13) that go back to the earliest part of her history.[11]

In support of his thesis, John Bright notes that the narrative in Exodus remembers a shameful servitude in Egypt from which only the power of God brought deliverance. He also mentions how this was not a heroic migration. The people continuously complained to Moses and yearned to return to the life they knew in Egypt (Exod 16:2–3; 17:1ff.; Num 20:2–5). This was not their finest hour. Following the miracle at the sea, the people were washed out of Egypt. It was harder to wash Egypt out of the people.

How Many People Left Egypt?

How many people left Egypt? Was it a small group or were there many thousands who traveled with Moses? The Book of Exodus states that the "Israelites journeyed from Rameses to Succoth, about six hundred *thousand* men on foot, besides children" (Exod 12:37). The Hebrew word used there for "thousand" is *elef*. This word, in some contexts, can mean thousand, but likewise it might mean "contingent," or "clan." Indeed, sometimes *elef* could mean contingent, clan, *or* thousand.[12] The problems surrounding 600,000 men, plus women and children, present an intractable difficulty: the Israelite population then would be well over two million people. Theoretically it is possible that seventy men (the number of the adult males in the tribes/clans who descended to Egypt at the time of Joseph) might over a period of 430 years (the traditional time given for the sojourn in Egypt [Exod 12:40]) increase to the figure of over two million. What is not possible to reconcile is that the total population of Egypt at this time is reckoned at less than five million. Further, the logistics of moving, communicating with, and organizing, much less sustaining, two million people *in the desert* is patently insurmountable. Two million people could not easily be moved in modern times without a massive support system, which requires a number many times that size. So, if not two million, then how many? If Exodus 12:37 should essentially be translated as the "Israelites journeyed from Rameses to Succoth, about six hundred *clans* on foot, besides children," then the more believable number might come up to three to five thousand people, a figure that can be organized and sustained in the desert, and moved with relative ease.[13]

Another question is the location of Mt. Sinai. A number of locales have been suggested for this venue, with no definitive answers.[14]

Documentary Sources

The Book of Exodus, like that of Genesis, is composed of various sources; those that refer to God by the Hebrew letters *Yud-Hey-Vav-Hey* (**J**), and those that address the deity with the name *Elohim* (**E**). In addition, there are sections attributed to the Priestly sources (**P**). Exodus, according to scholars who debate these issues, is quite a mixture of all of these sources. P dominates chapters 25–31 and 35–40, which essentially deal with the ritual matters of the tabernacle. P is also found elsewhere.[15]

3. SLAVERY-LIBERATION-REVELATION: EXODUS 1–20

Chapter 1 recounts the settlement of the Israelites in Egypt. Their number is listed as seventy people. Fertile and prolific, "the land was filled with them" (vs. 7). Disaster soon strikes: "Now, a new king arose over Egypt who did not know Joseph" (vs. 8). The Israelites are perceived as a threat to this dynasty, and so they are enslaved, forced to build "supply cities, Pithom and Rameses, for Pharaoh " (vs. 11). The threat to Israel escalates as Pharaoh tries to have all newly born male children killed.

Two women are noted briefly, the midwives Shiphrah and Puah, in Exodus 1:15–22. Some other women are mentioned surrounding Moses' birth, but, at that point, they are anonymous.

Chapter 2 describes the birth and early years of Moses. After he is born his mother seeks to protect him, but she can only hide him for three months. She then constructs a wicker basket and places him along the banks of the Nile, enlisting his sister to watch over him. No one less than the pharaoh's daughter finds the child, and she discerns his origins. His sister appears and volunteers to find a wet nurse for the boy. After he is weaned he is brought to the pharaoh's daughter, who adopts him and then names the child Moses (in Hebrew *Mosheh*), which is connected with the "Hebrew *m-sh-h*, 'to draw up/out (of water).'"[16]

Presumably reared in the Egyptian court, one day as an adult he goes to visit his kin and witnesses their labors. Seeing an Egyptian beating a Hebrew, Moses intervenes and strikes the oppressor. Moses kills him and buries him in the sand. The next day Moses revisits the area and sees two Hebrews fighting. When he questions their action, one of the men reprimands Moses, making it clear that his crime is known. Fearful for his life, Moses immediately flees Egypt and heads eastward to the land of Midian.

There he meets and marries Zipporah, the daughter of a Midian priest, and begins his family. The chapter ends with a post-script: Pharaoh dies; the Israelites cry out in their bondage; and God looks down upon the Israelites and takes notice of them.

Chapter 3 features Moses' commission. One day when pasturing the flocks he ventures westward toward the wilderness and comes to "Horeb, the mountain of God." An angel appears to him in a flame of fire in a bush, though the bush remains undamaged. When Moses approaches, God addresses Moses, explaining that this is holy ground. God identifies himself as the God of Abraham, the God of Isaac, and the God of Jacob. God then informs Moses that great changes are going to occur: Moses is going back to Egypt. He will act as God's agent to rescue the Israelites from bondage, with the intent of bringing them to a land flowing with milk and honey (vss. 8–10). Moses seeks to know God's name, and he is told, "I AM WHO I AM....This is my name forever, and my title for all generations" (Exod 3:14–15). Even as he asks about God's name, Moses voices doubts about this mission. God is insistent but acknowledges that this will be difficult. "I know, however, that the king of Egypt will not let you go unless compelled by a mighty hand. So I will stretch out my hand and strike Egypt with all my wonders that I will perform in it; after that he will let you go" (vss. 19–20).

Chapter 4 finds Moses still demurring, but to no avail. When Moses objects for the fifth time, in verse 13, God finally gets angry and says, your brother Aaron will meet you. He speaks fluently, and he can be the spokesperson. Moses takes leave of his father-in-law and, accompanied by his wife and children, travels to Egypt. Along the way, he meets Aaron. The chapter concludes with Moses and Aaron conferring with the elders of the Israelites and informing the people that God has remembered them.

Chapter 5 describes Moses and Aaron's initial encounter with the pharaoh. The well-known line "Let my people go" is immediately followed by Pharaoh's reply: "Who is the LORD, that I should heed him and let Israel go? I do not know the LORD, and I will not let Israel go" (Exod 5:1–2). Moses and Aaron insist that they are to take their kindred three days journey into the wilderness to sacrifice to God. Pharaoh is incredulous and takes out his anger on the Israelite slave population, demanding even more work from them. The people complain to Moses, who then turns to God and says, why have you placed me—and the people—in such an unfortunate position? This episode concludes as God says to Moses: wait and see what happens next! (Exod 6:1).

Chapter 6 begins with a restatement of much that appeared in chapters 3 and 4 (compare 3:1—4:17). God again states the divine name and the historical connections with the patriarchs, Abraham, Isaac, and Jacob. God promises to take the people and to bring them into the land promised to the ancestors. Exodus 6:14–25 is a subsection that breaks off the flow of the narrative. These verses are a genealogy that traces Moses' and Aaron's lineage to Levi, Jacob's son. The closing verses focus again on Aaron and Moses.

Chapter 7 continues the thread of chapter 6. God repeats the fact that Pharaoh will be obstinate and that God will perform signs and wonders in Egypt. In chapter 7, the first plague will afflict Egypt, the pollution of the Nile River. Moses performs this miracle in the sight of Pharaoh and his officials as they are standing by the Nile (vs. 20). Pharaoh's magicians, however, perform the same feat, and so Pharaoh turns his back and returns to his palace.

Chapter 8 initially details the second plague: frogs. Though Pharaoh's magicians again duplicate this plague, Pharaoh shortly capitulates, as he says (Exod 8:8 [8:4 H]), pray to God to take away the frogs for me and my people and I will let the people go. Though Moses does his part, Pharaoh reverses himself and hardens his heart. Moses retaliates with the third plague, that of gnats (vermin, or lice, vs. 16 [12 H]), but Pharaoh remains adamant. Plague four brings swarms of flies[17] to Egypt, and the ruler begs for relief, promising that the Israelites can depart for the wilderness to offer sacrifices to God. Only the area where the Israelites dwelled, Goshen, was exempted from the plague. Once the plague is over, however, again Pharaoh reneges.

Chapter 9 includes plagues five, six, and seven: pestilence (vss. 1–7), boils (vss. 8–12), and hail (vss. 13–35). The pattern is constant: Moses warns the pharaoh, but the Egyptian ruler refuses to let the people go. That the Israelites are excluded from these and subsequent plagues is either directly stated or inferred. In the midst of the hail Pharaoh summons Moses and Aaron and says, "This time I have sinned; the LORD is in the right and I and my people are in the wrong....Enough of God's thunder and hail! I will let you go" (Exod 9:27–28). Yet when the hail and thunder cease, he reverses himself again.

Chapter 10 features the eighth and ninth plagues, respectively locusts and a dense darkness. The chapter begins with God's words to Moses, "Go to Pharaoh; for I have hardened his heart and the heart of his officials, in order that I may show these signs of mine among them." This raises a difficult question. If God is stiffening or hardening Pharaoh's heart, making him more obstinate and obdurate, how can the monarch be held responsible for his actions in not letting the people go? With the first five plagues, Pharaoh made this decision on his own; only with the last five does divine causality apply. "This is the biblical way of asserting that the king's intransigence has by then become habitual and irreversible; his character has become his destiny. He is deprived of the possibility of relenting and is irresistibly impelled to his self-wrought doom."[18]

Chapter 11 announces the final, the tenth plague. Every first-born in Egypt will die, from Pharaoh's child to the child of the lowly slave, and the firstborn of the livestock as well. Only the Israelites will be spared this terrible punishment.

Suddenly the inexorable movement toward the final denouement with Pharaoh is interrupted by a description of the rites of the festival of Passover/*Pesach*. The first twenty-eight verses of chapter 12 leave the reader—and the Israelites—in suspense. It is a wonderfully dramatic moment.

The biblical traditions for the Passover/*Pesach* are set out: a lamb without blemish, whether a sheep or goat, is slaughtered and some of its blood is placed on the two doorposts and the lintel. Verse 13 explains that this blood serves to mark the Israelite houses, so that death will *pass over* these dwellings and they will be spared the plague that is coming to Egypt. The lamb is roasted and totally consumed that night.

In addition the Israelites are told to remove all leavening from their homes for seven days, and this will be known as the [festival of] Unleavened Bread (vs. 17). What probably are older nomadic shepherding and agricultural festivals involving respectively lambs and unleavened bread are combined to remember the miraculous escape from Egypt. The word *pass over/pasach* specifically is found in verse 27.[19]

With Exodus 12:29 the focus changes abruptly and moves from ritual to the drama of the unfolding narrative with Pharaoh and the Egyptians. The tenth plague has come. A loud cry goes throughout Egypt as death strikes, from the firstborn of Pharaoh to the firstborn of the prisoner in the dungeon, and the firstborn of livestock as well. Moses and Aaron are summoned, and Pharaoh capitulates a final time. "Rise up, go away from my people, both you and the Israelites! Go, worship the LORD, as you said. Take your flocks and your herds, as you said, and be gone" (Exod 12:31–32).

The early stages of the Exodus are recorded in verses 37ff. as the people journey from Rameses to Succoth. They bake unleavened bread, explains the text, because they did not have time to wait. Verses 43–51 return to some Passover ritual matters and then note this was the day that God freed the Israelites from Egypt.

Chapter 13 is a mixture of ritual and narrative. It deals with unleavened bread (*matza*, pl. *matzot*) and in verses 9–10, 16 touches on wearing phylacteries (*tefillin* in Hebrew).

Exodus 13:17 explains that God did not lead the people on the most direct route to the Promised Land, lest they run into opposition along the way. They were still untried and inexperienced in the ways of warfare, and they might panic and want to return to Egypt.

Chapter 14 details the miraculous events at the Sea of Reeds. Coincidentally, it *is* the Reed Sea, not the Red Sea, which is hundreds of miles away. The Hebrew is *yam suf,* Reed Sea (Exod 15:4, or Sea of Reeds, as a note in NRSV explains). God's redemptive powers were finely etched into the minds of the people. Reflecting the description found in Exodus 15, Psalm 66 explains, "Come and see what God has done: he is awesome in his deeds among mortals. He turned the sea into dry land; they passed through the river on foot. There we rejoiced in him, who rules by his might forever..." (Ps 66:5–7; cf. Josh 4:21–24; Isa 11:15–16; 51:9–11; Ps 114:1–3).

Initially they are told to circle back and encamp near Pi-hahiroth, not far from the sea. This is part of God's stratagem to wreak a final blow on Pharaoh. The Egyptian ruler will think that the Israelites are wandering aimlessly and that they are trapped in the wilderness. Pharaoh, accompanied by six hundred picked chariots and his army, gives chase. They soon catch up with the former slaves, who are then panicked. Would it not "have been better for us to serve the Egyptians than to die in the wilderness?" they ask Moses. Moses stills the people and tells them to watch what God is about to accomplish. Moses stretches his hand over the sea (vs. 21) as a strong east wind turns the water into dry land. The Israelites march through, even as the Egyptians are about to give chase. Then, when the Egyptian army is in the midst of this place, their chariot wheels become clogged and turn with difficulty. At dawn, Moses stretches his hand again, and the sea returns to its normal depth as the Egyptians drown in the waters (vss. 23ff.). The chapter ends on a note of triumph; the people fear and believe in God and in God's servant Moses.

Chapter 15 contains two songs or poems of praise, that of Moses (vss. 1–19) and that of Miriam (vss. 20–21). The songs celebrate God and the victory over the Egyptians. God is portrayed as a mighty warrior, battling the sea, an image that will be repeated in the Psalms (Ps 78:12f.; 77:16ff. [77:17ff. H]).

The words "Who is like you, O LORD, among the gods? Who is like you, majestic in holiness, awesome in splendor, doing wonders?" and "The LORD will reign forever and ever" (Exod 15:11, 18) are part of the daily Jewish liturgy.

Mention of Miriam at her triumphant dance and her song is the first time that Moses and Aaron's sister is named;[20] earlier (chapter 2) she was anonymous.

Miriam is titled a prophet at her appearance at the splitting of the sea (Exod 15:20). "Miriam's association with the Song at the Sea challenges several stereotypes about women in ancient Israel. It conveys an image of women as singers of war songs, which is supported by other biblical texts (Judges 5 [Deborah]; 1 Sam. 2:1–10 [Hannah])." Though references to Miriam are limited, at least in Numbers 12:2 and Micah 6:4 she "is grouped with Moses and Aaron in such a way as to suggest that the three of them formed a leadership triad."[21]

Chapter 16 finds the Israelites in the second month of their journey. They are heading toward the Wilderness of Sin, probably on the Sinai Peninsula. Again they start to murmur against Moses and his leadership, a theme that repeats itself with alarming frequency. Even before Moses can answer this accusation, God replies that bread will rain down from heaven. The next morning a layer of dew surrounds the camp, and when the dew lifts there is a "fine flaky substance, as fine as frost on the ground" (vs. 14). "When the Israelites saw it, they said one to another, 'What is it?' For they did not know what it was. Moses said to them, 'It is the bread that the LORD has given you to eat'" (Exod 16:15). In Hebrew, "What is it?" is *man hu,* which becomes the origin of the word *manna* (see vs. 31). The chapter closes with a note that the Israelites ate manna throughout their desert wandering.

Chapter 17 records some further travels; some more Israelite complaints, now about the lack of water; and the battle with the fierce desert tribe, the Amalekites. Joshua is mentioned for the first time toward the end of this chapter. At the conclusion of the forty years, he will become Moses' successor.

Chapter 18 features the return of Moses' father-in-law, here called Jethro. He is bringing Moses' wife and two sons with him.

Moses reports to Jethro all that happened in Egypt and God's triumph over Pharaoh.

The next day Moses turns to his duties as judge for the people. This takes a great deal of time, and there are long lines. Jethro chides Moses, suggesting that this wears out the people more than it is of help. It is also wearying on Moses. For the people's sake, as much as for his, he needs to find good people to help him. Moses takes his advice and leaves only the hard cases for himself. At the chapter's close, Jethro returns to his own country.

Chapter 19 commences as the Israelites come to the Wilderness of Sinai. It is now the third month. They are about to receive the Ten Commandments.

Up to this point, Israel's role has been passive. They benefited from God's acts, and very little has been asked of them. God sent Moses, and through Moses confronted Pharaoh. God brought plagues to the Egyptians. God hardened Pharaoh's heart and coerced him to let the Israelites leave. God created the miracle at the sea. God provided food for the people in the wilderness. Now things are about to change. Israel is going to learn that it has a reciprocal relationship with God, each side has obligations toward the other.

> The liberated multitude of erstwhile slaves must be united not only by a vital sense of a shared tragedy and a common experience of emancipation, but even more by bonds of perceived ideals—a vision of a new order of life, namely, the establishment of an essentially different kind of society from what had hitherto existed.
>
> The precondition for the fulfillment of this goal, indeed its instrumentality, is to be the forging of a special relationship between God and Israel. This relationship is to be sealed by a covenant.[22]

Standing before Mt. Sinai, the people are to consecrate themselves for three days. God says, "Now therefore, if you obey my voice and keep my covenant, you shall be my treasured possession...you shall be for me a priestly kingdom and a holy nation" (Exod 19:5–6). On the morning of the third day thunder and lightning as well as a thick cloud can be seen. The mountain itself is wrapped in smoke and shakes violently (vs. 18). Moses goes up to the top of the mountain and begins his dialogue there with God.

Chapter 20 commences as Moses reports the Ten Commandments to the people. See Text Study at the end of the chapter, "The Ten Commandments."

4. LEGISLATION: EXODUS 21–40

Chapter 21 and the next two or three chapters contain legislation that is called the Covenant Code.[23] That designation, or its alternative, the Book of the Covenant, is based on Exodus 24:4, 7. The chapter begins with laws affecting a male Hebrew (probably a euphemism for fellow Israelite) slave (vss. 2–6). This is followed by material dealing with the female slave (vss. 7–11). Verses 12–17 cover several capital offenses, and then come matters of bodily injury caused by humans. This section includes the well-known words, "eye for eye, tooth for tooth" (vs. 24). For a discussion of this material, see the chapter on the Book of Numbers, specifically the section "The Laws of Retaliation/*Lex Talionis*." The concluding verses of the chapter concern deaths caused by an animal (vss. 28–32) and laws pertaining to carelessness affecting animals (vss. 33–36).

Chapter 22 covers a variety of issues. "Laws dealing with property" is a wide category that Exodus 21:33—22:17 (22:16 H) addresses. Carelessness, theft, and then cases of trusteeship are found in here.

The rest of chapter 22 and the opening verses of chapter 23 include different kinds of provisions: social, ethical, moral, and religious (Exod 22:18—23:19 [22:17 H—23:19]). Among the legislation are matters of apostasy; concern for the strangers, widows, and orphans; and the poor in general. "The exploitation of these unfortunates was so tempting, and apparently so widespread and seemingly beyond the reach of the law, that the Torah…[emphasizes] the gravity of the sin in the sight of God…[who] champions the cause of the downtrodden."[24] (See also the chapter on Deuteronomy, "Themes in Deuteronomy—Humanitarian values.")

Chapter 23 commences with statements that people are to shun false reports, and they are to avoid joining the majority to do wrong. Justice is not to be perverted, and care must be shown animals belonging to your enemy. The land is to lie fallow in the seventh year, though the poor and wild beasts have a right to eat of the food therein. Work six days a week, but then comes a day of rest for the household, including animals. Verses 14–19a deal with religious agricultural matters. The last part of verse 19, "You shall not boil a kid in its mother's milk" (cf. Exod 34:26; Deut 14:21), remains enigmatic. It does become the basis for the rabbinic tradition of a separation between milk and meat products.[25]

The chapter concludes (vss. 20–33) with God explaining that an angel will be sent before the Israelites, whose function it will be to help the people conquer the Promised Land. They are told to obey the angel/messenger, and when they get to the land, they are utterly to demolish the sacred sites of the local inhabitants. The conquest of the land will be gradual.

Chapter 24 deals with the ratification of the Covenant Code. After Moses explains the code to the people, they reply (vs. 3), "All the words that the LORD has spoken we will do." Moses then writes down the code (vs. 4), and, following a sacrifice, Moses reads the Book of the Covenant (vs. 7); and the people reaffirm their commitment.

The next six chapters (25–31) find Moses on Mt. Sinai, a fact mentioned at the close of chapter 24. He will be there for forty days and nights.

In chapter 25, Moses begins to receive the instructions for the tabernacle. It will be a mobile sanctuary, which serves as the place where God will address Moses, and where various offerings will be brought. For a discussion about the ark and the tabernacle, see below, the Text Study "The Ark and the Tabernacle." The opening verses discuss materials to be used: gold, silver, and bronze (other translations, copper), various colored threads, different animal skins, as well as wood, oil, spices, and precious stones. Verse 16 explains that the "covenant," that is the Ten Commandments, are to be placed in the ark. That is the ark's sole function. The mercy seat (*qapporet/kapporet* in Hebrew) serves as a cover above the ark (vss. 17, 21), and at either end of this cover sit cherubim facing each other (vss. 18ff.). See Text Study in the chapter on the Book of Numbers, "The Cherubim." The cherubim, with wings outstretched toward one another, serve as a support for the invisible throne of God. It is there that God will address Moses once the ark is built (vs. 22; see also Exod 29:42). The seven-branched lampstand (Hebrew, *menorah*) is described in verses. 31–40.

Chapter 26 provides directions for various curtains associated with the tabernacle, with specific size and color, and decorated with images of cherubim.

Chapter 27: The altar is made of acacia wood, square in shape, about 7.5 feet x 7.5 feet, and it is 4.5 feet high (5 cubits x 5 cubits, 3 cubits high; roughly 2.3 meters x 2.3 meters, and 1.35 meters high). There are horns on the four corners, overlaid with bronze (some translations, copper). Verses 9–19 describe the enclosure for the tabernacle. Olive oil is used for lighting.

Chapter 28: Vestments for the high priest, with special attire or insignia including a breastpiece, an ephod (perhaps a kind of apron), a robe, a checkered tunic, a turban, and a sash are described. Verses 15ff. explain the high priest's breastpiece of judgment (NJPS, breastpiece of decision); and verse 30 makes specific mention of the *Urim* and *Thummim,* which were used for some form of predictive purposes. See Text Study below, "The *Urim* and *Thummim:* Device for Discerning God's Will."

Chapter 29 concentrates on the service for the ordination or installation of the priesthood, namely, for Aaron and his sons. The ritual is elaborate and involves animal sacrifices. It takes place over a seven-day period (vs. 35).

Chapter 30 features supplementary materials, including the taking of a census (vs. 11ff.). For a discussion about the implications of census taking, see the chapter on the Book of Numbers, "The Census." Other items mentioned include the bronze washstand/laver and various oils and kinds of spices and incense to be used for the sacrifices. It is for priestly use only (vs. 33.).

Chapter 31 mentions that Bezalel, son of Uri, son of Hur, of the tribe of Judah, is specially appointed by God, for he has ability, intelligence, and knowledge of every kind of craft. He will be assisted by Oholiab, son of Ahisamach of the tribe of Dan, who possesses similar skills. They will build or supervise the building of the various cultic objects. Beginning in verse 12 the Israelites are told again the importance of observing the Sabbath; it is a covenant for all time and a special sign between Israel and God.

Chapters 32–34 break up the flow of the instructions for the ritual objects for the tabernacle.

Chapter 32 begins with ominous words. "When the people saw that Moses delayed to come down from the mountain, the people gathered around Aaron, and said to him, 'Come, make gods for us, who shall go before us; as for this Moses, the man who brought us out of the land of Egypt, we do not know what has become of him.'"[26] Aaron's actions here are difficult to explain. In the event he capitulates to the people's demands and creates a molten calf from the gold he has collected from the people. He builds an altar before it and says, "Tomorrow shall be a festival to the LORD" (vs. 5). The next day the people rise up early and revel. Dramatically the next sentence switches scenes and focuses on Mt. Sinai. God speaks to Moses, and in an accusatory tone rebukes the people for their defection. God calls them stiff-necked and perverse. With divine fury, God makes Moses an amazing offer: let me destroy them, and I will start all over with you.

Moses' reply (vss. 12–13) is astonishing. He placates God and argues that God should be more patient. Remember what you promised the ancestors Abraham, Isaac, and Jacob! You vowed to give the land to their descendants. Besides, should the Egyptians say that it was with evil intent that you brought them to the mountains, to consume them? In the end, God relents. Moses then hurries down the mountain carrying the tablets of the Ten Commandments. When he sees the revelry and the calf, he is enraged and shatters the tablets at the base of the mountain. In short order he roundly rebukes the people and calls for the death of the apostates. Many are killed.

Chapter 33: Moses seeks reassurance from God that the deity will not turn away from the people. God agrees to this. Then Moses wants some further proof of God's commitment. "Show me your glory, I pray," Moses says to God (Exod 33:18). God replies that this request is not possible, for no human can see God and live. Yet, by way of a compromise, God promises Moses that he can stand atop Mt. Sinai, and there, protected in a cleft of a rock, God will pass by

Moses. God says to Moses, "I will cover you with my hand until I have passed by; then I will take away my hand, and you shall see my back; but my face shall not be seen" (vss. 22–23).

As chapter 34 begins, Moses, on God's instructions, cuts two tablets like the first, and God promises to inscribe them like the former ones. The next morning Moses climbs to the top of Mt. Sinai, and God's presence passes before him. God descends in a cloud and (in vss. 6–7) proclaims the thirteen divine attributes.[27]

Verses 10–28 "may be another tradition about the making of a covenant (v. 10), parallel to that of chapters 19–24. In the present context, however, it is understood as a renewal of the covenant after it was broken by the people (ch. 32)" (NRSV comment on Exod 34:10–28). There is material that inveighs against pagan worship, followed by a cultic calendar. Moses is on the mountain a further forty days and nights (vs. 28) and rewrites the Ten Commandments. When he returns from the mountain, Moses' face is radiant. The people are fearful, and so, when he is not communicating with God or reporting God's words, Moses wears a veil.

Chapters 35–40 return to matters surrounding the construction of the tabernacle.

Chapter 35 begins with a note to observe the Sabbath but then quickly turns to the voluntary gifts needed to build the tabernacle. Most of the chapter is an expansion of Exodus 25:1–9, and this is followed by a reiteration of the skills of the artisans Bezalel and Oholiab.

Chapter 36 continues to extol these two artisans and then continues with details about the tabernacle's creation.

Chapters 37 and 38 continue with great details about the manufacture of the tabernacle.

Chapter 39 discusses the intricacies of materials and construction of the priestly vestments.

Chapter 40 deals with the final details of the erection and furnishing of the tabernacle and the installation of the priesthood. Exactly nine months after the Israelites arrived at Sinai, the tabernacle was completed. It was the first day of the second year of the Exodus (vs. 17; cf. Exod 19:1). Moses himself sets up the tabernacle and its fixtures. When Moses finished this work the cloud covered the tent of meeting because the glory of God filled the tabernacle. The cloud of God was on the tabernacle by day, and a fire was in the cloud at night.

5. EXODUS IN THE CHRISTIAN SCRIPTURES

The Christian scriptures feature dozens of references to the Book of Exodus. Beginning with Matthew, and throughout the Gospels, Exodus is featured prominently. Exodus is alluded to or quoted from directly in Acts, in many of the Epistles, and likewise in Revelation.

Jesus and Moses

In many ways, the figure of Jesus in the Christian scriptures is patterned on the life of Moses in the Book of Exodus. E. P. Sanders, in writing about Jesus, explains that "Matthew saw Jesus as a second, superior Moses (as well as son of David), and he cast a good deal of his opening chapters in terms of the stories about Moses." He goes on to say that Joseph and Mary's flight to Egypt and then eventual return (Matt 2:14–21) was a conscious reminder of Israel's history and Exodus from Egypt. "In Matthew 5, Jesus goes up on to a mountain (as did Moses when he received the law), and while there he comments on some of the ten commandments and other parts of the Mosaic law (Matt. 5:21–48)." Sanders also suggests that there are connections between the ten miracles found in Matthew 8–9 and the miracles Moses performs in Egypt in chapters 7–11 surrounding the ten plagues.[28]

Jesus and Moses are directly connected in Matthew 17, the episode of the Transfiguration (cf. Mark 9:2–8; Luke 9:28–36). Jesus takes his disciples Peter, James, and John and goes *up a mountain* to pray. While he is praying, his appearance changes and his clothes become a dazzling white. As the disciples gaze at the scene, Moses and Elijah suddenly appear, speaking to Jesus. Jesus' changing appearance and the brightness of his clothes are reminiscent of

Moses' experiences on Mt. Sinai (Exod 34:29ff.). When Moses descends from the mountain he does not realize that his face is shining, the result of his having spoken with God. That Moses and Elijah, both of whom are associated with mountains where they encounter God, are in attendance with Jesus reinforces the message about Jesus' uniqueness. Matthew (as Mark and Luke also) portrays Jesus as even greater than Moses, for out of a bright cloud comes a voice, "This is my Son, the Beloved; with him I am well pleased; listen to him!" (Matt 17:5). (See also earlier, "Deuteronomy in the Christian scriptures.")

For Matthew, Moses is a "type," a precursor of Jesus. This view is not always shared among the Gospel writers. Neither Mark, Luke, nor John has an infancy narrative in which Joseph and Mary flee to Egypt. Further Luke has Jesus preach the Beatitudes on a plain or level place, as opposed to a mountain (Luke 6:17ff.). While there are many parallels between Moses and Jesus, there also are clear disparities: Moses is often accompanied by his brother, Aaron, who becomes the high priest; there is no parallel figure for Jesus. Moses marries; Jesus does not. Moses dies in private, his burial place unknown. Jesus' very public death and placement in the tomb are vital parts of the Christian story.

Chosen for Holiness

The early Christian church appropriated for itself the notion of chosenness and chosen for holiness. In the Epistles, speaking to the faithful in Ephesus, Paul says, "Blessed be the God and Father…who…chose us in Christ before the foundation of the world to be holy and blameless before him in love." Paul then continues, "You were taught…to clothe yourselves with the new self, created according to the likeness of God in true righteousness and holiness" (Eph 1:3–4; 4:22, 24).

Redemption

Redemption is at the heart of Christianity. In the Christian scriptures, Jesus' death and resurrection are required for human redemption.

Salvation and redemption are two words which express the liberation of human persons by God. These words imply the
poles of sin and grace, alienation and reconciliation....
Christians believe that God has redeemed people through the
death and resurrection of Jesus....Redemption through Jesus'
Cross and Resurrection is a once-for-all historical event. Yet, it
is also an eschatological event. Thus, it is present as well as
future. Although God has already redeemed people in the
Cross and Resurrection, Christians believe that they must also
appropriate that redemption in the present. They do this in
baptism and in following Jesus....Yet, redemption also calls for
response; it demands that graced and redeemed persons sur-
render themselves to God in faith and follow Jesus as his disciples. This means that Christians take on Jesus' own way of
life, that they too live in obedience to the Father and in soli-
darity with others.[29]

Passover and Easter

The clearest connections between the Book of Exodus and
Christianity center on the holy days of Passover and Easter. Easter
commemorates the last days of Jesus on earth in the passion narrative. It centers on the Last Supper, Jesus' arrest, crucifixion, and
concludes with the celebration of his resurrection. Though this holiday is termed *Easter* in the English language, its Passover connections are underscored more clearly in Romance languages. The
word for *Passover* in Hebrew is *Pesakh (Pesach, Pesah),* and in
French Easter is known as *Pâques;* in Spanish and Portuguese it is
Pascua.

The great Passover themes of sacrifice, redemption, and
renewal are paralleled in Easter.

In the final week of his life, Jesus comes to Jerusalem to celebrate Passover. As portrayed in the Synoptic Gospels* (Matthew,
Mark, and Luke) the Last Supper in the upper room—or guest
room—is a Passover Seder (Matt 26:17–30; Mark 14:12–26; Luke
22:7–23). As cast in Christianity, the Last Supper (also called the
Lord's Supper) is taken beyond the traditional understanding of the
Jewish Passover. At that Passover in Jerusalem Jesus takes both
wine and bread and shares them with his disciples. He tells them,

"Do this in remembrance of me" (Luke 22:19). Paul reiterates this idea when he describes that final meal and writes specifically, "For as often as you eat this bread and drink the cup, you proclaim the Lord's death until he comes" (1 Cor 11:26). Both of these statements echo the words in Exodus concerning the Passover: "This day shall be a remembrance for you. You shall celebrate it as a festival to the LORD; throughout your generations you shall observe it as a perpetual ordinance...you shall observe the festival of unleavened bread...throughout your generations" (Exod 12:14, 17).

At the supper Jesus refers to the cup of wine as the "blood of the covenant" (Matt 26:28; cf. vs. 29). Though he does not make that direct connection, the phrasing "blood of the covenant" echoes the confirmation of the covenant at the time of Moses as described in Exodus 24:8.

At the Last Supper there are specific references to wine and bread (presumably unleavened bread), though there is no mention, as one might expect, of the lamb of Passover as delineated in Exodus 12:21ff. Jesus, however, earlier had been described as the "Lamb of God" by John the Baptist (John 1:29, 36).

Jewish tradition links the lamb of the original Passover ("Your lamb shall be without blemish" [Exod 12:5]) with Abraham's son Isaac as the "perfect sacrifice" on Mt. Moriah as described in Genesis 22. Referring to the words "Your lamb shall be without blemish," the rabbis explain that a lamb is chosen because it serves as a reminder of Isaac. They quote Genesis 22:8: "Abraham said, 'God himself will provide the lamb for the burnt offering, my son.'"[30] The thematic connections between Abraham's willingness to offer/sacrifice his "only son" (by Sarah) and God's willingness to offer/sacrifice his "only son" (Jesus) are well known. Likewise, that Christianity saw Isaac's willingness to be that sacrifice as a prefigurement of Jesus' taking on that role is well understood. The parallels between the story of the binding of Isaac and "the Gospel story are easy to make, and John assumes them in referring to Jesus as lamb. The church father Origen (185–255) has interpreted the lamb that Abraham sacrificed instead of his 'only son' Isaac as a Christian 'prefiguration' of God's sacrifice of his 'only begotten son' Jesus (Genesis Homily, 8)."[31] In Romans 8:32 Paul states that God "did not withhold his own Son, but gave him up for all of us" (cf. John 3:16, "For God so loved the world that he gave his only Son").

Earlier Paul had praised Abraham as the person of faith, for Abraham, hoping against hope, believed he would be the father of many nations (Rom 4:16ff.).

There are several parallels between Easter and Passover, and they echo the events in Exodus.

1. Freedom/Redemption

In Judaism, Passover celebrates freedom—freedom from physical, psychological, and social bondage. It is centered on the experience of the Israelites but has application for all humanity. On another level, Passover also hints at the ultimate redemption of all humans.

In Christianity, the holiday celebrates the physical resurrection of Jesus, and through his triumph over death, the promise of redemption and resurrection for those who believe in Jesus.

2. A Communal Celebration

The celebration of the first Passover was both public and family oriented. Families were to take a lamb and slaughter it, roast it over a fire, and then consume it with bitter herbs and unleavened bread. If the family were not large enough, they were to join with another family (Exod 12:1ff.).

Over time, this became the Passover Seder, celebrated today as a special meal in Jewish homes on the first night, or the first two nights, of Passover. There the past is recalled, and the family and guests eat special foods, including bitter herbs and unleavened bread. Cups of wine are also part of the meal.

In Christianity, the Lord's/Last Supper is replicated in the liturgy of the church. It has been transformed into the Eucharist service, also known as holy communion, the Mass, or the divine liturgy. As part of the Eucharist service, bread and wine are distributed to the worshippers, as a remembrance of Jesus and the Lord's/Last Supper.

In the Gospels (Matt 4:1) Jesus is led by the Spirit into the desert, where he remains for forty days without eating. This episode probably is an echo of Moses' forty days atop Mt. Sinai. Moses "was there with the LORD forty days and forty nights; he neither ate bread nor drank water" (Exod 34:28).

Much more could be said in terms of how the Book of Exodus is reflected in the Christian scriptures.[32]

6. EXODUS IN RABBINIC LITERATURE

There are several midrashic collections accessible in English. Among them are *Midrash Exodus Rabbah*, the *Mekilta [Mekhilta] of Rabbi Ishmael*, and the *Midrash Tanhuma on Exodus*. The *Pirke de Rabbi Eliezer* takes a narrative approach to the period in Egypt, the Exodus itself, and the Israelite's life in the desert as described in Exodus and the later books of the Torah.

Moses' Human Side

Moses is regarded as "the" prophet par excellence. The Torah itself highlights Moses' unique character. The closing words of Deuteronomy state, "Never since has there arisen a prophet in Israel like Moses, whom the LORD knew face to face" (Deut 34:10). In Judaism Moses often is called *Moshe Rabbenu*, "Moses our teacher," an honorific title even as it is one of affection. Moses is praised as a very humble person, yet for all that, the rabbis also understood that Moses was human, and as such was far from perfect. Moses had his faults. At times, he both doubts God's word and defames Israel.

At the episode at the burning bush God commissions Moses to go to Egypt and plead the case for the Israelites. Moses is reluctant to take on this task and needs active encouragement from God. God says that the people "will listen to your voice" and that the ruler of Egypt will favor the people leaving. Moses is not convinced. He says to God, "But suppose they do not believe me or listen to me?" (Exod 4:1). God then consciously mocks the serpent magic practiced in Egypt, where snakes were hypnotized into rigidity and then picked up by their tails. God reverses the trick by having Moses turn his staff into a snake and then grasp it by the tail to become Moses' staff once more. Noting that Moses had challenged God's statement ("But suppose they do not believe me or listen to me?"), the rabbis say that for his lack of faith, God tells Moses he deserves to be beaten with his own rod. Your words, Moses, are like the serpent's in the Garden of Eden. As that snake was punished, so in time will you be. Indeed, the rabbis liken the snake to Pharaoh in Egypt. Now he bites Israel, but in the future, like a piece of wood he will be unable to do so. The reference to Pharaoh as a serpent is not poetic imagination, for the prophet Ezekiel (Ezek 29:3) describes the Egyptian ruler as a great dragon sprawling in the Nile.[33] As much as Moses was the revered leader and the greatest teacher of Judaism, Moses was neither divine nor semidivine.

Moses' Staff

Moses' staff has an interesting history. The rabbis regarded that staff as the same one as Aaron's, mentioned later in the Bible (Exod 7:9ff.), and also as the same "staff of God" mentioned in Exodus 17:9. It is one of the ten ordinary objects that play an extraordinary role in human affairs. All of these objects were created, according to the rabbis, on the twilight of the original Shabbat.[34] "This is the rabbinic way of stating that what appears to be a miraculous suspension of the laws of nature was providentially integrated into the cosmic order at Creation."[35] According to another rabbinic source, it is the same staff that has God's seventy names emblazoned upon it.[36] See also "Aaron's Budding Staff" in the chapter on Numbers below (Numbers in Rabbinic Literature).

Coincidentally, a miraculous staff will also become part of Christian legend. Even as Aaron's staff sprouted almond blossoms (Num 17:8 [17:23 H]) so will there be a similar miracle performed with several Christian bishops ("The Blossoming Rod").[37]

Each Creature Has Its Place

Do not think that creatures like serpents, scorpions, flies, gnats, frogs, or hornets do not have their purpose, explains the midrash. On the sixth day of creation, God saw everything that he had made, and indeed, it was very good. So each creature has its definite place in the scheme of things.[38]

God Redeemed with the Israelites

In one of the most amazing passages in the midrashic literature, the rabbis suggest that God needed to be redeemed from Egypt with the Israelites.[39] In the view of the rabbis, God voluntarily went into exile in Egypt with the Israelites. Quoting Genesis 46:4, "I myself will go down with you to Egypt," the rabbis find parallel statements for God volunteering to be with Israel in Babylonia and Persia as well.[40] God chooses self-exile with the people Israel and awaits redemption to this very day.[41]

If God is in voluntary exile and will be redeemed only when all people are redeemed, then one answer to those in pain is that God, far from being absent or uncaring, is present in our lives. God is, or can be, with us *there* in our pain and suffering. If God is in voluntary exile with those who suffer or are in pain, God says to us, "We are in this together, and I, God, am in some measure dependent on you to do your part! We need one another to effect redemption! We are in a partnership; you *cannot* do it by yourself, and I *will not* alone do it for you. I am present, and I will help you, but *you* need to begin the process." This has tremendous implications for those who, when experiencing pain, would ask "where is God?" God's refusal to provide sudden and miraculous cures for us when we are suffering does not mean that God does not care about human lives. Rather, God suffers along with us.

Rewards and Punishments

The Bible is replete with examples of people being repaid according to their acts. Cain is a farmer, dependent on the soil; his punishment is to be a ceaseless wanderer. Jacob takes advantage of his father's lack of sight and then is deceived in the dark by his father-in-law, Laban. Jacob, described as a homebody, is forced into exile for twenty years. Young Joseph gloats of his position over his brothers only to be at their none-too-tender mercies. As a pharaoh ordered the drowning of the Israelite children, so, the rabbis point out, will Pharaoh's firstborn die, and he himself will drown in the sea.[42] The rabbis also explain that when the angels on high saw the Egyptians drowning, they rejoiced, breaking forth in song. God rebuked them, saying, "The work of my hands is drowning in the sea, and you desire to sing songs!"[43] God does not rejoice at the death of sinners, but that they should return from their ways and live (cf. Ezek 18:31–32).

Pharaoh's daughter, according to the rabbis, was his firstborn. She escapes death because she is rewarded for her acts of kindness with Moses, and so was worthy to inherit the world to come.[44]

Women Have an Honored Role

Though women today are reclaiming their rightful place as co-equal partners with men in religious life, in the past they often were relegated to a second-class role. That being said, there are examples where the rabbis specifically honor women. In several places in the midrashic literature, the rabbis differentiate between the terms *B'nai Israel* (Israelites; literally, children/people of Israel) and *Beit Yaakov* (House of Jacob). Though they appear to be synonymous terms, the rabbis explain that the term *B'nai Israel* refers to males and *Beit Yaakov* refers to females. In Exodus 19:3 the text reads: God told Moses, "Thus you shall say to the house of Jacob, and tell the Israelites." Why, ask the rabbis, did God command the women first? Because, they answered, women are prompt in the fulfilling of commandments. Further, they introduce their children to the study of Torah.[45]

Those Present and Those to Come/ Seventy Languages

The midrash suggests that when God gave the Torah on Mt. Sinai this revelation was not given merely to those who were physically present. According to the rabbis, future generations of prophets and scholars were there as well. They quoted the words that begin the Ten Commandments: "Then God spoke *all* these words..." (Exod 20:1). Then, they use as a proof text verses in

Deuteronomy ("I am making this covenant...not only with you who stand here with us today before the LORD our God, but also with those who are not here with us today," Deut 29:14–15 [13–14 H]). The rabbis explain that "with us today" in the latter part of the verse refers to those who one day will be created. Though they did not physically exist at the time of Sinai, still they have a share in the Torah. For example, among other texts, the midrash quotes the prophet Isaiah, who clearly states: "From the beginning...from the time it came to be I have been there" (Isa 48:16).[46]

The rabbis take this idea a step further and point out that God's words were heard in seventy voices, seventy languages, so that all the nations of the world could understand. God's teaching is a universal message; it is not for Israel alone.[47]

Plan Ahead

Though many a midrash has a valuable kernel, at times the rabbis stretch to find meaning in the text. In Exodus 26:15, wood is needed to build the tabernacle. The rabbis wonder, how is it that this particular wood was available to the Israelites? It was a miracle, they explained.

> Where did the boards come from? Our father Jacob planted them when he went down to Egypt. He said to his children: My children, you are going to be redeemed from here; and after you are redeemed the Holy One is going to say to you: Make me a tabernacle. Just arise and plant cedars. When he tells you to make a tabernacle, the cedars will be available in your hands. Immediately they did as their father told them. They arose and planted cedars.[48] [The rabbis regard cedar trees as generic lumber.]

The Reason the Ark Is Built of Acacia Wood

The ark is built of acacia wood. Hebrew word for *acacia* (*shittim*) is the exact same word as the place-name *Shittim* in Numbers 25:1ff., where the Israelites sin by associating with Moabite women who lead them to idol worship. The rabbis explain that these acacias for the tabernacle will heal the breach brought about by the Israelites' future apostasy. The rabbis also indicated that God, in the world to come, will bring healing through acacia wood. To support this they quoted the prophet Joel, "In that day...a fountain shall come forth from the house of the LORD and water the Wadi Shittim" ("water the Wadi of the Acacias," so NJPS; Joel 3:18 [4:18 H]).[49]

7. TEXT STUDY

A. Exodus 20:1–17. The Ten Commandments

"More people praise the Bible than read it. More read it than understand it, and more understand it than conscientiously follow it."[50] As this is true of the Bible as a whole, so likewise it is true of the Ten Commandments.

Few people realize that the Ten Commandments appear twice in the Torah, once in Exodus 20 and again in Deuteronomy 5, with minor differences in language. For examples, see the discussion on the Ten Commandments in the chapter on Deuteronomy.

The Ten Commandments start out with God setting the basis for the relationship with Israel. It is a matter of reciprocity: I, God, rescued you from the brutality of Egyptian slavery. As I have established my credentials, now this is what I expect from you: do not worship other gods; do not misuse my name; do keep the Sabbath; and so forth. This language of establishing the basis for the contractual relationship is reflective of other ancient Near Eastern law codes, the most famous of which is the Code of Hammurabi.[51]

The specific numbering of the verses of the Decalogue, the Ten Commandments, differs between Jewish and most Christian Bibles. In the accepted Jewish counting there are thirteen verses, and seventeen in the Christian version. (In Jewish Bibles the prohibitions against murder, adultery, theft, and false witness are all part of vs. 13. In Christian versions, they are numbered vss. 13–16.) Most Jews offer this division of the commandments:

1. I am the LORD your God, who brought you out of the land of Egypt, out of the house of slavery.
2. You shall have no other gods before me. You shall not make for yourself an idol...
3. You shall not make wrongful use of the name of the LORD your God...
4. Remember the Sabbath day...
5. Honor your father and your mother...
6. You shall not murder.
7. You shall not commit adultery.
8. You shall not steal.
9. You shall not bear false witness against you neighbor.
10. You shall not covet...

On the other hand, ancient Jewish writers, including Philo of Alexandria and Josephus, as well as the New Jewish Publication Society (NJPS) version, suggest that the first commandment ends with the words "You shall have no other gods before me," and the second commandment begins with the words, "You shall not make for yourself an idol..."[52]

Of the Ten Commandments the most radical is the fourth, Remember the Sabbath day. The concept of a Sabbath day, a day of rest for *all* people, is so inculcated into our society that we often fail to understand how revolutionary a concept this was in its time. The idea that all people, the entire household, including slaves and strangers, as well as animals, were divinely mandated with a day of rest was unknown up to this time. "The Sabbath is wholly an Israelite innovation. There is nothing analogous to it in the entire ancient Near Eastern world....Further, its intrinsic sacred character derives from God. By following a pattern of living and observance in conformity with that intrinsic holiness, Israel transforms its mundane existence into a spiritual existence one day a week....Human liberty is immeasurably enhanced, human equality is strengthened, and the cause of social justice is promoted by legislating the inalienable right of every human being, irrespective of social class, and of draft animals as well, to twenty-four hours of complete rest every seven days."[53] The only exception to resting on the Sabbath was in order to save a human life. In the Talmud, the rabbis make clear that protecting life is a religious duty that supersedes Sabbath rest.[54]

Often people misquote or misunderstand Exodus 20:13, translating it as "You shall not kill." That is not its intent; rather the commandment says, You shall not murder. As the note in NRSV explains, "This commandment forbids murder (see Gen 9.5), not the forms of killing authorized for Israel, e.g. war or capital punishment." Indeed slaughtering animals is a form of killing, which most people agree is not the intention of this commandment.

Two other of the commandments are also often misunderstood. The last command, which says "you shall not covet," surely means more than just desiring or being envious of your neighbor's house, his wife, slaves, or anything that is your neighbor's. You cannot stop your mind from thinking. Jealousy is a very human emotion. It is when you take that envy or desire and turn it into action, taking something that does not belong to you, that problems arise. Coveting, then, in this context really is a synonym for "stealing."[55]

This then begs the question, what is meant by the earlier command, "You shall not steal"? Traditionally Judaism understood this to mean, you shall not steal a fellow human being, you shall not *kidnap*.[56] Modern scholars also have supported the view that in this context *steal* means *kidnap*, because otherwise it overlaps with the meaning of *not coveting*.

B. Exodus 25:1–22.
The Ark and the Tabernacle

In the modern world we take for granted formal places of religious worship, be they synagogues, churches, mosques, or temples. Generally these buildings have three basic functions; they are a place for the faithful to worship, to study, and to meet socially. While people speak of God filling the world and being beyond the world, these places of worship are concrete locales where believers join in community, where they come to offer their prayers. In a broad sense, the tabernacle filled a similar role: it was the place where God "connected" with the people.

About a third of the Book of Exodus deals with a detailed description of the tabernacle: the ark, the sanctuary, and various pieces of ritual furniture, such as the table, the wash basin, and the altar. As moderns, we regard the words of verbal or written prayer as the standard way of communicating with God. In today's world, it is true that Judaism, as Christianity, Islam, Buddhism, and Hinduism, have certain religious rituals that are also performed. Among other examples, there are the Jewish blessings over Light, over Wine and Bread on the Shabbat (Sabbath), and there is communion within Christianity. Yet it is largely verbal or written communication, whether literally spoken or communicated in the heart, that serves as our primary link to God. It was different in the past. The ancient world employed a radically dissimilar system to connect with the gods, or, within the world of ancient Israel, with the one God. Animal and grain sacrifices were understood as the formal—and normal—way of expressing religious feeling.

In Exodus 25:8 God instructs Moses that the people are to make God a sanctuary, "so that I may dwell among them." A few verses on, God says to Moses that an ark of the covenant is to be built. "There I will meet with you....I will deliver to you all my commands for the Israelites" (Exod 25:22). God understood that the people needed a real place, a concrete image, a physical location where they could believe God dwelt among them. It was strange and difficult enough to accept that God was invisible, that God was "being" itself ("I AM WHO I AM/I AM WHAT I AM/I WILL BE WHAT I WILL BE" [Exod 3:14]). They had lived in Egypt for so long; they had seen temples and shrines there. The people needed a tangible symbol of God's presence. The sanctuary, the tabernacle, or tent served that purpose. Stated succinctly, the tabernacle was God's dwelling place on earth.

Nahum Sarna points out that the two terms used for the sanctuary, the *Mishkan* ("tabernacle" or "dwelling") and the *'Ohel* ("tent"), are used synonymously; they are used indiscriminately and are interchangeable.[57]

The sanctuary area was 100 cubits x 50 cubits, roughly speaking 150 feet x 75 feet (approximately 50 meters x 25 meters). Surrounding the perimeter, serving as an outer enclosure, were hangings of fine twisted linen. They were attached to wood poles, some 7 to 8 feet high, spaced at intervals of 7 to 8 feet. There were three major zones in ascending order of importance: the outer court; the holy place; and the holy of holies.

In the outer court stood the altar for the burnt offerings and a laver or wash basin.

The holy place was a rectangle made up of wood planks or frames, some 45 feet x 15 feet (30 cubits x 10 cubits). In the holy place stood the seven-branched menorah or lampstand, as well as a table and the altar of incense. In the holy of holies some 15 feet x 15 feet (10 cubits x 10 cubits) was the ark of the covenant, itself about 3 feet to 4 feet x 2 feet to 2.5 feet x 2 feet to 2.5 feet (2.5 cubits x 1.5 cubits x 1.5 cubits).

According to the text, each day a lamb was offered on the altar of the burnt offerings, both morning and evening. In addition, a grain offering and a libation of wine were offered (Exod 29:38–42). The priests wash their hands and feet at the wash basin before entering the holy place or before performing some ritual matter. On the table in the holy place every Sabbath twelve loaves ("bread of display/show bread") were placed. The lamps of the menorah were lit each night and burned until morning.

Aromatic incense was burned on the altar of incense, both morning and at sundown (Exod 30:1–10; 37:25ff.; 39:38; 40:27).

In the holy of holies, the two tablets of stone were set in a rectangular chest, the ark. Cherubim resided atop the ark.

The two stone tablets, the "tablets of the covenant," were placed in the holy of holies. They were the Ten Commandments, the written reminder of God's presence. They were the link between Moses, the people, and God on Mt. Sinai. The ark was seen as God's footstool, literally as well as figuratively. This is attested to later in the Bible as when King David says, "I had planned to build a house of rest for the ark of the covenant of the LORD, for the footstool of our God" (1 Chr 28:2; see also Ps 99:5; 132:7). In the mind of the people, God's invisible but heavenly throne was situated above the ark. As mentioned above, it was at the ark that God told Moses they would meet. "There I will meet with you....I will deliver to you all my commands for the Israelites" (Exod 25:22). God's presence was manifest there at the cherubim above the ark. In several places, God is spoken of as being enthroned on the cherubim. "The ark of God, the LORD, who is enthroned on the cherubim which is called by his name" (1 Chr 13:6; cf. 2 Sam 6:2; Ps 80:1 [80:2 H]). (For a discussion about the cherubim, see the Text Study in Numbers, "The Cherubim").

The German Jewish scholar Martin Buber (early to mid-twentieth century) suggested that there is a broad parallel between God's creation of the world in six days and then blessing the seventh day, and the seven stages in building the tabernacle, ending with Moses blessing the work. The key words "made," "completed," and "blessed" are found in both narratives in a similar order. Stated briefly, there is reason to believe that the description of the building and completion of the tabernacle (in Exodus 25 and 39) purposely were patterned on the narrative of the creation of the world.[58]

Creation Narrative	**Building of Tabernacle**
1. So God *made* the dome and separated the waters (Gen 1:7)	And have them *make* me a sanctuary (Exod 25:8)
God *made* the two great lights (Gen 1:16)	They shall *make* an ark (Exod 25:10)
God *made* the wild animals (Gen 1:25)	You shall *make* a table (Exod 25:23)
	You shall *make* a lampstand (Exod 25:31)
2. For in *six days* the LORD made heaven and earth, the sea… (Exod 20:11)	The glory of the LORD settled on Mount Sinai…*six days* (Exod 24:16)
3. [God] rested on the *seventh* day (Exod 20:11)	On the *seventh* day [God] called to Moses (Exod 24:16)
4. The heavens and the earth were *finished*…And on the seventh day God *finished* the work… (Gen 2:1–2)	The work of the tabernacle… was *finished* (Exod 39:32) So Moses *finished* the work (Exod 40:33)

5. God *saw* everything that he had made (Gen 1:31)	Moses *saw* that they had done all the work (Exod 39:43)
6. Indeed *[v'hiney]*, it was very good (Gen 1:31)	...*[v'hiney]* they had done (Exod 39:43)
7. God *blessed* the seventh day (Gen 2:3)	Moses...*blessed* them (Exod 39:43)

C. Exodus 28:30.
The *Urim* and *Thummim:*
Device for Discerning God's Will

God often spoke to Moses giving specific instructions. There also were times when people wanted to make inquiries of God, to discern the divine will. As part of the vestments worn by the high priest there was a "breastpiece of judgment" (Exod 28:15). Above the breastplate, or more likely breastpiece, were twelve stones, each stone inscribed with the name of one of the tribes. Aaron wore the breastpiece continually. Attached to the breastpiece was a pouch, which contained two objects, the Urim and the Thummim. The Bible makes limited reference to these Urim and Thummim. In Numbers 27:21, and again in 1 Samuel 28:6, these objects appear as ways that someone can inquire about God's will on a certain matter. The meaning of these two words is unknown. The Talmud suggests that the words are connected with *'or* ("light") and *tam* ("complete"; and, by extension, "true.")[59] In 1 Samuel 14:37–41 King Saul seeks to know who is responsible for certain deeds, and by asking yes/no questions an answer is given via these objects. How the objects work is unclear. They are mentioned only twice more in the Torah (Lev 8:8 and Deut 33:8), but those passages merely explain that they are to be worn. The shape of the objects, how they indicated their answers, and what happened to them are unknown. After the time of David, there is no indication that they were ever used again, and the references to them in Ezra (2:63) and Nehemiah (7:65) are of a theoretical nature. The Mishnah explains that "with the death of the first prophets, the Urim and Thummim ceased."[60] Umberto Cassuto suggests that they had limited application. Only the leader of the people could make inquiry from them, and that was restricted to matters of public concern. The inquiry related to matters of conscience or to some future event for which there was no other way objectively to find an answer. Questions were framed with an either/or response; yes or no. Only one question could be asked at once. It is likely that they were two lots, one for a positive and one for a negative answer.[61]

Notes

1. It is no small irony that in Hebrew the name for the Book of Exodus is *Sh'mot,* literally, "names." Technically these names refer to the children of Jacob who descended to Egypt at the time of Joseph. While we have their names, many other important names are missing. In Exodus 1 we learn that a new king arose over Egypt, but aside from referring to him as Pharaoh, no specific identification is offered in the Torah. In Exodus 2, Moses' parents and his sister are unnamed, as is Pharaoh's daughter. Though Pharaoh's daughter is nameless in the Torah text, according to the midrash, her name was Bithiah (*Midrash Exodus Rabbah 1.26; Pesikta Rabbati, Piska* 17.5). Moses' parents are eventually named in Exodus 6:20, Amram and Jochebed, and Miriam's name is introduced in Exodus 15:20. In Exodus 2:23 it states that the (unnamed) king of Egypt died, and presumably was succeeded by another, again anonymous, pharaoh, the ruler who refused to allow the Israelites to leave. Even God maintains anonymity, for when Moses asks, "'What is [your] name?'...God said to Moses, 'I AM WHO I AM....This is my name forever, and this my title for all generations'" (Exod 3:13–15). An alternative name for this book is *Sefer Yetziyat Mitzrayim* (the "book of the going out of Egypt").

2. Were they Israelites, people of Israel, tribes of Israel, clans of Israel, or did they call themselves the "children of Israel"? Indeed, did they refer to themselves as Hebrews? The Hebrew term is *B'nai Israel,* and while its most literal translation is "children of Israel," modern convention most often uses the terms *Israelites* or *Israelite people.* The word for "Hebrew" (*Ivri* in Hebrew) is a term that is used very sparingly in the Torah, indeed it has limited use in the Bible. The first time it appears is as a description of Abram/Abraham in Genesis 14:13. The three main uses of the word *Hebrew* suggest that it is an ethnic term. It is found in the chapters surrounding the story of Joseph and is used as a contrast to *Egyptians.* Similarly in early Exodus, it is used in opposition to Egyptians. Finally, in the Book of Samuel it is used to contrast Hebrews/Israelites with

Philistines. There is great scholarly debate as to whether the Hebrews are the same as the 'Apiru, a kind of social entity, perhaps nomadic mercenaries. In any case, as Sarna points out, by the end of the second millennium BCE, the 'Apiru disappear from history. Nahum Sarna, *JPS: Exodus,* (Philadelphia: Jewish Publication Society, 1991), 266, Excursus 1.

3. There are other ways to describe the major divisions of the book. One suggestion separates Exodus into two halves. In the first section, there is the period of slavery/liberation/revelation, including the Ten Commandments: chapters 1–20. The other half features various kinds of legislation, with a major section dealing with the Tabernacle: chapters 21–40. An alternative division of the Book of Exodus suggests that the initial section tells the story of Israel in Egypt, the oppression, the struggle for freedom, the liberation, and concurrently God's faithfulness, compassion, and power (chapters 1–17). This is followed by the account of the covenant at Sinai and the explanations about these laws, making the people God's kingdom of priests and a holy nation (chapters 19–24). The final section features chapters 25–31 and 35–40, which cover the instructions for the erection of the Tabernacle and its completion. Chapter 18 (Jethro's visit) and chapters 32–34 are explained as separate items inserted into the flow of the broader narrative/text. See Moshe Greenberg, "Exodus, Book of," in *Encyclopedia Judaica* (Jerusalem: Keter, 1971), 6:1051.

4. It does not follow directly on the closing words of Genesis but rather paraphrases the narrative found in Genesis 46:8–27, which gives the names of the seventy family members that settled in Egypt.

5. What was Egypt like at this time? The Book of Exodus commences with the clans/tribes moving south to Egypt from the land of Canaan during the time of the great drought. It further makes mention that a "new king arose over Egypt, who did not know Joseph" (Exod 1:8). This king/pharaoh is not named, but one commonly held theory is that this really refers to a change in dynasty rather than a change in pharaoh, or a new set of rulers over Egypt. Many scholars point out that for about two hundred years (c. 1750–1550 BCE) a group of nonnative Egyptians ruled Egypt, people known as the Hyksos. Probably from Asia Minor, they had overwhelmed the Egyptian armies and dominated Egyptian life for two centuries. It is likely that the Semitic clans/tribes of Jacob/Israel moved to Egypt at this time. In any case, native Egyptians regained control under the leadership of King Ahmose of Thebes, about 1550 BCE. This was the beginning of the eighteenth dynasty.

Egypt prospers at this time and expands her empire to the south, Sudan, the west, Libya, and then the northeast, Palestine, the land that will become Israel, and also into Syria. This period sees the building of cities in Palestine such as Bet Shaan, Megiddo, Jerusalem, Hazor, and Jericho. This is the Late Bronze Age. Egypt is nominally in charge of these areas but allows local rulers to remain in place as long as they retain loyalty to Egypt.

By about the year 1300 another new dynasty arises, the nineteenth, led by Seti I and his son, Rameses II. This dynasty moves its capital farther north, closer to the Nile Delta and its connection to the Sinai desert, and therefore closer to Palestine and Syria. Egyptian records speak of building projects, which could have been the "store cities," "garrison cities," or "supply cities" of Pithom and Rameses mentioned in Exodus 1:11. As a note in the NRSV (to vs. 11) points out, this work was carried out by the corvée or forced labor gangs, as were the pyramids, which had been built a thousand years before the Israelite clans ever settled in Egypt.

6. William W. Hallo, "Exodus and Ancient Near Eastern Literature," in *The Torah: A Modern Commentary,* ed. W. Gunther Plaut (New York: Union of American Hebrew Congregations, 1981), 370.

7. A couple hundred years later, in a passage reminiscent of the aforementioned quote from Exodus, God tells the prophet Samuel that he is to select Saul as king. "Tomorrow...you shall anoint him to be ruler over *my people* Israel. He shall save *my people* from the hand of the Philistines; for I have seen the suffering of *my people* because their outcry has come to me" (1 Sam 9:16). Likewise in the Psalms: "May the LORD give strength to *his people!* May the LORD bless *his people* with peace!" (Ps 29:11).

8. The covenant with God is for all time. "Throughout Israel's history—despite the people's sin and rebelliousness—God never abandons his chosen. From Bible times to the present day...the Bible is clear: the preservation of the people of Israel from generation to generation has reflected God's faithfulness, grace, and ultimate purposes in history...Thus he kept his word...and remained faithful to those covenant promises he made to his own people...." Marvin R. Wilson, *Our Father Abraham: Jewish Roots of the Christian Faith* (Grand Rapids, MI: Eerdmans, 1989), 258.

God's covenant with the Jewish people is not only eternal, it is irreversible. No matter what the circumstances, no matter whether Israel is suffering or in forced exile from the Land, the covenant remains in place. God has not and will not abandon this relationship with Israel. "It is especially important that this idea of covenant be understood in the Jewish-Christian dialogue. Any suggestions by Christians that God's covenant with Israel has been transferred to a 'new Israel' is obviously offensive to Jewish beliefs. Any statement implying that God's covenant with the Jewish people has been discontinued or has been replaced by a covenant with others is totally unacceptable to Jewish religious belief, and goes against the Bible itself" (Marc Angel, "Covenant," in *A Dictionary of the Jewish-Christian Dialogue,* Expanded Edition, ed. Leon Klenicki and Geoffrey Wigoder, Stimulus Book [Mahwah, NJ: Paulist, 1995], 34).

9. See David J. Zucker, *Israel's Prophets: An Introduction for Christians and Jews* (Mahwah, NJ: Paulist, 1994), 106–10, 114.

10. A person can believe that there is but one God, but that this one God can have a special relationship with more than just one people. In the following statement on revelation from a Christian viewpoint, normative Judaism's quarrel is that the writer claims that Christianity's message is superior. Christianity's message is unlike that of Judaism. It is distinct and unique in its own right. It has a different purpose than that of Judaism, but it is offensive to claim that it is better than/superior to the message of Judaism. Writing about the Christian revelation, the author explains that this "is not another revelation, but a fuller revelation. There is *superiority* [my italics] of this mode of revelation in Christ over all other modes, because Christ is *one* with his Father (Luke 10:22–24; John 17:6–8). So, those who share in his Spirit have a full knowledge of God (Matt 11:27; 1 Cor 2:10ff.; 12:3). For such a Spirit is none else but God's Holy Spirit, so that God subjectively reveals through his Spirit the One he is, objectively, in Christ" (André Lacocque, "Revelation," in *A Dictionary of the Jewish-Christian Dialogue,* ed. Klenicki and Wigoder, 169).

11. John Bright, *A History of Israel* (Philadelphia: Westminster, 1959), 110–11. For an alternate view, see Israel Finkelstein and Neil Asher Silberman, *The Bible Unearthed* (New York: Free Press, 2001).

12. For example, in Judges 6:15 the word *elef* clearly means "clan"; so also in 1 Samuel 10:19. In 1 Samuel 23:23, "contingents," "clans," or "thousands" might be the correct translation. NRSV has the word *thousands* at this point, and NJPS has the word "clans": "I will search him out among all the thousands [clans] of Judah."

13. See *JPS: Exodus,* 62; cf. James King West, *Introduction to the Old Testament,* 2nd ed. (New York: Macmillan, 1981), 165; Bright, *History of Israel,* 121; Plaut, ed., *The Torah,* 1034.

14. J. Philip Hyatt, *Exodus: New Century Bible Commentary* (Grand Rapids, MI: Eerdmans; London: Marshall, Morgan & Scott, 1980 [1971], 203ff.

15. One suggested division (following the research of S. R. Driver) is clearly outlined in Greenberg, "Book of Exodus" in the *Encyclopedia Judaica,* 6:1057–58.

16. Sarna, *JPS: Exodus,* 10.

17. "The plague cannot be identified with certainty because Hebrew *'arov* occurs only in the present context...the Septuagint and Philo specify [it] as the dog fly. This would be the stable fly...a vicious, bloodsucking insect that can multiply prodigiously....It is known to transmit anthrax and other animal diseases" (Sarna, *JPS: Exodus,* 42).

18. Sarna, *JPS: Exodus,* 23. See also Plaut, ed., *The Torah,* 416f.; Brevard S. Childs, *The Book of Exodus: A Critical, Theological Commentary* (Philadelphia: Westminster, 1974), 170–75.

19. In Exodus 12:13 God says, "I will pass over [*u-fa-sah-ti*] you." The Hebrew for "I will pass over" shares the same root as the word *Pesach/Pesah/*Passover *[p/f-s-h].*

20. "The entire story of the Egyptian oppression, from the midwives who frustrated Pharaoh's intent to the enforced labor of the Israelites, is told in terms of its relationship to Miriam, Aaron, and Moses. The historicity of these three figures was an article of faith long before the close of the biblical period. References to them in pre-exilic* prophecy (Mic. 6:4; Jer. 15:1), in the Deuteronomic history (Josh. 24:5; I Sam. 12:8) and in the Psalms (105:26; 106:16) show how deeply embedded was the belief in their crucial role in transforming the twelve tribes into one people" (Hallo, "Exodus and Ancient Near Eastern Literature," 368).

21. Drorah O'Donnell Setel, "Exodus," in *The Women's Bible Commentary,* ed. Carol A. Newsom and Sharon H. Ringe (London: SPCK; Louisville, KY: Westminster John Knox, 1992), 31, 32. Certainly, in the rabbinic period Miriam is regarded as one of the key figures during the period of the sojourn in the desert (see "Numbers in Rabbinic Literature" in the chapter on Numbers).

22. Nahum M. Sarna, *Exploring Exodus* (New York: Schocken, 1986), 130.

23. There is some disagreement among scholars about which materials are to be included in this Covenant Code. For example NRSV (comment to Exod 20:22 [20:19 H]) suggests the closing verses of chapter 20 and all of chapters 21–23; see also West, *Introduction to the Old Testament,* 183ff. Lawrence Boadt (*Reading the Old Testament: An Introduction* [Mahwah, NJ: Paulist 1984], 181) begins about the same place but favors the inclusion of chapter 24. Sarna (*JPS: Exodus,* 117) favors chapters 21:1—24:18.

24. Sarna, *JPS: Exodus,* 138.

25. Ibid., 147.

26. How is one to respond to the apostasy of the people? They had so recently committed themselves to following God's laws. At the ratification of the Covenant Code they had said, "All the words that the LORD has

spoken we will do" (Exod 24:3). Yet against this, Moses *has been* away on the mountain, day and night for nearly six weeks! (cf. Exod 24:18). Their fears are not unreasonable. Who knows what has happened to Moses? This is a low point in Israelite history, just as is the similar apostasy in Numbers 13–14 when the people doubt their ability to conquer the land. It is to the Bible's credit that these "forgettable" moments were recorded and not carefully excised from the record.

27. (1 and 2) The Lord, the Lord (God is merciful both before and after humans have sinned and repented); (3) God (God is ruler); (4) compassionate; (5) gracious; (6) slow to anger; (7) abounding in kindness; (8) truth; (9) extending kindness; (10, 11, and 12) forgiving iniquity, transgression, and sin; (13) does not remit all punishment. See Plaut, ed., *The Torah*, 663.

28. E. P. Sanders, *The Historical Figure of Jesus* (London, New York: Allen Lane/Penguin, 1993), 87–88. See also the parallel passages here and elsewhere cited in Craig S. Keener, *A Commentary on the Gospel of Matthew* (Grand Rapids, MI and Cambridge, UK: Eerdmans, 1999).

29. Celia Deutsch, "Salvation," in *A Dictionary of the Jewish-Christian Dialogue*, ed. Klenicki and Wigoder, 183–85. See also John R. W. Stott, *The Cross of Christ* (Downer's Grove, IL: InterVarsity, 1986), 175ff.

30. *Midrash Exodus Rabbah* 15.12.

31. Steven Kepnes, "'Turn Us to You and We Shall Return': Original Sin, Atonement, and Redemption in Jewish Terms," in *Christianity in Jewish Terms*, ed. Tikva Frymer-Kensky et al. (Boulder: Westview, 2000), 299.

32. For a scholarly approach to this subject, one excellent source is Childs, *Book of Exodus*.

33. *Midrash Exodus Rabbah* 3.12.

34. *Mishnah Avot* 5.6.

35. Sarna, *JPS: Exodus*, 23 n. 20.

36. *Pesikta de-Rab Kahana: Rabbi Kahana's Compilation of Discourses for Sabbaths and Festal Days*, trans. William G. Braude and Israel J. Kapstein (Philadelphia: Jewish Publication Society, 1975), *Piska* 3c.

37. Theodor H. Gaster, *Myth, Legend, and Custom in the Old Testament* (Gloucester, MA: Peter Smith, 1981), 301.

38. *Midrash Exodus Rabbah* 10.1.

39. Ibid., 15.12.

40. Ibid., 15.16.

41. Babylonian Talmud *Megillah* 29a.

42. *Midrash Exodus Rabbah* 20.4.

43. Babylonian Talmud *Megillah* 10b; *Sanhedrin* 39b.

44. *Pesikta Rabbati, Piska* 17.5; *Pirke de Rabbi Eliezer,* chapter 48; *Midrash Exodus Rabbah* 20.4.

45. *Midrash Exodus Rabbah* 28.2.

46. Ibid., 28.6.

47. Ibid., 5.9; cf. 28.6.

48. *Midrash Tanhuma, Exodus and Leviticus,* S. Buber Recension, trans. John T. Townsend (Hoboken, NJ: Ktav, 1997), 7.9, Exodus 26:7ff., part III.

49. Ibid.

50. Samuel Sandmel, *The Hebrew Scriptures: An Introduction to Their Literature and Religious Ideas* (New York: Knopf, 1963), 3.

51. See West, *Introduction,* 178ff.; Boadt, *Reading the Old Testament,* 186ff.

52. For a discussion of these points and an interesting introduction to the Decalogue, see Umberto Cassuto, *A Commentary on the Book of Exodus* (Jerusalem: Magnes Press, The Hebrew University, 1983), 251.

53. Sarna, *JPS: Exodus,* 111, 112.

54. Babylonian Talmud *Yoma* 85a–b.

55. For an alternate view, see Jeffrey Tigay's comments on the parallel verse in Deuteronomy (*The JPS Torah Commentary: Deuteronomy* [Philadelphia and Jerusalem: Jewish Publication Society, 1996], 72).

56. That is the meaning suggested by the *Mekilta de Rabbi Ishmael, Nezikin* 5.77, and Babylonian Talmud *Sanhedrin* 86a.

57. Sarna, *Exploring Exodus,* 197. For a schematic drawing of the tabernacle, see Plaut, ed., *The Torah,* 601; Sarna, *JPS: Exodus,* 155; or Sarna, *Exploring Exodus,* 192. For a visualization of the tabernacle, see *Views of the Biblical World* (Chicago and New York: Jordan, 1959), 1:160–69.

58. The scheme that follows in the text is slightly adapted from Nehama Leibowitz, *Studies in Shemot: The Book of Exodus* (Jerusalem: World Zionist Organization, 1976), 477–82; Sarna, *Exploring Exodus,* 213f.

59. Babylonian Talmud *Yoma* 73b.

60. *Mishnah Sotah* 9:12.

61. Cassuto, *Exodus,* 378–82.

Leviticus

1. INTRODUCTION

The English term for this book, *Leviticus*, is derived from the Greek *Levitikon*, a word that refers to the matters of the Levites, the priests. In the Hebrew Bible this book is termed *Vayikra*, literally, "and he summoned" (or "and he called"), taken from the opening verse of the book, "The LORD summoned Moses and spoke to him...."

In the Talmudic period, the rabbis referred to Leviticus as the Priest's Manual, *Torat Kohanim*, because it is devoted to the proper application of religious practices, the rituals of ancient Israelite society. While this is the Priest's Manual, the laws do not apply solely to the priests; they touch on the whole Israelite community. The priests (the Levites) have multitask roles. Their primary role is to teach the people what is and what is not acceptable practice. The priests were charged with determining what was holy and what was mundane. Their role was to distinguish between items that were clean and unclean (Lev 10:10; cf. 14:57). What is of major concern is that through the people's defilement, God's tabernacle may become defiled (Lev 15:31). Should such defilement occur, the priests are authorized to clear that violation, to purge the sanctuary so that it is once more pure.

In the ancient Near East, there were specific roles for humans in relationship to the plentiful gods. This was true of the Babylonians and Sumerians, Akkadians and Egyptians. People believed that the gods provided rain in its season, a fruitful harvest on the land, fecundity among the flocks, and fertility within human society as well. For their part, humans were expected to provide food to the gods at regular intervals. The gods were dependent upon these offerings: meat, fowl, meal and oil offerings. The most elaborate offerings involved meat. The priests brought these offerings to tables set before the gods. Curtains were then drawn. After a set time, the curtains were removed, and any food left over went to the ruler or to the priests. On special occasions, the laity would share the leftovers, feeling privileged that they had shared food with the gods.

Though it cast its religious observance in a different fashion, clearly ancient Israel was affected by these practices. It was a part of the cultural milieu in which it lived. In Israelite religion, there was a threefold division within the world: God, humans, and the world of nature. Laws addressed these various realms. God could only excuse offenses against God; those "against human life could not be absolved by material compensation"; and likewise offenses against nature needed some payment or reimbursement. The killing of an animal, spilling its blood, was a kind of affront to God and to nature. By turning this into a sacrifice, the consumption of the food was sanctified. The levitical legislation provided a framework where God, the priesthood, and the laity each could have their needs met. In the early chapters of Leviticus, legislation is found that specifies "which parts of the animal belonged to God and which to the priests." Further, it is clear that only the balance, if any, was available to the individual Israelite who brought that sacrifice. This was then extended to the meal offerings as well.[1]

In addition to concern with food items, the priesthood also acted as a kind of department of public health. They would not have thought of skin diseases, fungus, menstruation, and genital discharges as related to health and hygiene. These were matters that caused impurity and therefore needed appropriate rituals to counteract their effect, which broadly meant that the person had to make atonement for introducing impurity into the camp.

"A paramount concern for the preservation of cosmic harmony in nature and society, as well as for the holiness and purity of individuals, led Israelite priests to make rules governing day-to-day activities of priests and other Israelites, including women," explains Judith Romney Wegner. "From this perspective, the largest and most important subgroup in Leviticus is *the entire class of women*. Women are perceived as a special class because of their role in protecting the holiness and purity of individual males with whom they have sexual contact, and thus the community as a whole."[2]

The priesthood was also concerned with bringing sanctity to the community. Sanctity took on various forms, relations between humans, but also the proper way to sanctify the annual calendar through specific holy days and festivals.

The Book of Leviticus is concerned with ritual purity to be sure, but in addition to ritual matters, there are also important sections dealing with morality, specifically chapters 18–20. In the ancient world, rite and right (in the sense of righteousness) were intertwined; they were inseparable parts of the same cloth.

Nearly half (247) of the traditional 613 laws/commandments that are found in the Bible are located in Leviticus. About the same proportion of material discussed in the Talmud relates to legislation in Leviticus. "Furthermore, Leviticus was traditionally the first book taught to school children (Lev. R. [*Midrash Leviticus Rabbah*] 7:3), stemming probably from the historical fact that the priestly school preceded the lay school in origin."[3]

The Book of Leviticus is both the central book of the Torah and its shortest work. It consists of a mere twenty-seven chapters and clearly is linked to both the closing chapters of Exodus (25–31; 35–40), and the opening ten chapters of Numbers. In Exodus and Numbers, the priestly sections largely describe the furniture of the sacrificial system. Leviticus explains what people are to do, how it is done, and which sacrifices they are to bring.

In terms of its "sources" Leviticus is very homogeneous; it is all part of the Priestly (**P**) school.

Just as there are several different possibilities for dividing the books of Genesis and Exodus, so scholars are of various minds about Leviticus.[4] Baruch A. Levine suggests,

> Allowing for some anomalies, we can divide Leviticus into two principal parts: Chapters 1–16 consist of manuals of practice addressed to the priesthood, and chapters 17–27 consist of priestly teachings addressed to the Israelite people. The former division represents *torat kohanim* in the sense of instruction *for* the priests, whereas the latter division expresses the notion of instructions *by* the priests. The former division

focuses on officiation and purification as particular concerns of the priesthood, whereas the latter section emphasizes holiness as the common concern of all Israelites.[5]

2. INSTRUCTIONS FOR THE PRIESTS: LEVITICUS 1–16

A Short Guide to Sacrifices (Lev 1–7)

The first seven chapters of Leviticus introduce various kinds of sacrifices. Chapters 1–5 are directed to the people, and chapters 6–7 are instructions for the priests to carry out these sacrifices. For hundreds of years, the ancients regarded these voluntary offerings as the norm, the established practice for communicating with the gods, and within the Israelite community, for communicating with the God of Israel. As explained earlier, animal and grain sacrifices were the proper way to communicate with God. The priesthood was society's accepted "infrastructure" that mediated between humans and the deity. The rites and rituals described in the early chapters of Leviticus became the background for the priesthood in Jerusalem at the time of the Temple.[6]

From the time of Moses, and as long as the Temple stood, the sacrificial system was the primary way to engage God. All those elaborate animal- and grain-centered rituals ended abruptly for the Jewish community when the Temple was razed to the ground. Judaism's central shrine and sanctuary no longer existed. Yet, as explained in an earlier chapter, many customs and rituals that had been part of the Temple were purposely transferred to the synagogue, which, as an institution, had been standing alongside the Temple for hundreds of years. Prayer, the "service/sacrifice of the heart," took the place of animal and grain sacrifices.[7]

Though the ancient sacrifices mentioned in Leviticus have no present-day application, they do tell us about the thinking of the ancients. There were three principal forms of sacrifices. These were the (totally) burnt offering, the grain offering, and the sacrifice of well-being. These different kinds of sacrifices could be offered each in its own right or in some combined form. Further, each could be a private or a public offering, and apply to a variety of settings. Sacrifices could not be offered for premeditated or intentional sins.

The ancient laws of sacrifice are much more complicated than presented below, but this offers a brief overview.

1. The burnt offering, the *'olah*. Chapter 1 begins with the burnt offering, a sacrifice totally consumed except for the hide of four-legged animals. A burnt offering would be a male species from the herd or flock, or it could be a fowl. The animal was slaughtered, sectioned, and then placed on the altar as an offering. Blood from the animal was sprinkled on the altar. The smoke went up to the heavens, where, it was believed, God appreciated the pleasing odor (Lev 1:9).

The individual donor would place his hand upon the victim and indicate that this was the designated animal and it was for a particular rite. Placing one's hand on the actual victim has a psychological effect on the donor. The victim is not theoretical; it is real and present. It involuntarily gives its life to make expiation for the donor. When the sacrificial ritual was completed—the smoke going heavenward—God had accepted the ransom. The animal was completely consumed; no part was eaten by the donor or the priests.

2. The grain offering, the *minhah*. Chapter 2 discusses different kinds of grain offerings. Often the grain was semolina flour (NRSV translates as "choice flour"); olive oil was added, as well as frankincense. Most grain offerings were made of unleavened dough. It might be baked or fried in an oven or on a griddle. Some was turned to smoke and offered to God; the rest was eaten by the priests.

3. The sacrifice of well-being, *zevah shelamim*. The sacrifice of well-being, or "sacred gift of greeting," is a kind of tribute offering. This sacrifice is introduced in chapter 3. It is a gift of greeting, linking the priests, the donors, and God. The fatty parts are offered up as smoke; blood is dashed on the altar; and then the rest of the sacrifice is boiled in pots. Unlike the burnt offering and the meal offering, which were "most holy" and did not leave the area of the sanctuary, the well-being offering also could be eaten by laity, and away from the sanctuary precincts. In 1 Samuel 9:12–25 there is an account of a sacrifice of well-being.

4. The sin offering, *hattat,* is introduced in chapters 4–5. When a person inadvertently did wrong, the offender had to bring a sacrifice. If the offender was the chief priest or the collective body of Israel, a bull was sacrificed. Part of the animal was sacrificed, and the rest was placed outside of the camp. None was to be eaten. If a chieftain or a commoner had sinned, a goat or female sheep could be offered; some of the animal was burnt, and the priests ate the rest.

5. The guilt offering, *'asham,* is also described in chapter 5. This offering can refer to misappropriation of property or sins of omission or commission. Note: in the Hebrew Bible, chapter 5 has twenty-six verses; in NRSV and many other Christian Bibles it has only nineteen verses. Chapter 6:1 in the Hebrew Bible corresponds to 6:8 in NRSV. The verses in chapter 7 correspond in each version.

Chapters 6 and 7 give directions to the priests and explain some of their specific duties in terms of sacrifices.

Consecration of Priests and Sanctuary (Lev 8–10)

Aaron, Moses' older brother, and Aaron's four sons, Nadab, Abihu, Eleazar, and Ithamar, were appointed as priests in Exodus (chapter 28). Directions were given there (chapters 29 and 40) for their consecration, including the fabrication of the special vestments they were to wear. Chapters 8–10 in Leviticus now return to those details. There is a serious breach in the proceedings, when Aaron's eldest sons, Nadab and Abihu, bring "unholy fire." See the Text Study section at the end of this chapter, "A Mysterious Death," for further discussion of this matter.

Laws of *Kashrut:* Permitted and Forbidden Foods (Lev 11)

The word *kashrut* or *kosher* refers to foods that Jews, by biblical and rabbinic tradition, are permitted to eat. *Kashrut* or *kosher* means "fit" or "proper," but those specific words are not found in the Book of Leviticus. The biblical legislation dealing with proper food is found in Leviticus 11 and Deuteronomy 14. These two chapters are similar but not the same. Deuteronomy 14 presents statements about humans, vessels, and food that is contaminated by being in contact with animals that are impure. The essential issue is holiness, not health (see Lev 11:44–45; Deut 14:21).[8] "The basis for these laws is not irrational taboo, but the covenant relationship, which sets Israel apart for the service of God (Ex 19.3–6). As a holy and consecrated people (Ex 22.31), Israelites must avoid all impurity in order that the holy God may tabernacle [i.e. dwell] in their midst (15.31; 18.1–5; 20.22–26; 26.11–12)."[9]

Stated succinctly, all foods are either vegetable or animal. The laws of *kashrut* do not address vegetation at all. The actual legislation is more detailed, but in the Torah, permitted foods are four-legged animals that have a split hoof and regurgitate their food (chew the cud). These would include cattle, sheep, and goats. Fish need to have both fins and scales. This eliminates all crustaceans (shrimp, lobsters, crabs, and so on), as well as eels, octopuses, and frogs. Fowl need to be domestic birds, primarily chickens, turkeys, and ducks. Generally speaking, permitted animals are herbivorous. In addition to the restrictions just listed, eating blood is forbidden (see Gen 9:4; Lev 17:10–14); and likewise the Torah dictates, "You shall not boil a kid in its mother's milk" (Deut 14:21; cf. Exod 23:19; 34:26). The Torah does not give any reason other than this is God's requirement, and the people are to follow these laws because they are to be holy. Note: in postbiblical writings these laws are expanded to include the proper way to slaughter an animal to minimize pain to that animal. The Talmud discusses the laws of *kashrut* in great detail.

Matters of Impurity (Lev 12–15)

Leviticus as a whole is concerned with matters of purity and impurity. A major part of the responsibilities of the priesthood was to deal with the area of public health. Chapter 12 addresses the category of parturition, laws dealing with childbearing. The child was born absolutely pure, without any traces of sin (a matter, which, in time would become a major difference between the thinking of Judaism and Christianity). The woman who bears the child, however, remains in a period of ritual impurity for set amounts of time depending upon the gender of the child. The mother of a newborn was in a state of impurity or infirmity just as if she were menstruating. If she bears a male child, she is impure for seven days and remains in a state of impurity for thirty-three days. For a female child, the times are doubled. Being impure meant that she could not engage in sexual relations nor enter the sanctuary. No reason is given for the difference in restrictions due to gender.

Chapters 13 and 14 deal with skin diseases, and with mold, mildews, or rots on certain items or buildings. A common, but inaccurate translation for the Hebrew *tsara'at* is "leprosy." Leprosy, or Hansen's disease, has specific symptoms, and they do not conform to the descriptions in Leviticus 13 and 14. NRSV inexplicably uses the term *leprous* but then in a footnote indicates that in relation to humans this is a "term for several skin diseases; precise meaning uncertain." In the context of clothing, notes in NRSV explain that *leprous* refers to mold or mildew, and in relation to houses, the disease means rot or mold.

Chapter 15 addresses various discharges from sexual organs. The legislation deals with normal seminal ejaculation and menstruation as well as matters of illness and infection. In Leviticus 15 illness and impurity are used in a synonymous manner.

Yom Kippur: The Day of Atonement (Lev 16)

In postbiblical Judaism the Day of Atonement/*Yom Kippur* would become the most solemn day of the Jewish year and the culmination of the ten-day period of the High Holy Days, which begins with the New Year/*Rosh Hashanah.* The major focus of chapter 16, however, concentrates on the expiatory rites to maintain a pure sanctuary. The sanctuary has to be absolutely pure, lest God withdraw the divine presence. At the culmination of these rites is the ritual wherein the high priest makes confession for the people over a specially designated goat (see the discussion about "the scapegoat" below). The goat is then dispatched to the wilderness, carrying away the sins of the people.

"The distinctive rites prescribed here involve rare practices called rites of riddance, which effect the removal and destruction of impurity."[10] It was the priesthood itself that constituted the greatest threat to the sanctuary's purity, because the priests were the people who officiated there. In addition, if either individual Israelites or collective Israel transgressed laws of impurity, this could also affect the sanctuary.

The rituals are complex and begin with the high priest. He bathes himself in water and then dons special sacral linen clothing. He will offer a bull as a sin offering on behalf of himself and his household, and later a ram on behalf of himself and the people.

The most fascinating part of this ritual is that the high priest takes two male goats and lets them stand before the tent of meeting. He casts lots, or dice, over the goats. One lot is designated for the deity, and the goat on which the lot falls is taken and slaughtered. The other lot is for Azazel. "Aaron shall present the goat on which the lot fell for the LORD, and offer it as a sin offering; but the goat on which the lot fell for Azazel shall be presented alive before the LORD to make atonement over it, that it may be sent away into the wilderness to Azazel" (Lev 16:9–10).

This is followed by the slaughtering of the bull and its preparation for sacrifice. Next comes an elaborate ritual involving incense and sprinkling blood around the cover of the ark and the horns of the sacred altar. In so doing, the high priest makes expiation for himself, his household, and for the whole house of Israel.

Now the high priest approaches the goat and confesses the sins of the people. He had already confessed his own sins and those of his household; that wrongdoing had been atoned. The live goat takes away the sin of the common people, not that of the priesthood. Having confessed the people's sin over the goat, the goat is then led into the wilderness to a place of no return.

What is this all about? The shortest answer is that we do not know. It is likely that Azazel was regarded as a demon living in the wilderness and that he perhaps took the shape of a goat. By some kind of sympathetic magic, sending the goat to the wilderness carried sins back to him.

The Scapegoat

It is suggested that William Tyndale, the sixteenth-century translator of the Bible into English, first used the term *scapegoat* for this animal that carried away the people's sins. The KJV translates the Hebrew term *Azazel* as "scapegoat" in verses 8, 10, and 26, as does the NIV. The NEB uses the term "the Precipice," with a note indicating "Or for Azazel." The NRSV, the NAB, and the NJPS use the term *Azazel,* though NRSV features a note, "Traditionally rendered *a scapegoat.*" NAB has a note, "The ancient versions translated this word as 'the escaping goat,' whence the English word 'scapegoat.'"

Over the years, the term *scapegoat* has changed radically in its meaning. In common usage, a guilty party *without admitting its wrongdoing or culpability* lays blame on someone or some group that is innocent, and the innocent person or group suffers; it is "scapegoated."

In the legislation in Leviticus, it is clear that the people have sinned, and they admit their guilt through the confession of the high priest. They claim their guilt and see it carried away by the innocent goat. The goat is not blamed, nor is it deemed wicked. The goat simply carries the peoples' sin to the place of no return. "The essential point about the scapegoat is that it removes from the community the taint and impurity of sins *which have first to be openly and fully confessed.* There is no question of transferring to it either blame or responsibility; the sole issue is how to get rid of the miasma of transgressions which one freely acknowledges."[11]

The ritual of Leviticus 16 was replicated during Temple times but ended with the destruction of the Temple by the Romans. As explained earlier, for close to two thousand years, verbal prayer has replaced the ancient concept of animal and grain sacrifice. Leviticus 16 continues to be read as the Torah portion on Yom Kippur in many synagogues, and even those that read alternate chapters, such as Leviticus 19, will still make reference to the ancient rites. For a cogent discussion of the scapegoat ritual, see Baruch Levine's commentary on Leviticus.[12]

3. INSTRUCTIONS BY THE PRIESTS TO THE PEOPLE: LEVITICUS 17–27

The Holiness Code (Lev 17–27)

Chapters 17–26 form a section known as the Holiness Code. A continuing theme in these chapters is that God has chosen Israel and demands holiness of Israel. "You shall be holy to me; for I the LORD am holy, and I have separated you from the other peoples to be mine" (Lev 20:26). Throughout these chapters, again and again, God explains, do such and such, "for I am the LORD your God."

Chapter 17 serves as a prologue to the code, and most of chapter 26 is an epilogue.

Chapters 18 and 20 concentrate on permitted and prohibited sexual unions. Incest is prohibited; people are not to marry near kin. The legislation in chapter 18 is, like much of the Ten Commandments, apodictic. It states that one is to do this or not do that, without giving a long explanation. In chapter 20, a fuller explanation is given. This form of law is known as casuistic, and follows a pattern of "If such and such…" or "When such and such…," and often concludes with some "…then so and so" statements. The only other place in the Torah dealing with similar laws about incest and sexuality is Deuteronomy 27:20–23.

In addition to prohibiting marriage of close family relations, the code enjoins against homosexuality and bestiality. These practices are seen as following the ways of the nations around Israel (Lev 18:24).

Chapter 18:21 (cf. 20:4–5) inveighs against Molech worship, which seems to be a reference to child sacrifice (see 2 Kgs 23:10).

Chapter 19 is unique. The laws there have been termed the highest development of ethics found in the Bible. Much of the legislation is in the apodictic mode: short statements simply to be followed. (See the Text Study section below, "A Code of Ethics.") The list of duties mixes cultic requirements with ethical observances.

The opening lines set forth the context: you, Israel, shall be holy, for I, God, am holy. Imitate God! The next verses speak of honor due parents, Sabbath observance, and prohibition of idol worship. Following a few verses dealing with the sacrifice of well-being, *zevah shelamim* (see above, "A Short Guide to Sacrifices"), Israel is told in concrete ways how to protect the poor and the aliens in the community. Next come statements not to steal, lie, or deal falsely with one another. All this in a dozen verses! Further laws in chapter 19 protect the wage earner from exploitation, provide safeguards for the physically infirm, honor the aged, and call for honest business practices.

Chapters 21–22 are addressed to the priesthood and either repeat or elaborate on material introduced earlier in Leviticus.

Chapter 23 focuses on the festival calendar of the biblical world. The chapter deals with Sabbath observance; Passover/*Pesach*—the feast of Unleavened Bread; the seven-week period between Passover and the holiday of Weeks/*Shavuot;* and the holiday of Weeks/*Shavuot* (also known as Pentecost), the late spring/early summer harvest. This is followed by mention of the holiday that is now celebrated as the New Year/*Rosh Hashanah.* Set on the first day of the seventh month, technically in Leviticus it is not called the new year but rather is described as a day of complete rest, "a holy convocation commemorated with trumpet blasts" (Lev 23:24). Next comes a reference to the Day of Atonement/*Yom Kippur* (technically called *Yom Kippurim*); and the chapter ends with a description of the festival of Booths/*Succot,* the late summer/early autumn harvest.

Chapter 24 covers a variety of laws, but primary among them are the lighting of lights in the sanctuary from evening to morning. In addition mention is made of the rows of bread—sometimes called the bread of display, or the showbread. Then come some laws dealing with blasphemy, and the chapter ends with some laws similar to Exodus 21:22–25, the laws of retaliation, or *lex talionis*.

The Laws of Retaliation/*Lex Talionis*

Leviticus 24:17–22 features laws found in other parts of the Torah: Exodus 21:22–25, but also Genesis 9:6; Exodus 21:12–14, 18–21, 35–36; and Deuteronomy 19:21. These laws deal with the proper punishment for a variety of situations, which range from humans injuring other humans to animals causing human injury. The best known of these laws contain the words "eye for eye, tooth for tooth." It is questionable, though possible, that in the biblical period these words were ever taken literally, much less applied. In all probability, monetary compensation took the place of physical retribution. These laws reflect similar laws found in ancient law codes, such as that of Hammurabi or of Eshnunna. Yet, a major difference in the biblical law is that, aside from slaves where special rules apply, all people, female and male, rich and poor, were treated equally. In these other codes, the punishment differed depending on your economic or social class. If you were of the aristocracy, you had special privileges. The one exception was intentional homicide.

In the postbiblical rabbinic period these matters, and specifically how monetary compensation was to take the place of physical retaliation, are extensively discussed in the Mishnah and the Talmud.[13]

Chapter 25 explains about the sabbatical law and the law of Jubilee. These were agricultural laws, which dictated that the land could be farmed six years in a row but then the soil had to lie fallow for a year. In that sabbatical year all forms of farming—sowing, reaping, pruning, and picking of vines—were prohibited. In the fiftieth year, seven years times seven, a Jubilee (Hebrew, *yovel*) was declared, and Israelites who had been indentured servants earned their freedom, and likewise tenured land returned to the original owners.

The theory behind this release of indentured servants and property reverting to the original owners was that wealth was to be redistributed on a regular basis. No records exist suggesting that this was more than an ideal.

Chapter 26 is filled with blessings and curses. It serves as an epilogue to the Holiness Code. Verses 3–13 are the blessings, followed by verses 14–45, which spell out the disasters that will befall Israel if they do not obey God's commands.

Finally, chapter 27 serves as a kind of add-on to the Book of Leviticus. It describes how the sanctuary is to be funded. This chapter deals with vows, gifts, and dues in relation to the upkeep of the sanctuary.

4. LEVITICUS IN THE CHRISTIAN SCRIPTURES

In the Gospel of Matthew, Jesus is asked, "Teacher, which commandment in the law [Torah] is the greatest?" (Matt 22:36). Jesus replies, quoting Deuteronomy 6:5, "You shall love the Lord your God with all your heart, and with all your soul, and with all your mind." He then continues, "And a second is like it: 'You shall love your neighbor as yourself'" (Matt 22:39). Even though Jesus then says clearly, "On these two commandments hang all the law and the prophets" (Matt 22:40), few Christians know that Jesus is quoting Leviticus 19:18 when he says, "You shall love your neighbor as yourself."

Jesus actually quotes this verse twice earlier. He does so in a slightly modified form in Matthew 5:43 as part of the famed Sermon on the Mount. Then in Matthew 19:19 someone comes up to Jesus and asks about eternal life, and after citing several of the Ten Commandments, Jesus says, "You shall love your neighbor as yourself." Variants of this latter episode are found in Mark 12:28ff. and Luke 10:25ff. In Romans, Paul suggests that all commandments are summed up in the verse from Leviticus 19:18 (Rom 13:9; cf. Gal 5:14; Jas 2:8).

In the Epistle to the Hebrews, Jesus is portrayed as a high priest that holds his priesthood permanently, thereby eternally available to make intercession for believers. These passages echo the legislation found in Leviticus 16 where the high priest intercedes for the Israelite congregation. The epistle describes Jesus in these terms: "We have this hope, a sure and steadfast anchor of the soul, a hope that enters the inner shrine behind the curtain, where Jesus, a forerunner on our behalf, has entered, having become a high priest forever…" (Heb 6:19–20). Likewise, the epistle presents Jesus as the permanent high priest, ever able to save, who unlike his counterparts in Leviticus needed to bring daily sacrifices.

> Jesus has also become the guarantee of a better covenant…he holds his priesthood permanently, because he continues forever. Consequently he is able for all time to save those who approach God through him, since he always lives to make intercession for them….Unlike the other high priests, he has

no need to offer sacrifices day after day, first for his own sins, and then for those of the people; this he did once for all when he offered himself." (Heb 7:22, 24–25, 27; cf. 9:11ff.)

At the point of Jesus' death it is stated that the curtain of the Temple was torn in two (Matt 27:51; Mark 15:38; Luke 23:45). This is a reference that has as its antecedent the curtain in the wilderness sanctuary (cf. Exod 26:31ff.).

The curtain also is mentioned in the atonement sacrifice on Yom Kippur (Lev 16:15ff.).

5. LEVITICUS IN RABBINIC LITERATURE

The three major rabbinic midrashic collections available in English that center on Leviticus are *Midrash Leviticus Rabbah, Midrash Tanhuma Leviticus*, and the *Sifra* to Leviticus.

Linking the Ten Commandments and the Holiness Code

The rabbis clearly understood that the ethical injunctions found in Leviticus 19 were linked in spirit to the Ten Commandments found in Exodus. Using the principle that similar wording suggests connections, the two documents are connected.

Taking each of the Ten Commandments in order, verses in Exodus and Leviticus are then connected.

1. "I am the LORD your God" (Exod 20:2); "I am the LORD your God" (Lev 19:3).
2. "You shall have no other gods" (Exod 20:3); "Do not turn to idols" (Lev 19:4).
3. "You shall not make wrongful use of the name of the LORD your God" (Exod 20:7); "And you shall not swear falsely by my name" (Lev 19:12).

4. "Remember the Sabbath day" (Exod 20:8); "Keep my Sabbaths" (Lev 19:3).
5. "Honor your father and your mother" (Exod 20:12); "You shall each revere your mother and father" (Lev 19:3).
6. "You shall not murder" (Exod 20:13); "You shall not profit by the blood of your neighbor" (Lev 19:16).
7. "You shall not commit adultery" (Exod 20:14 [20:13 H]); "Both the adulterer and the adulteress shall be put to death" (Lev 20:10). [Technically the example comes from Leviticus 20, not Leviticus 19, but proximity allows for "poetic license" in this case.]
8. "You shall not steal" (Exod 20:15 [20:13 H]); "You shall not steal" (Lev 19:11).
9. "You shall not bear false witness" (Exod 20:16 [20:13 H]); "You shall not go around as a slanderer" (Lev 19:16).
10. "You shall not covet...anything that belongs to your neighbor" (Exod 20:17 [20:14 H]); "Love your neighbor as yourself" (Lev 19:18).[14]

God's Direct Involvement with Miriam's Illness

In the view of the rabbis, at times God chose to be directly accessible to humans, literally assuming a hands-on approach to life. They gave the following example. Leviticus 13:12–13 states that if someone has a skin eruption "from head to foot, so far as the priest can see, then the priest shall make an examination." The rabbis infer that this involves an examination of parts of the body that are normally clothed. They then raise the question, who examined Miriam when she was ill (Num 12:10–15)? According to Jewish law, they explain, a person can examine someone else, but not oneself. If you say it was Moses, even Moses was not qualified to do so, for he was not a priest. If you say it was Aaron, Aaron was ineligible because you may not examine a relative. The answer, the midrash explains, is that God said, "I am a priest, I shut her up and I shall declare her clean." That is the meaning of the verse (in Num 12:14) "The LORD said to Moses...'Let her be shut out of the camp for seven days, and after that she may be brought in again.'"[15] See also "Miriam's Words" in the Text Study in the chapter on Numbers.

Giving "Thanks" Is Timeless

The rabbis suggested that in the messianic age—when humans would be free from sin—that a certain class of sacrifices would continue to be offered. "Though all sacrifices may be discontinued in the future...the offering of thanksgiving will continue...[such as Lev 7:12] though all prayers may be discontinued, the prayer of thanksgiving will never cease."[16]

Sins Committed against God; Sins Committed against Humans

In the view of the rabbis, the holy day of Yom Kippur would absolve a person of sins committed against God, but not wrongful acts against humans. They cite Leviticus 16:30, "From all your sins you shall be clean before the LORD." The rabbis explain, "For transgressions against God, the Day of Atonement [*Yom Kippur*] effects atonement; but for transgressions between humans, the Day of Atonement does not effect atonement until one first reconciled with that person."[17]

Premeditated Sins Are Not Forgiven by *Yom Kippur*...

Intentionality is a factor. You cannot consciously sin with intent to repent at a later point. The rabbis explain, "If one says 'I will sin and repent, I will sin and repent,' [God] will not give that person an opportunity to repent. [If that person says] 'I will sin and the Day of Atonement will effect atonement' then the Day of Atonement will not effect atonement."[18]

Study Takes the Place of the Temple Sacrifices

In the post-Temple world, the rabbis explained that study of Torah takes the place of the sacrificial cult. In Leviticus 17:2 the Hebrew says, "This is what [or "This is the thing," Hebrew, *davar*] the LORD has commanded." The rabbis then point out that the word *davar* can mean either "what" (or "thing") and "word." Hence, they explain, God commanded that the "word," that is to say "study," or "study of the words of Torah" could take the place of actual sacrifice.

> [(Lev. 17:2:) THIS IS THE THING.] The Holy One foresaw that the Temple was going to be destroyed; so the Holy One said: As long as the Temple exists, you shall sacrifice within it, <and> there will be atonement for you; but when the Temple does not exist, how will there be atonement for you? Occupy yourselves with the words of Torah, because they are comparable with offerings, and they will atone for you. Thus it is stated (ibid.) THIS IS THE THING (literally: WORD)...The words of Torah resemble all the offerings.[19]

6. LEVITICUS IN ONGOING JEWISH TRADITION

The cult of animal and grain sacrifice spelled out in Leviticus was the basis for the worship offered at both the first and later the second Temple in Jerusalem. That change to a specific central location did not happen in a vacuum. Though Jerusalem was the designated capital of the united kingdoms, following the schism at the time of Rehoboam and Jeroboam, there would be two sanctuaries, two shrines. One was for the northern kingdom, Israel, in Samaria at Beth El (and also at Dan), and the other for Judah, in the south, at Jerusalem. Even so, before Jerusalem became the capital, there were competing priesthoods, in Shiloh and elsewhere. It took years before the Jerusalem Temple was regarded as the place of centralized worship. As noted earlier, when the Romans destroyed the Temple in 70 CE, verbal prayer and study replaced the cult of animal and grain sacrifice.

The rabbinic period in Judaism and the establishment of the synagogue as the place where the community engaged with God are not the subject of this book. It is important to note, however, that a fair amount of the Mishnah and the Talmud are devoted to ritual matters first addressed in Leviticus. These include such subjects as sacrifice and what is termed matters of family purity: menstruation, bathing, childbirth, circumcision, and likewise matters of diet: the laws of *kashrut*.

In the Mishnah and Talmud, there also are many tractates devoted to the proper form of blessings, holy days, and ritual life. The antecedents for this postbiblical legislation in many cases is the Book of Leviticus.

Even following the completion of the Talmud, these matters engaged the Jewish community, and do so today. The fact is that Judaism, for thousands of years, right up to the present, continues to celebrate the holy days and festivals detailed in Leviticus. These days, the weekly Sabbath/*Shabbat,* Passover/*Pesach,* Weeks/*Shavuot,* Booths/*Succot,* to say nothing of the Day of Atonement/*Yom Kippur,* link present-day Judaism with that of the past. Details of the celebration may change. Judaism does not have an active priesthood, nor have Jews brought animal and grain sacrifices for two thousand years. Likewise, Jews do not bring the produce that they have grown to a central shrine. The spirit of those festivals, however, is reflected in their modern-day expression. Dietary laws, concerns for the physically disabled, respect for the elderly—these laws in modern guise continue to inform Jewish life. The past is actively alive in the present.

7. TEXT STUDY

A. Leviticus 10:1–7. A Mysterious Death

One of the ongoing mysteries of the biblical period is the unsettling account of the death of the sons of the high priest Aaron. Aaron's two oldest sons are Nadab and Abihu. They, like Aaron, had been specifically selected by God to serve as priests at the sanctuary (cf. Exod 28:1ff.). Then, according to the text, inexplicably they offered "unholy fire" (in some translations, "strange fire" or "alien fire") before God, fire that God (apparently) had not authorized. Consequently, fire comes forth and consumes them. By way of explanation—or perhaps chastisement—Moses turns to Aaron and says, "'This is what the LORD meant when he said, "Through those who are near me I will show myself holy, and before all the people I will be glorified."'" And Aaron was silent" (Lev 10:3).

What is this all about? What is this "unholy" ("strange" or "alien") fire? What does Moses mean by his cryptic statement? Why is Aaron silent? Why does Moses instruct Aaron and his remaining sons, Eleazar and Ithamar, not to mourn publicly, lest they also die. Why is the community of Israel, instead, to "mourn the burning that the LORD has sent" (Lev 10:6)?

One explanation for these strange events comes after several chapters. In terms of the narrative text, the opening verses of Leviticus 16 seem to follow this episode in Leviticus 10. The intervening materials dealing with ritual impurity are an item in their own right. Leviticus 16:1–2 follow logically from the death of the two men. Verse 1 gives a different explanation why Nadab and Abihu die: "they drew near before the LORD and died." Consequently, Moses instructs Aaron, do not come into the sanctuary without permission. The inference is that Aaron's sons acted impulsively, without authority, and now Aaron is warned not to do likewise.

Leviticus 10:1 features the two men each taking his censer (or firepan) and making an offering. They seem to be offering something new, something that was not authorized. "The priestly ideal is one of conformity, not of innovation."[20]

Some traditional commentaries rationalize the death of Nadab and Abihu by suggesting that these two sons of Aaron were especially beloved of God. "Through those who are near me I will show myself holy" (Lev 10:3). God loved them, therefore God took them.

In the Babylonian Talmud *Zevahim* 115b the rabbis explain that Moses turned to Aaron and said, "'Oh my brother, your sons died only that the glory of the Holy One may be sanctified through them.' When Aaron saw that his sons were honored by God, he was silent, and was rewarded for his silence." What is that reward? In Leviticus 10:8–11 God directly addresses Aaron instead of speaking through Moses.

When God speaks to Aaron at this point, the subject is that when priests are performing their duties they are to refrain from drinking alcohol. On the assumption that these incidents are connected, another explanation is that Nadab and Abihu were acting improperly; they were intoxicated with alcohol when they brought their fire, and therefore this resulted in God's admonition to Aaron in verses 8–11.

It is also possible that Aaron's older sons were challenging the authority of Moses and Aaron. Perhaps they thought, "We, too, can offer sacrifices." If this is so, then they were punished for their presumption. Moses might have been wary of a challenge to his authority, for later in that same chapter, Moses criticizes Aaron's remaining sons for what he, Moses, perceives to be an infraction of the rules (Lev 10:16ff.). In the event, Aaron comes to his sons' rescue, and Moses then appears to apologize. The rabbis take this opportunity to teach a moral lesson: a truly great person is not ashamed to admit publicly when a mistake is made. "Moses issued a proclamation throughout the camp and said: I misinterpreted the law and my brother Aaron came and put me right."[21]

B. Leviticus 19:1–4, 9–18, 32–37.
A Code of Ethics

As explained above, the list of duties found in Leviticus 19 mixes cultic requirements with ethical observances. Throughout the chapter, the message repeats: you, Israel, shall be holy, for I, God, am holy. Imitate God! Though there are also cultic issues in

Leviticus 19, the present focus is on the social-ethical teachings of that chapter.

1. Verse 3 (parents, Shabbat). While in the Ten Commandments honor for father precedes that of mother, here she comes first, and the verb is "revere," a different quality than honor. Just as reverence for parents is a quality basic to a good and moral life, so equally humans need to honor the sanctity of the Sabbath. Humans are not machines; humans need a day of rest.

2. Verse 4 (idolatry). In like manner, just as reverence of parents and recognition of a day of rest is basic to a moral society, so people are reminded: do not turn to idolatry. Only God is God. The theme "I am the LORD your God" is offered for emphasis.

3. Verses 9–10 (protect the impoverished). Biblical society did not have Social Security. There were no government safety nets to provide for and protect the poor. The average Israelite lived under straitened circumstances. The laws of Exodus 21, which refer to people who needed to become indentured servants or who literally sold their daughters into servitude, reflect a society where poverty is widespread. Here, in this beacon of moral teachings, those fortunate enough to own land and benefit from the produce of the earth are told to share some of their wealth. The Bible does not specify what the space or quality of the edge of the field should be. In the Mishnah, the teachings of the rabbis of roughly two thousand years ago, a minimum of one-sixtieth of the yield of the harvest is suggested. They add that, in addition, the resources of the owner and the needs of the impoverished need to be taken into consideration.[22]

4. Verse 13 (the laborer). Here again the level of poverty dictates that the laborer is paid immediately. He may need the wages to buy food, to support his family that very night.

5. Verse 14 (the deaf, blind). The deaf and blind need special consideration. Do not take advantage of their infirmities to cheat them or to mock them. Again comes the refrain, do this because I am the LORD.

6. Verse 15 (equal justice, judge fairly, honesty). Justice needs to be blind. Do not favor people just because they are poor, nor, similarly, should you pander to the rich because of their wealth.

Judge fairly, be honest in all your dealings (see vss. 35–36, do not cheat in measurements or weights).

7. Verses 17–18 (no grudges, love your neighbor). These verses are connected. Do not allow jealousies or envy to annoy and irritate. Be direct and straightforward in your dealing with your kin. Do not hold grudges. Then, the famous line, "love your neighbor as yourself," immediately precedes the signature line, "I am the LORD." Notice: it does not say, "love your Jewish neighbor," or "love your neighbor who is just like you," nor does it say, "love your likable neighbor." Verse 17 contrasts with verse 18: hate versus love. A subtle message here is that you have to love yourself before you can love your neighbor. Self-love in the sense of self-respect is an important quality for an orderly society. Clearly self-love is not to be taken to an extreme. You need to treat your neighbor as you would want to be treated yourself.

8. Verse 32 (the aged). Just as the deaf and the blind need special consideration, so do the aged and the elderly. You show deference to the aged by caring for them with compassion. Again comes the signature line, I am the LORD.

9. Verses 33–34 (strangers). Strangers are to be protected. You were strangers in Egypt; you were exploited, degraded, and despised. God expects better of you. You know first-hand what it means to be the "other"; treat people with respect. "I am the LORD your God!"

10. Verse 37 (keep and observe). The verbs *keep* and *observe* in the Hebrew serve to reinforce each other, hence the translation, "You shall keep…and observe them" (alternate translation, "You shall faithfully observe," NJPS), and then one more time, to emphasize the message, "I am the LORD."

Notes

1. William W. Hallo, "Leviticus and Ancient Near Eastern Literature," in *The Torah: A Modern Commentary*, ed. W. Gunther Plaut (New York: Union of American Hebrew Congregations, 1981), 742–43.

2. Judith Romney Wegner, "Leviticus," in *The Women's Bible Commentary*, ed. Carol A. Newsom and Sharon H. Ringe (London: SPCK; Louisville, KY: Westminster John Knox, 1992), 36, 38.

3. Jacob Milgrom, "Leviticus, Book of," in *Encyclopedia Judaica* (Jerusalem: Keter, 1972), 11:138–39.

4. Hallo suggests an 11:5:11 approach: consumption of food—chapters 1–11; requirements for purification—chapters 12–16; and finally sanctification, chapters 17–27. Hallo, "Leviticus," 740. Another, more detailed suggestion makes these divisions: chapters 1–7 as the sacrificial system itself followed by the induction service for the priesthood, chapters 8–10. In this latter section there is the episode of the "unholy fire" (or "alien fire" or "strange fire") offered by Nadab and Abihu, and it ends with the consumption of the initiatory offerings. Chapters 11–16 in this schema deal with various laws of impurities, including animal impurities; impurities that directly affect humans (childbirth, skin diseases, fungi in houses, genital discharges), as well as impurities that touch the sanctuary or the nation as a group. Chapters 17–26 are deemed the Holiness Source, and, finally, chapter 27 describes the commutation of gifts to the sanctuary (Milgrom, "Leviticus," 139).

5. Baruch A. Levine, *The JPS Torah Commentary: Leviticus* (Philadelphia: Jewish Publication Society, 1989), xvi.

6. The Jerusalem Temple, first built by Solomon circa 950 BCE, stood for nearly four hundred years. Destroyed by the Babylonians early in the sixth century BCE, a second Temple was built in the late sixth century and lasted well over five hundred years, only to be destroyed by the Romans in the year 70 CE.

7. Rabbi Yohanan ben Zaccai, a rabbi who lived at the time of the Roman destruction of the Temple, is credited with saying that acts of loving kindness are as equally desirable as bringing daily sacrifices (*Avot de Rabbi Natan,* chapter 4). A similar idea is reflected in the Christian scriptures. In Mark 12:32ff. a scribe says to Jesus that affirmation of God's unity, to love God with one's heart and strength (Deut 6:4–5), and to love one's neighbor (Lev 19:18)—"this is much more important than all whole burnt offerings and sacrifices." (See comments in "Deuteronomy in Rabbinic Literature" below). Coincidentally, the Talmud suggests that study itself is a greater act than bringing daily sacrifices (Babylonian Talmud *Megillah* 3b). Further, it is stated that God gives credit to those who study Torah, as if they had brought the Temple sacrifices (Babylonian Talmud *Menahot* 110a).

8. Cf. Levine, *JPS: Leviticus,* 243ff.

9. NRSV comment to Leviticus 11:44–45.

10. Levine, *JPS: Leviticus,* 99.

11. Theodor H. Gaster, *Festivals of the Jewish Year* (New York: William Sloane, 1953),142.

12. Levine, *JPS: Leviticus,* 250–53.

13. Cf. *Mishnah Baba Kamma* 8.1; Babylonian Talmud *Baba Kamma* 83b–84a and elsewhere. See also the discussion on Exodus 21:23ff., "Lex Talionis," in Sarna, *JPS: Exodus,* 125ff.; and "Retaliation and Compensation in Biblical Criminal Law," in Levine, *JPS: Leviticus,* 268–70.

14. *Midrash Leviticus Rabbah* 24.5; cf. *Midrash Tanhuma* Leviticus, 7.3, Leviticus 19:1ff., part III.

15. *Midrash Leviticus Rabbah* 15.8.

16. Ibid., 9.7.

17. *Mishnah Yoma* 8.9.

18. Ibid.

19. *Midrash Tanhuma* Leviticus, 6.16, Leviticus 17:1ff., part III.

20. Bernard Bamberger, commentary on Leviticus 10:1, in *The Torah,* ed. Plaut, 800.

21. *Midrash Leviticus Rabbah* 13.1.

22. Cf. Levine, *JPS: Leviticus,* 127.

Numbers

1. INTRODUCTION

Numbers, the fourth book of the Torah, derives its English name from the Latin *Numeri*, which is a translation of the Greek *Arithmoi*. These *numbers* refer to a census of the Israelites taken early on in the work. There will be several censuses in the book. In Hebrew, the more common name for Numbers is *Bemidbar* ("in the wilderness/desert"), from the first important words in the book—"The LORD spoke to Moses in the wilderness of Sinai." In the Talmud, the book is called *Sefer Ha-Pekudim* ("the book of the census").

Numbers begins in the second year following the Exodus from Egypt (specifically in the fourteenth month of that forty-year journey). The Book of Numbers concludes during the last year of the desert experience, just prior to entering the Promised Land. These statements, while true, are also misleading. The Israelites were in the desert wilderness for forty years, but they were not continuously on the move for all of that period. Much of their time, possibly as much as thirty-eight years, was spent at one oasis or group of oases called variously Kadesh (Num 13:26; 20:1), Kadesh-Barnea (Num 32:8), and Meribath-Kadesh (Num 27:14). This is located some fifty miles south of present-day Beersheba.[1] According to this theory, the Israelites arrived at Kadesh at the end of the second year of their sojourn (Num 13:26), and they would remain there for well over three decades. The Book of Numbers does not state that explicitly, but it can be derived from the fact that they leave Kadesh the same year that Aaron and Miriam die (Num 20:1, 22ff.). A bit later, Numbers explains that Aaron died in the fortieth year following the Exodus (Num 33:38).[2]

141

Numbers is a mixture of narrative and legislation. In that sense, it is similar to Exodus.[3] Lists are a recurring item in this book. Names of the tribal leaders and accounts of their actual numbers; lists of various encampments (though it does not state how long they stayed at each locale; cf. Num 21:10ff.); and there also are lists of the places where the spies went to reconnoiter Canaan, the Promised Land (Num 13:21ff.).

One of the most famous sets of verses in the Bible, the so-called Priestly blessing, appears in Numbers. "The LORD bless you and keep you; the LORD make his face to shine upon you, and be gracious to you; the LORD lift up his countenance upon you, and give you peace" (Num 6:24–26).

Numbers also contains the words that are featured prominently in Jewish liturgy: "How fair are your tents, O Jacob, your encampments, O Israel" (*Ma tovu oha-lekha Yaakov, mish-keno-tekha Israel;* Num 24:5). In addition, it is in Numbers that the narrative is told of Balaam, and his miraculously Hebrew-speaking animal (Num 22).

Finally, it is in Numbers that the five daughters of Zelophehad are confirmed in their request to inherit their father's estate (Num 27:1–11).

The simplest way to divide the book of Numbers is to place a line between the generation that left Egypt (Num 1–25) and those who would enter the land (Num 26–36).[4] That first generation had so discredited itself with lack of faith in God's direction that, with the exception of Moses and the faithful spies, Joshua and Caleb, they all died in the wilderness. The last remnant of the Egyptian-born generation die in the fortieth year following the Exodus from Egypt.

Another way to characterize the Book of Numbers is in terms of subject matter. A striking feature of the book is that two kinds of writing, law and narrative, are skillfully interwoven with each other, one following the next.[5]

2. THREE WEEKS AT SINAI: NUMBERS 1–10

The Census

It is time now to begin the journey to the Promised Land. In Numbers, the people need to transform themselves into an organized military camp. On the way to Canaan, they will pass through difficult terrain, and they will encounter hostile tribes and nations. They must be prepared for this journey. To organize properly they have to have an accurate count of their actual population.

God instructs Moses and Aaron to begin this mammoth task. Yet, they are not to work alone. Associated with them will be a God-mandated senior representative from each of the twelve tribes (Num 1:4). This enumeration went on simultaneously, each tribe doing its own internal count. The presence of someone representing the tribe, or perhaps reporting for the tribe to Moses and Aaron, has the ring of authenticity. On one hand, this information was necessary for military purposes. On the other hand, there may have been a reluctance to gather these numbers. Plaut writes that there was "until quite recently an ambivalence toward counting people and toward knowing their ages. For there was a feeling that knowing a person's 'number' was equivalent to knowing his essence, and such knowledge was ultimately a divine prerogative (e.g., knowing when 'someone's number was up')."[6]

This explanation puts the reluctance toward gathering an accurate census in theological terms. Earlier, in Exodus 30:11ff., there was an enigmatic statement that when a census would be taken people were to pay a half-shekel so that "no plague may come upon them for being registered." Rich and poor pay the same half-shekel; it is an atonement for their lives. Somehow, taking this count of the population presented a danger to people.[7]

Chapter 1 lists the twelve tribes and their representatives. The order of the tribes differs here from the birth order of Jacob's sons, and it differs from the order found in Genesis 49 and Exodus 1.

Verse 10 refers to the "sons of Joseph," Ephraim and Manasseh. There is no single tribe of Joseph, but rather his two sons each head up separate tribal units. Conspicuously missing from the list is the tribe of Levi, named for Jacob's third son. The Levites will be counted, but separate from the rest of the Israelites. The Levites have special duties: they are associated with helping with the sanctuary and public health issues.

In 1:46 the census states that the total number of Israelite men twenty years and over comes to 603,550, and this figures does not include the Levites! Taken literally, these numbers would provide innumerable difficulties. As discussed in the chapter on Exodus, it would not be hard to extrapolate that when the women and children are added, the total Israelite camp would number between two and three million people. The mere logistics of communicating with, organizing, and moving them, much less sustaining such numbers, and under desert conditions, is insurmountable. Absent a massive support system, which would put an enormous strain on a society even in modern times, it is impossible to take these figures at face value.

Various answers are suggested for these figures. As explained in the chapter on Exodus, the Hebrew term *elef* may mean "contingent," or "clan" and not necessarily "thousand." Likewise, the Hebrew *revavot* in this case must mean something other than "ten thousand."[8] Yet even if the figure in Numbers 1:21, which says 46,500, were to be understood as 46 contingents, numbering 500 fighting men above the age of twenty, there still would be enormous problems. Taking the composite number, 500 men for the tribe of Reuben, 300 for Simeon, 650 for Gad, and so on, the total comes to 5,550 fighting men. Conservatively, this would mean that there were well over twenty thousand Israelites in the desert for the forty-year sojourn, again a difficult figure to sustain.

In chapter 2, the tribes are given their marching orders. They are to place themselves around the sanctuary (the tent of meeting), with the various tribes in specific directions: north, south, and so on.

The next two chapters (3 and 4) are devoted to organizing the priesthood. Aaron and his sons are in a prominent position. The Levites are counted. There are specific directions how to move the sanctuary: how sacred objects are to be covered and then put into their proper place for transport.

Next (in chapters 5–6) comes some legislation that deals with matters of impurity. The majority of chapter 6 focuses on the voluntary role of the Nazirite. A man or a woman could choose to take on additional restrictions, extra vows of abstinence, and thereby be in a specially purified state. Long hair, refraining from the consumption of alcohol, and avoiding the dead were the primary aspects of the Nazirite (Num 6:2–21). Chapter 6 concludes with the priestly blessing (see Text Study below, "The Priestly Blessing").

Chapter 7, the longest in the Torah, details the tribal leaders' gifts for the sanctuary. It concludes with a one-line statement that when Moses went into the tent of meeting to speak with God, Moses would "hear the voice speaking to him from above the mercy seat that was on the ark of the covenant from between the two cherubim" (Num 7:89). (See Text Study below, "The Cherubim.")

Chapters 8:1–10:10 deal with varied items: the seven-branched menorah/lampstand, purification rites and age limits for the Levites, and final preparations before setting out on the journey. It includes notification of the second Passover and, finally, the construction of two silver trumpets to summon the community for special events, or setting them in motion.

3. FORTY-YEARS SOJOURN: NUMBERS 11–20

When the Israelites leave Sinai they expect shortly to enter Canaan, the Promised Land. As they set out, Moses turns to his father-in-law and invites him to join with the people. Moses explains that the people will be generous with him, but he declines, saying that he wants to return to his native land.[9]

Soon the people begin to complain; this will be a recurring theme. God is incensed and sends out a fire. The people are fearful, and Moses intervenes on their behalf. They—or at least some of the people—are slow learners. Voices are raised; people complain about their diet. "If only we had meat to eat! We remember the fish we used to eat in Egypt for nothing, the cucumbers, the melons, the leaks, the onions, and the garlic; but now our strength is dried up, and there is nothing at all but this manna to look at" (Num 11:4–6). Once again, God is displeased, but this time Moses displays his human side. He turns to God and says, I cannot do this. You have given me an impossible burden.

God's reply is to provide extra support for Moses. Seventy elders of the people are taken from the camp and gathered around the tent (of meeting). God takes some of the spirit that is on Moses and places it on the elders. The seventy then prophesy (or speak in ecstasy), but this is a one-time occurrence (Num 11:16–17, 24–25). Next, we learn that two men, Eldad and Medad, had remained behind, and then suddenly they began to speak ecstatically within the camp. Someone comes to Moses to alert him about this. Moses is not upset. "Are you jealous for my sake? Would that all the LORD's people were prophets, and that the LORD would put his spirit on them" (Num 11:29). It is unclear if these two men were part of the original group chosen who just did not go to the tent, or if they simply began to prophesy.

Why the number seventy? Surely, seventy-two would, in principle, make more sense, six elders per tribe. There *is* precedent for the number seventy. Traditionally there are seventy nations (Gen 10) and likewise there were seventy elders who accompanied Moses, Aaron, Nadab, and Abihu at Mt. Sinai (Exod 24:9).[10]

Choosing seventy elders to help Moses unfortunately deals with only part of the problem. The people clamor for meat, which God provides for them. A wind blows in a large number of quails, which fall beside the camp. Some of the people start to devour them. The people are gluttonous, and God's anger again is unleashed, bringing a very great plague.

Challenges to Moses' control are not limited to the riffraff. In chapter 12 Moses' own siblings question his authority. In verse 2 Miriam and Aaron ask, "Has the LORD spoken only through Moses? Has he not spoken through us also?"

The answer is not long in coming. God orders the three to congregate at the tent of meeting. There, God chastises Miriam and Aaron and explains that the relationship between God and Moses is unique. God says: "With him I speak face to face—clearly, not in riddles; and he beholds the form of the LORD. Why then were you not afraid to speak against my servant Moses?" For some reason only Miriam is directly punished: she is afflicted with some disfiguring skin disease. Only after Moses intercedes on her behalf does God relent, though she is quarantined for a week (see Text Study at the end of this chapter, "Miriam's Words").

Despite these setbacks, these murmurings and complaints, the generation that left Egypt still fully expects that it will enter the Promised Land. This is Moses' expectation, and apparently God's expectation as well. In chapter 13, God instructs Moses to send out scouts to reconnoiter, to spy out, the land of Canaan. As expected, there is one leader per tribe, twelve spies in all. They are listed, and among them are Caleb, son of Jephunneh from the tribe of Judah, and Joshua, son of Nun from the tribe of Ephraim. Moses gives explicit instructions: "Go up there into the Negeb, and go up into the hill country, and see what the land is like, and whether the people who live in it are strong or weak, whether they are few or many?" He also wants to know if the land is good or not. Are the walls of their cities fortified? Is the land rich or poor? Are there trees or not? Finally, Moses admonishes them, "Be bold, and bring some of the fruit of the land" (Num 13:17–18, 20).

For forty days they follow their mission, and then, bearing a large cluster of grapes, as well as pomegranates and figs, they return to the Israelite camp at Kadesh. It is a wonderful place, they report. The land flows with milk and honey. Yet, the towns are large and fortified. A whole variety of people live there.

Caleb tries to play down the difficulties and suggests that this is the time to attack. His advice is shouted down. His fellow spies say, compared to the people who live there "we seemed like grasshoppers." As chapter 14 begins, the people are terribly disheartened and immediately lose courage. "Would that we had died in the land of Egypt! Or would that we had died in this wilderness!...Let us choose a captain, and go back to Egypt" (Num 13:33; 14:2, 4). Joshua then raises his voice in support of Caleb. Their arguments fall on deaf ears; the people are adamant in their fear.

This apostasy, this failure of nerve, in later years was seen as the low point in Israel's early history, matched in its faithlessness and disloyalty only by the episode of the golden calf (Exod 32–33). As the people are about to stone Moses and Aaron, and probably Caleb and Joshua as well, God's glory appears to all Israel at the tent of meeting. God addresses Moses and declares divine displeasure. "How long will they [the people] refuse to believe in me?...I will strike them with pestilence and disinherit them, and I will make of you a nation greater and mightier than they."

Moses pleads for the people, and God relents to the extent that they are not to be wiped out. Nonetheless, as a punishment, they shall bear their iniquity—a year for each day that the spies were on their mission: forty years. The full generation that came out of Egypt, excepting Moses, Caleb, and Joshua, will die in the desert.

Chapter 15 notes various laws, including a form of thanksgiving offering when entering the new land, and describes what happens if one inadvertently forgets to follow a commandment, and if someone defiantly reviles God. The chapter ends (vss. 37–41) with the laws of fringes *(tzitzit)*, lines that have been incorporated into the Jewish daily liturgy, following the *Sh'ma [Shema]*, the affirmation of God's unity, itself a quotation from Deuteronomy 6:4.

As chapter 15 regarded matters of law, so chapters 16 and 17 follow with narrative (see end of the "Introduction" section above). The Torah now presents the most famous, indeed the most serious, rebellion against Moses' and Aaron's authority: the rebellion of Korah, Dathan, and Abiram. In all probability there are multiple stories woven together (see Text Study below, "Korah's Rebellion").

The primary villain is Korah, the son of Izhar. Like Aaron and Moses, Korah is a Levite. Accompanied by two hundred fifty prominent Israelites, Korah turns to Moses and Aaron and says, "You have gone too far! All the congregation are holy, everyone of them, and the LORD is among them. So why then do you exalt yourselves above the assembly of the LORD?" (Num 16:3). Like any demagogue, Korah is purposely vague. He does not give details; he claims holiness for the whole congregation and suggests that Moses and Aaron falsely exalted themselves. He insinuates that the primacy of the Aaronite family over other Levites (Num 3:5–10) is capricious.

Moses is appalled. He replies that on the next day God will decide which faction is in the right: Korah and company or Moses and Aaron. Moses chastises the Levites and asks rhetorically, is it not enough that God has designated you as a group to assist in the work of the sanctuary, do you also seek the responsibility of the priesthood?

The next day Moses suggests that if Korah and his rebels die a natural death, then God is not siding with Moses. Yet if God creates something new, the ground opening up and swallowing up the rebels so they go to Sheol* alive, then the people will know that God is with Moses.

> As soon as he finished speaking all these words, the ground under them was split apart. The earth opened its mouth and swallowed them up, along with their households—everyone who belonged to Korah and all their goods. So they with all that belonged to them went down alive into Sheol; the earth closed over them, and they perished from the midst of the assembly...and fire came out from the LORD and consumed the two hundred fifty men. (Num 16:31–35)

The versification for chapters 16 and 17 differs between Jewish Bibles and most Christian Bibles (including NRSV, NEB, NIV, and KJV, but not NAB). In Jewish Bibles there are but thirty-five verses in chapter 16 and twenty-eight verses in chapter 17. Most Christian versions have fifty verses in chapter 16 and thirteen in chapter 17, following the tradition of the Septuagint.

In both versions, chapter 17 features the story of Aaron's miraculous staff. As a proof of his being chosen by God, at one point the staff produces blossoms and bears ripe almonds (Num 17:8 [23 H]).

Chapters 18 and 19 return to matters of legislation. The responsibilities of Aaronite priests and other Levites are discussed in chapter 18, while chapter 19 deals with legislation outlining the rites for purification for someone who has come into contact with a corpse. This subject has been dealt with previously (Lev 21:1–4; Num 6:6–13), but here the Torah goes into much greater detail. The chapter specifically mentions a "red heifer" or a "red cow." The Hebrew is *parah adumah*. The word *adumah* is the feminine version of the more common term *adom,* which generally means "red," or perhaps "ruddy." Hebrew does not have a word for the color "brown," but that is probably what is meant in this context, a brown cow which is uniform in its color, without specks of white or black.

The priest takes the cow and slaughters it, and then the cow is totally burned. The priest then needs to wash himself, and he is ritually impure until evening. The ashes are taken and mixed with water. The person who takes the ashes also washes himself and is impure until evening. This water then is used to purify someone who has touched a corpse. Just how these ashes, which contaminate both the priest and the person who moves them, can purify someone ritually defiled by touching a corpse defies logic. It is a mystery that has been part of Jewish tradition for over three thousand years.[11]

Chapters 20–21 return to narrative sections. Numbers 20:1 begins with a mystery. It states, "The Israelites, the whole congregation, came into the wilderness of Zin in the first month, and the people stayed in Kadesh. Miriam died there and was buried there." It says "the first month," but of which year? A few verses later, Numbers 20:22 explains that the Israelites then set out from Kadesh and came to Mount Hor, where Aaron dies. As noted previously, a later chapter mentions in passing that Aaron died in the fortieth year of the wilderness sojourn (Num 33:38–39). So it would seem that Numbers 20 takes place at the end of the wilderness sojourn. The problem is that some verses in Numbers and Deuteronomy appear to contradict this understanding. See the Text Study section below, "The Kadesh Mystery."

In any case, the dividing line for the fortieth year is Numbers 20:22, when the Israelites (for the first or second time) leave Kadesh for Mount Hor. A few of the generation that left Egypt are still alive, but they will die out by the end of chapter 25. Their deaths represent the end of the old generation, and to mark that fact, Numbers 26 begins with a call for a new census.

4. HEADING TOWARD THE PROMISED LAND: NUMBERS 21–36

As Israel heads in a general northerly direction in chapter 21, it encounters Canaanites in the Negeb (the Negev), and Israel defeats the king of Arad. With a lamentable consistency, the people again complain about Moses' leadership, and God sends poisonous (or fiery) serpents that bite the people. To ward off this evil Moses is instructed to erect a pole with a poisonous (fiery) snake on it, for anyone who sees this bronze (or copper) serpent will live (vss. 6–9). The journey continues through Transjordan, and in vs. 14 there is an intriguing reference to a long lost work, the Book of the Wars of the LORD. Like the Book of Jashar mentioned in Joshua 10:13 and 2 Samuel 1:18, nothing more is known of this work. Chapter 21 then ends with successful battles against the monarchs Sihon of Heshbon and Og of Bashan.

Chapter 22 finds the Israelites in the area of Moab, east of the Jordan River near Jericho. The Moabites fear the Israelites. The Moabite king, Balak, the son of Zippor, sends emissaries to engage the foreign priest–diviner–prophet, Balaam, the son of Beor, who lives in Pethor, located on the Euphrates River. This is a huge undertaking. The two locales are over four hundred miles distant, and there certainly were not direct routes. Balak wants to hire Balaam to curse Israel. Chapters 22–24 form a wonderful story within a story.[12]

The figure of Balaam is complicated. His reputation is powerful. Whomever he blesses is blessed; whomever he curses is cursed (Num 22:6).

Balaam communicates with God and follows what God tells him (vs. 12–13), namely, not to go with Balak's emissaries, who in fact return to Moab.

King Balak is not to be put off; he sends a second delegation to convince Balaam. Again Balaam says, I will not move without God's consent (vss. 15–19). This time God agrees, but then inexplicably is incensed at Balaam's leaving. God sends an angel to deter Balaam. The story is a gem and well worth reading in its entirety. The section where Balaam's donkey speaks with a human voice to rebuke his ungrateful master is a wonderful tale of irony. To King Balak's dismay, Balaam ends up blessing Israel; and by the end of chapter 24, Balaam sets off for his journey home.

The opening verses of chapter 25 record Israel's apostasy at Shittim, where certain Israelites sexually consort with Moabite women. Reference is made to the Baal of Peor. Baal is the name of a major pagan god; in Canaanite religion it was the god of storm and fertility. Peor may be a locale, a pagan cult site (cf. Deut 3:29, where Beth-peor is mentioned). A plague erupts, and in the midst of this an Israelite man takes a Midianite woman and appears to be engaged in sexual congress. Phineas *(Pinhas)* in a burst of zeal takes a spear in hand and impales the two in the midst of their activity. Though many die, the plague is ended.

Chapter 26 commences with the second major census in Numbers. These figures catalog the generation that will occupy the Promised Land. Each clan and the number of its able-bodied men are listed. In 26:33 the pattern is altered when mention is made of five women, daughters of Zelophehad. They appear in the beginning of the next chapter.

Zelophehad's five daughters—Mahlah, Noah, Hoglah, Milcah, and Tirzah—are daring women. As chapter 27 commences, they stand before Moses and the whole congregation of Israel, at the tent of meeting, and call for justice. Their father died without male heirs. The women demand that they be accorded the right of inheritance. This is one of those wonderful defining moments of history. Though no mention is made of Moses' reply, it is clear that he is stumped. There is no known precedent for such a request. Wisely Moses seeks divine direction, and God says, "The daughters of Zelophehad are right in what they are saying; you shall indeed let them possess an inheritance among their father's brothers and pass the inheritance of their father on to them" (Num 27:7).

Chapter 27 concludes with God instructing Moses that he is soon to die. He will not enter the new land. Moses voices a concern that God appoint a new leader, so that the people will not be "like sheep without a shepherd." Joshua is chosen to succeed Moses and is commissioned.

Chapters 28–29 return to matters of the cult. These chapters deal with the proper offerings of lambs, rams, bulls, and goats for daily, Sabbath, new moon, and festival services.

Chapter 30 deals with legislation about the annulment of vows and obligations made by women—young women in their father's home, married women, and widows.

Chapter 31 is a detailed account of the war against Midian, including the division of spoils.

Chapter 32 covers the allotment of land in the area of Transjordan, land that will go to the tribes of Reuben, Gad, and Manasseh.

Chapter 33 primarily names the encampments along the journey from Rameses to Succoth and on through forty more places (including Kadesh and Mount Hor, vs. 37), and brings the Israelites to the plains (steppes) of Moab.

Chapter 34 describes the ideal boundaries of the Promised Land. It includes much of the Negeb, as well as land westward to the Mediterranean (the Great Sea), northward to the mountains of Lebanon, and eastward along the Salt Sea (Dead Sea). Forty-eight levitical towns are designated in chapter 35, including six cities of refuge for cases of humans killing humans, but only if this is unpremeditated killing (vss. 6–15). Next, there is legislation that deals with deliberate murder as well as involuntary manslaughter. Finally, chapter 36 returns to the matter of Zelophehad's daughters, and they marry their cousins, so that the land remains within the clan holdings.

5. NUMBERS IN THE CHRISTIAN SCRIPTURES

In his letter to the community in Rome, early on Paul wishes them "Grace to you and peace from God" (Rom 1:7), which echoes the Priestly blessing (Num 6:23ff.). As a book, Numbers is a limited source for quotations in the Christian scriptures. There are references, but few compared to other books of the Torah. The author of Hebrews knows Numbers. He makes reference to Aaron's rod that budded (Heb 9:4; Num 17:8ff. [17:23ff. H]) and for some reason suggests that this rod was contained in the ark (the Torah suggests it was placed "beside" or before the ark. See "Aaron's Budding Staff" below in the section on Numbers in Rabbinic Literature). He also knows the tradition of the heifer that purifies the ritually unclean (Heb 9:13; Num 19:17ff.), and the rebellious times in the desert (Heb 3:8ff.; Num 16).

John's Gospel mentions the bronze (or copper) snake at the time of Moses (John 3:14; Num 21:9). The First Epistle to the Corinthians refers to the poisonous (fiery) snakes (1 Cor 10:9; Num 21:6). Balaam and his donkey (Num 22:22–30) earn a reference in the epistles (2 Pet 2:15–16; Jude 11), and at one point Balaam is mentioned alongside Korah's rebellion (Jude 11). Balaam, Balak, and sexual immorality are examples in Revelation 2:14 (Num 22:4–5; 31:16; cf. Jude 11). Luke's "seventy others" appointed by the Lord (Luke 10:1–12) has the feel of Numbers 11:16ff. Another image from Numbers is suggested in the Gospels: Moses' concern that the people should be like "sheep without a shepherd" (Matt 9:36 and Mark 6:34; Num 27:17).

6. NUMBERS IN RABBINIC LITERATURE

The most accessible midrashic collection on Numbers in English is *Midrash Numbers Rabbah*. One might also consult *Sifré to Numbers: An American Translation and Explanation*. The *Pirke de Rabbi Eliezer* also features several references to Balaam.

Great Is Peace

In the rabbinic mind, peace is a great gift, perhaps the greatest gift. Several midrashic sources extol peace, based on Numbers 6:26, "The LORD…give you peace." By way of an example, mention is made of Abraham, who is regarded as the quintessential man of faith. Traditionally he endures ten trials, the final of which is the threatened loss of his son Isaac in Genesis 22. As his final reward God tells Abraham, "You shall go to your ancestors in peace" (Gen 15:15). The Torah itself is likened to peace, for it says in Proverbs 3:17, "All her paths are peace" (the literal subject in Proverbs is "wisdom," which the rabbis associate with the Torah). Isaiah 32:18

foretells a future world where God's people "will abide in peaceful habitation."[13]

In Jewish tradition at the center of the daily, Shabbat, and festival services is a set of prayers known as the *Amidah*. The theme of the final prayer is peace.

Likewise, the final words of the blessing recited after eating food is also devoted to peace.

Miriam's Well

The rabbis stated that, because of Miriam's merit, a well of water followed the Israelites in the desert.

> Three good leaders had arisen for Israel, namely Moses, Aaron and Miriam. For their sake three good things were conferred [upon Israel], namely the Well, the Pillar of Cloud and the Manna; the Well, for the merit of Miriam; the Pillar of Cloud for the merit of Aaron; the Manna for the merit of Moses. When Miriam died the well disappeared, as it is said [in Num 20:1] "Miriam died there" and immediately follows [the verse in Num 20:2] "Now there was no water."[14]

According to the rabbis, this well was so special it was created on the eve of the first Sabbath.[15]

Controversies

Controversy and disagreements can be for a greater good, or they merely can be self-serving. The rabbis speak of controversy "for the sake of heaven," and they give the example of the debates between the great Pharisaic schools of Hillel and Shammai (first century BCE). Those "not for the sake of heaven" are like the rebellion of Korah in Numbers 16.[16]

Aaron's Budding Staff

Aaron's miraculously budding staff (Num 17:8ff. [17:23ff. H]) has quite a history. Some associate it with the staff carried by Judah (Gen 38:18); others associate it with the staff that Moses carried (see "Moses' Staff" in Exodus in Rabbinic Literature above). According to a midrash, God placed the divine name on the staff. Every king, the midrash continues, held that same staff, until the Temple was destroyed. Then it was divinely hidden away and will be seen next in the hand of the messiah.[17]

Bashing Balaam

Shakespeare suggested, "The evil that men do lives after them, The good is oft interred with their bones."[18] The bard was referring to Caesar, but he could have written similarly of Balaam, or so is Balaam's reputation in both rabbinic literature and the Christian scriptures. On many occasions he is termed "Balaam the Wicked."[19] On three occasions in the Christian scriptures he is held up as an example of malice (2 Pet 2:15; Jude 11; Rev 2:14).

Balaam's reputation has mixed reviews in the Bible. He is castigated in Deuteronomy 23:4–5 (5–6 H); Joshua 24:10; and Nehemiah 13:2. In Numbers his reputation is sullied (Num 31:16). Yet in the eighth century BCE the prophet Micah speaks well of Balaam, "Remember now what King Balak of Moab devised, what Balaam son of Beor answered him" (Mic 6:5).

Balaam is not without praise in the rabbinic world. He is called a world-class philosopher.[20] Balaam also is compared to Moses, sometimes with Moses having superior characteristics, and sometimes with Balaam having superior characteristics. He is also termed the prophet to the nations.[21] On the whole, however, he is wicked Balaam.

A strong case can be made that Balaam is scorned unfairly. He becomes the whipping child for any and all foreigners who would speak ill of Israel. The literal reading of the text suggests that, if anything, he is sympathetic to Israel, and a loyal follower of God. Twice he tells Balak's emissaries that he will not act without God's consent (Num 22:8, 18–19; cf. 23:26; 24:12ff.). Balaam declines the bribe offered by Balak. When he stands viewing Israel, God's spirit comes upon Balaam and willingly, almost joyfully, he praises Israel, and does so effusively, much to the fury of Balak (Num 24:1ff., 10). This hardly seems like the acts of someone who is predisposed against

Israel. Not only does Balaam praise and bless Israel, he prophecies the destruction of Moab by Israel! (Num 24:17).

7. TEXT STUDY

A. Numbers 6:22–27. The Priestly Blessing

The Priestly blessing, or the Aaronide (or Aaronic) blessing, is one of the most recognizable prayers in the Bible. This blessing has been incorporated into many Jewish and Christian congregations as the closing benediction of the service. When, thousands of years ago, the Temple stood in Jerusalem, the priests on a daily basis would recite these words of blessing for the people. The priests stood on a raised platform in order to be seen. The Aramaic word for this platform is *dukhan,* and in Yiddish, this particular prayer is referred to as the *dukhanen.* In Orthodox Jewish services, this prayer is recited publicly by men who claim their lineage from the priesthood *(kohanim).*

The priests do not bless the people, rather the priests are the conduits of the blessing, which comes from God.

There are six parts to these blessings: bless and keep; shine and be gracious; lift divine countenance (i.e., to look, to look with favor, more colloquially, "to bestow favor") and give peace. Many midrashim extol peace as the ultimate blessing. See Numbers in Rabbinic Literature above, "Great is Peace."

B. Numbers 12. Miriam's Words

Miriam and Aaron complain that Moses has married outside of the Israelite community. Then they challenge Moses' leadership. God chastises them and punishes Miriam. Aaron begs Moses to intervene. Moses does, but God says Miriam needs to suffer some reproof.

This passage has been criticized, for in "the course of emphasizing Moses' unique position, the narrator uses Miriam as a foil. This is the same Miriam who led Israel in song after the deliverance at the Reed Sea (Ex. 15:20–21)....The lineage of Miriam is a lineage of generations of women who have been rejected or humiliated for doing exactly the same thing as their male counterparts."[22]

There are many parts, and many possible levels of meaning, to this short episode.

1. Verse 1: An ethnic slur? Miriam and Aaron appear to criticize Moses for "marrying out" of the Israelite community. A *Cushite* is a term for a darkly pigmented person. Whether the word Cushite refers to an Ethiopian or a Midianite, on the face of it, this is an ethnic slur.[23] Since Miriam is the one who is punished for the words, the rabbis focus on her. One frequently found teaching says that Miriam slandered Moses. Then, offering a wordplay on the term *leprous* or skin disease *(metsora')*, the rabbis suggest that the chief cause of leprosy/skin disease is slander or defamation. Miriam was *metsora'* because she brought forth a bad name, *motsi shem ra'*, that is, she slandered.[24]

Another, less well known midrash suggests that while Miriam clearly was criticizing Moses, the issue was not a racial slur. Quite the contrary! Miriam was defending Moses' wife, Zipporah, who only coincidentally was dark skinned. Miriam's issue is that Moses *married* her, but that since he was on Mt. Sinai, Moses kept himself celibate. He denied Zipporah marital rights.[25]

2. Verse 2: Challenging Moses' leadership. Miriam and Aaron clearly are suggesting that they, too, are prophets (Exod 7:1; 15:20) and that Moses is not the only one who hears God's voice. Ironically, God overhears their statement and is quick to act.

3. Verse 3: Moses' humility and devotion are highlighted here.

4. Verses 4–9: God distinguishes the special relationship enjoyed by Moses. Other prophets get their messages through visions or dreams, but Moses is different. Moses and God speak "face to face" [alternately, "mouth to mouth"] and Moses "beholds the form of the LORD." For a discussion about different kinds of prophecy and different words for a prophet, see Zucker, *Israel's Prophets.*

5. Verses 10–14: Miriam's being "as white as snow" is a wonderfully ironic twist. Whatever was the intention of her initial criticism of Moses, Miriam used the term *Cushite,* which infers dark

pigmentation. It is not accidental that, by way of contrast, a disease that is white in color afflicts her.

What is harder to explain is why Aaron is not similarly afflicted. He seems equally guilty of the accusation against Moses in verses 1–2. One source suggests that initially he was afflicted but then was freed from this condition.[26] There also is irony in that Aaron, who just claimed that he and Miriam share power with Moses, now has to grovel before Moses and plead on behalf of Miriam.

Moses' prayer is the shortest prayer in the Bible: "O God, please heal her." Ironies continue. He who has just been challenged by his siblings and then powerfully affirmed by God now is called upon to plead with God on behalf of the perpetrators. His prayer is terse. Is this because of the urgency of the situation? Alternatively, does this reflect his personal reluctance to pray on her behalf? In any case, God insists that Miriam be quarantined for a week. This is less than either a life-long sentence of leprosy/skin disease or even the normal quarantine period (cf. Lev 13:5; 14:1–20).

6. Verses 15–16: The people are clearly committed to Miriam. She is a significant figure for them. They refuse to continue on their travels until Miriam is once more part of the camp.[27]

C. Numbers 16. Korah's Rebellion

Korah's rebellion detailed in Numbers 16 actually is an amalgam of several different stories skillfully interwoven so that it appears as one episode. In all probability there are at least two (maybe more) sources of the insurrection.

1. Verses 1–11: The Korah-led revolt challenges Moses and Aaron for aggregating too much power to themselves. Korah, a Levite himself, organizes 250 important leaders to confront Moses. Good leader that he is, Moses takes charge; he sets the conditions for the test. He explains that the next day Korah and his associates are to bring censers and to put fire and incense in them. Moses tells the rebels that at that time God will decide who is really chosen. He chastises them saying, God has selected you to perform duties at the tabernacle, to assist the priests. "Yet you seek the priesthood as well?"

2. Verses 15–22: This is both a reply to Korah's challenge, and a description of what took place on the next day. Korah and his com-

pany stand before the tent of meeting with their censers, fire, and incense. God is impatient with this controversy and wants to annihilate the whole congregation. Moses and Aaron plead on behalf of the congregation at large and say, do not judge the whole by the actions of a few people.

3. Verses 28–35: Moses continues to lay out the conditions for the test. If these people die a natural death, says Moses, then God has not sent me. If, however, the ground opens up and swallows them and they go down to Sheol (the biblical term for the underworld), then God has rejected them. An earthquake comes, and Korah, his household, and their goods are swallowed up. Then a divine fire consumes the 250 leaders who had been offering incense.

4. Verses 1, 12–14, 23–27: In verse 1, the names of Korah and Dathan and Abiram get melded together. This is true also of verses 24 and 27. In all probability there was an introductory verse to the Dathan and Abiram story, which was woven together with the Korah introductory verse, resulting in verse 1. The Dathan and Abiram narrative is told in verses 12–14 and then continues in verses 23–27. It is unclear what happens to them. Did the earth swallow them up as well? According to Deuteromony 11:6 (and later in Psalm 106:17) they and their household were swallowed up. While those passages refer to Dathan and Abiram's rebellion, no mention is made of Korah. In Numbers 27:3 Korah is mentioned without reference to Dathan and Abiram.

5. In verse 1 there is a reference to On, the son of Peleth. This is the single reference to him. He simply drops out of sight. The rabbis suggest that his wife saves him from infamy. She says, "What good will it do to follow Korah? We will be subservient to him, as we are now to Moses and Aaron." In a variation of this story, his wife gets him inebriated and puts him to bed. Then she and her daughter sit in front of their home and carry on as if he died. When the rebels come to his home to collect him for the confrontation with Moses and Aaron, they assume his death is real and turn away. The net result is that his life is saved.[28]

D. Numbers 20:1–22. The Kadesh Mystery

In Numbers 20:1 it states that the "Israelites, the whole congregation, came into the wilderness of Zin in the first month, and the people stayed in Kadesh. Miriam died there, and was buried there." Yet, what year was this? The third year? Alternatively, the fortieth year? A few verses later, Numbers 20:22 states that the Israelites then set out from Kadesh and came to Mount Hor, where Aaron dies. A later chapter mentions in passing that Aaron died in the fortieth year of the wilderness sojourn (Num 33:38–39).

Three possibilities exist.

1. The Israelites traveled to Kadesh at the end of the second year or the beginning of the third year. In Numbers 32:8 Moses explains he sent the spies out "from Kadesh-barnea to see the land." Indeed in Numbers 13:26 the spies bring their report to the Israelite encampment in Kadesh. The people's lack of faith in being able to capture the land of Canaan immediately results in their being punished: that generation is to die in the wilderness. At this point they leave Kadesh, and then years later, they return there. Since Numbers 20:22 states that the Israelites went from Kadesh to Mount Hor, where Aaron died (in the fortieth year), the "first month" mentioned above (Num 20:1) then would be the first month of the fortieth year.

2. A second possibility is that the Israelites trekked for forty years, with many stops along the way, and then they reached Kadesh in the wilderness of Zin, where Miriam died. From Kadesh they took the final leg of their journey, via Mount Hor, where Aaron died, and then they reached the plains (or steppes) of Moab. The detailed itinerary listed in Numbers 33:3–49 supports this argument, for it mentions Kadesh toward the end of a long list of encampments. In this case, again the "first month" mentioned above (Num 20:1) would be the first month of the fortieth year.

3. In the third possibility, Miriam died at the beginning of the third year of the desert wandering. The twelve spies brought their report to the Israelite encampment at Kadesh. The statement in Numbers 20:3, where the people, once more complaining, make reference to the death of their brothers, presumably the rebellion of Korah in Numbers 16, a few months earlier, supports this argu-

ment. These people are still ungrateful and yearn for Egypt, as verse 5 indicates. They sound like the generation that left Egypt. Moses calls them "rebels" (vs. 10). In this case the "first month" mentioned above (Num 20:1) would be the first month of the third year.

A major problem is that while in Deuteronomy 1:46 it states that the Israelites stayed in Kadesh "many days" in the next chapter it says that the journey *after they left* Kadesh took thirty-eight years. "And the length of time we had traveled from Kadesh-barnea until we crossed the Wadi Zered was thirty-eight years, until the entire generation of warriors had perished from the camp, as the LORD had sworn concerning them" (Deut 2:14).

Some Solutions

It may be that chapter 20 represents two different traditions. One tradition had the Israelites at Kadesh early in the wilderness wandering. A separate tradition had them encamped at Kadesh toward the end of the desert sojourn.

A convincing argument is that there were two different locales named Kadesh. The encampment at the first Kadesh included the episode of Moses sending out the spies and the spies returning there with their report. This is supported by the statements in Numbers 32:8 and Numbers 13:26. The second Kadesh is featured in Numbers 20. It is the beginning of the fortieth year. Miriam dies there, and not long thereafter Aaron dies. The people who complain about their "brothers" are of the generation that left Egypt, but they are elderly.

In chapter 20 Moses and Aaron are both told that they will not enter the Promised Land (vs. 12). To have been told this at the beginning of the third year does not make sense. It would undercut their motivation and authority. Further, the argument for a late date for this encampment at Kadesh is supported by a rabbinic tradition that throughout the desert travels wherever Miriam went, a well followed, providing water for the people (see "Miriam's Well" above in the section Numbers in Rabbinic Literature). Numbers 20:1 records Miriam's death, and verse 2 states, "Now there was no water for the congregation." The inference is that up until that point there had been water.

That there are two different places named Kadesh is not hard to grasp. There are many states in the United States that have cities named Springfield or Aurora. There is no reason to think that in biblical times there were not two locales named Kadesh. Alternately, the Israelites encamped at Kadesh, and then years later return to the same oasis.

As mentioned earlier, the dividing line for the fortieth year is Numbers 20:22, when the Israelites (for the first or second time) leave this Kadesh for Mount Hor. A few of the generation that left Egypt are still alive, but they will die out by the end of chapter 25. Their deaths mark the end of the old generation, and to commemorate that fact, Numbers 26 begins with a call for a new census.

E. Numbers 7:89. The Cherubim

The word *cherubim* (Hebrew, *keruvim;* the plural form of the word *cherub*) appears throughout the Jewish Bible, literally, from Genesis through Chronicles. Cherubim are found in each of the three major sections, Torah, Neviim, and Ketuvim (Teaching, Prophets, and Writings). More than any other book, the prophet Ezekiel mentions cherubim, especially in chapters 10 and 28. We first learn about cherubim in the Torah in early Genesis. Cherubim are set by God to guard the Garden of Eden (Gen 3:24). Other cherubim are found on top of the holy ark in the Book of Exodus (as here in Num 7:89). They are gold cherubim with wings spread out toward each other, and upon which God's presence rests (Exod 25:18–20; 37:7–9). Cherubim are a form of angels. Neither the cherubim guarding Eden nor those atop the holy ark looked like the popular modern versions of those figures depicted in Renaissance art. They are not pink-skinned, winged, chubby, or cuddly, curly-haired cherubs.

The cherubim found upon the ark with their outstretched wings will be replicated in Solomon's Temple in Jerusalem, where they will be much larger. The portable ark of the wilderness wandering as described in Exodus 25:10 was but 3 feet to 4 feet x 2 feet to 2.5 feet x 2 feet to 2.5 feet (2.5 cubits x 1.5 cubits x 1.5 cubits). There the cherubim were built of acacia wood. The cherubim built in the Temple were made of olive wood; they were 15 feet (10 cubits) high, and each of the wings was 7.5 feet (5 cubits) in length, with 15 feet (10 cubits) between wingtips. These cherubs had either two or four wings and were overlaid with gold (1 Kgs 6:23–28).

In the description of the prophet Ezekiel (Ezek 10) the cherubim have four faces. He explains that they are the same faces he saw in chapter 1 by the River Chebar. There they had the faces of a human being, a lion, an ox, and an eagle (Ezek 10:21f.; cf. 1:10). They have four wings each; two reach out for the other, and with two they cover their bodies. In chapter 41 the cherubim have the face of a human and a young lion (Ezek 41:19).

Cherubim were part of the decorative art of the curtains associated with the wilderness ark (Exod 26:31; 36:35) and the curtains of the tabernacle (Exod 26:1; 36:8). They also appeared on the inner and outer walls of the Temple (1 Kgs 6:29) and the doors of the sanctuary (1 Kgs 6:32, 35) and the frames (1 Kgs 7:29, 36).

In the Talmud there is some disagreement as to whether there were cherubim in both the First and Second Temples or only in the First.[29] It is also said that if the people adhered to the divine will, then the cherubim would be turned to each other; if the people did not do so, the cherubim were turned away from each other.[30] The talmudic rabbis suggest that on the three pilgrimage festivals (Booths/*Succot* in the autumn, Passover/*Pesach* in the spring, and Weeks/*Shavuot* in the early summer) the curtain of the ark would be removed for the Israelites. An explanation was given that the cherubim represented the love between God and Israel. Then, in a very anthropomorphic image, the rabbis suggest that the cherubim were shown to the people with the cherubs' bodies interlocked. The people were told, "You are beloved before God as with a man with a woman."[31]

Notes

1. Martin Noth, *Numbers: A Commentary* (Philadelphia: Westminster, 1968), 106.

2. Contradictory material, however, raises questions about the extended stay at Kadesh. The Text Study on Numbers features a discussion about this "Kadesh Mystery."

3. The books of Exodus and Leviticus set the stage for the narrative and legislation sections of Numbers. Exodus begins with the Israelites in Egypt. It pictures their suffering and then the wonders of God's miracles that lead to their freedom: the redemption from Egypt. This is followed by

the theophany at Sinai, where the people pledge themselves to God. God's revelation includes Moses receiving the Ten Commandments on Mt. Sinai. The Israelites learn about religious aspects of being God's chosen, including clear instructions on how to build the portable sanctuary. In Leviticus, there is instruction for both the people at large and the priesthood. It features material on sacrifices, the investiture of the priesthood, matters of impurities, the building of the sanctuary, laws dealing with Sabbath and festivals, and laws setting out ethical standards.

4. Another suggestion offers a fourfold division of the book:

A. Numbers 1:1—10:10 covers the initial census at the wilderness of Sinai. It continues with a section on the priestly service, and then varied kinds of legislation, including vows of abstinence, the famous Priestly blessing, and offerings for the tabernacle. It concludes with the matter of the silver trumpets. In terms of linear time, this section is just under three weeks long. Numbers 1:1 mentions specifically the first day of the second month of the second year of the Exodus, and the next section begins on the twentieth day of the second month of the second year (Num 10:11).

B. Numbers 10:11—22:1 features Israel on the march. The Israelites leave the Sinai desert and eventually travel to the area of Paran. Along the way there are several rebellions against the leadership of Moses and Aaron, the most famous led by Korah, Dathan, Abiram, and their followers (Num 16). They eventually get to Kadesh, where according to one theory they reside for many years. In linear time, this section lasts about thirty-eight years.

C. They leave Kadesh (Num 20:22), and in the fortieth year of the desert sojourn, they begin their projected assault on the land of Canaan. It is unclear which route they took, for some of the material is contradictory or at least incomplete. Numbers 33:38 attests that Aaron died in the fortieth year after the Israelites left Egypt. His death took place after the Israelites left Kadesh and were at the border of Edom at Mount Hor (Num 20:22). Numbers 20:22—22:1 take the Israelites along the Moabite border. Their march leads them eventually to the area of Moab, not far from Jericho.

D. Numbers 22:2—25:18 is the Balaam–Balak episode and its aftermath. Balak, king of Moab, sends for the prophet/diviner Balaam with the intent of putting a curse on Israel, thereby defeating them. His plan comes to naught; it is a resounding failure, though a few Israelites do succumb to pagan temptation. Phineas (Hebrew, *Pinhas*) is elevated in status for his zeal. Presumably the last of the generation that left Egypt dies by this time.

Finally, Numbers 26:1 [25:19 H]—36:13 sees Israel ready, poised to enter the land of Canaan. Another census is held, some initial land distribution is articulated, and the Israelites receive details about levitical towns and cities of refuge. These last two sections together comprise the remaining months of the fortieth year.

5. Numbers 1:1—10:10 law; 10:11—14:45 narrative. Numbers 15 law; 16–17 narrative. Numbers 18–19 law; 20–25 narrative. Numbers 26:1—27:11 law; 27:12–23 narrative. Numbers 28–30 law; 31—33:49 narrative. Numbers 33:50–56, 34–36 law (Jacob Milgrom, *The JPS Torah Commentary: Numbers* (Philadelphia: Jewish Publication Society, 1990), xv.

6. W. Gunther Plaut, *The Torah: A Modern Commentary*, ed. W. Gunther Plaut (New York: Union of American Hebrew Congregations, 1981), quoting Matitiahu Tsevat, 1035.

7. When the United States has conducted its decennial census as mandated by Congress, census takers have reported people reluctant to answer questions. Some wish to preserve their privacy for a variety of issues, often stemming from the view that such knowledge is an unwarranted governmental intrusion in one's private life.

8. Plaut, *The Torah*, 1034.

9. In Numbers 10:29 Moses' father-in-law is named Hobab, son of Reuel the Midianite. In Exodus he was identified as Jethro (Exod 3:1; 4:18 [or Jether]; 18:1), and also as Reuel (Exod 2:18). Various theories have been offered for these discrepancies (see Milgrom, *JPS: Numbers*, 78f.).

10. Seventy descendants of Jacob came to Egypt (Exod 1:5; Deut 10:22). It is true that Moses had selected advisors to share his burden earlier (Exod 18:21ff.) but there the number is not given. Rabbinic tradition offers a resolution to the problem of why seventy instead of seventy-two. When God instructed Moses to choose seventy people, Moses fretted over this decision. "If I choose six per tribe, I will have too many. If I choose only five per tribe, I will lack ten people. If I choose six from some tribes, and five from others, this will spark jealousy." What did Moses do? He selected six people from each tribe. Then he wrote the word *elder* on seventy separate slips, and left two slips blank. He took all seventy-two slips and put them in an urn. Moses then let the elders each choose a slip. If the word *elder* was written there, Moses explained that God had chosen that person, and if it was blank, that too was divinely fixed (Babylonian Talmud *Sanhedrin* 17a; *Midrash Numbers Rabbah* 15.19).

In the Bible the number seventy appears as a generalized figure meaning "many," the way in English one might say "dozens." Yet it also has sacred and symbolic meaning (Exod 24:1; Judg 9:2, 5; 2 Kgs 10:6; Jer 25:12).

11. In a midrash a rabbi argues that "these laws are decrees from God and we have no right to question them" (*Midrash Numbers Rabbah* 19.8).

12. "The action moves swiftly....Balaam consents only when he receives the Lord's permission and, further, warns Balak that he will speak

only as the Lord directs him. On these occasions, involving a sacrificial ritual and change of site, Balaam blesses the Israelites instead of cursing them. And in a fourth oracle he predicts the eventual doom of Moab at the hands of Israel: Balak's curse, intended for Israel, will instead be inflicted by Israel on Moab" (Milgrom, *JPS: Numbers,* 185).

13. *Midrash Numbers Rabbah* 11.7 end.

14. Babylonian Talmud *Ta'anit* 9a. Cf. Babylonian Talmud *Shabbat* 35a; *The Midrash on Proverbs,* ed. Burton L. Visotzky (New Haven and London: Yale University, 1992), chapter 14, beginning.

15. *Mishnah Avot* 5.6.

16. Ibid., 5.17.

17. *Midrash Numbers Rabbah* 18.23.

18. *Julius Caesar,* Act III.

19. *Mishnah Avot* 5.19; Babylonian Talmud *Sanhedrin* 105a–106b; *Pesikta De-Rab Kahana,* supplement 1.4; *Pirke de Rabbi Eliezer,* chapter 47.

20. *Pesikta De-Rab Kahana* 15.5.

21. *Midrash Numbers Rabbah* 14.20; *Sifre: A Tannaitic Commentary on the Book of Deuteronomy,* trans. Reuven Hammer (New Haven and London: Yale University Press, 1986), *Piska* 357; *Tanna Debe Eliyyahu: The Lore of the School of Elijah,* trans. William G. Braude and Israel J. Kapstein (Philadelphia: Jewish Publication Society, 1981), *Eliyyahu Rabbah* 142 (Chap [28] 26).

22. Katherine Doob Sakenfeld, "Numbers," in *The Women's Bible Commentary,* ed. Carol A. Newsom and Sharon H. Ringe (London: SPCK; Louisville, KY: Westminster John Knox, 1992), 48.

23. Martin Noth suggests that Cush is connected to Cushan, a reference in Habakkuk 3:7 (*Numbers,* 94).

24. *Midrash Leviticus Rabbah* 16.1–6, and many other places.

25. Jacob Neusner, *Sifré to Numbers: An American Translation and Explanation, Vol. 2, Sifré to Numbers* Ninety-nine (Numbers 12.1–16, Horowitz, pp. 97–99), Brown Judaica Series (Atlanta: Scholars Press, 1986), 115–16; *Midrash Tanhuma Leviticus* 5.6, Leviticus 14:1ff., part VI.

26. Babylonian Talmud *Shabbat* 97a.

27. Grateful thanks to Rabbi Bonita E. Taylor for suggesting this insight. For a detailed analysis of this incident, see Milgrom, *Numbers,* 93–99.

28. *Midrash Numbers Rabbah* 18.20; Babylonian Talmud *Sanhedrin* 109b–110a.

29. Babylonian Talmud *Yoma* 54a, cf. 21a.

30. Babylonian Talmud *Baba Batra* 99a.

31. Babylonian Talmud *Yoma* 54a.

Deuteronomy

1. INTRODUCTION

Deuteronomy is the fifth of the five books of the Torah. The title comes from the Greek *Deuteronomion*. In Hebrew the Book of Deuteronomy is known as *Devarim* ("words," "matters," "things"), taken from the opening line of Deuteronomy, "These are the words that Moses spoke to all Israel...."

Deuteronomy is a reaffirmation and a review of the covenant between God and Israel. Deuteronomy means "second law." This term is based on a line within the book itself. Deuteronomy 17:18 states that the future ruler of Israel "shall have a copy of this law *[mishneh ha-Torah]* written for him in the presence of the levitical priests." The Hebrew *mishneh ha-Torah* ("a copy of this law/teaching") was translated as *deuteronomion* and (mis-) understood as "second law," in the sense of an *additional* law. In its context, most scholars believe it means a copy, not an additional law.

On the other hand, it could be argued that the Ten Commandments at Sinai represented the first covenant with Israel and that an additional covenant was concluded at Moab (cf. Deut 5:31 [5:28 H]; 29:1 [28:69 H]).[1]

In Hebrew, the word *Torah,* especially in this context, means "teaching," and not "law," which is much too narrow a translation.[2] *Mishneh ha-Torah* might better be translated as "a copy of this teaching" (so NJPS), or "a copy of this instruction." As noted in the introductory chapter to this book, the word *Torah* has many nuances.

Among the first five books of the Bible, Deuteronomy is unique in its emphasis on teaching and learning. In Deuteronomy, when referring to instructions, the term *torah* is used frequently.[3]

Deuteronomy is a series of addresses, discourses, or sermons spoken by Moses. They are unequal in length. Traditionally scholars speak of three addresses, though there is not full agreement on what constitutes the parameters of the second and third discourse.[4]

Themes in Deuteronomy[5]

Most scholars today accept that Deuteronomy, though ascribed to Moses, actually reflects a time many centuries later in Israelite history. Israel has matured; it has become more settled and a more sophisticated society. The concepts found in Deuteronomy suggest a date of composition in the eighth to seventh centuries BCE.

Monotheism

The deity depicted in Deuteronomy is not God amongst many gods, God is God alone! The deity of Israel is more than merely the "God of gods and Lord of Lords, the great God, mighty and awesome" (Deut 10:17). God is the "living God" (5:26 [5:23 H]). This is the deity that "created human beings on the earth....there is no other besides him" (Deut 4:32, 35). The people are reminded that when they stood at Sinai, they "heard the sound of words but saw no form; there was only a voice....Since you saw no form when the LORD spoke to you...take care and watch yourselves closely, so that you do not act corruptly by making an idol for yourselves, in the form of any figure" (Deut 4:12, 15–16).

Allegiance to God

The statement affirming God's unity is a central concept in Judaism. It is as close to a credo as one finds. Recited twice daily, in the evening and morning services, it forms part of the introductory prayers before the reading of the Torah on the Shabbat. Known as the *Sh'ma (Shema)*, the Hebrew word for "hear," it is the most famous line in Deuteronomy: "Hear, O Israel: The LORD is our God, the LORD alone" (Deut 6:4). In Deuteronomy this affirmation is followed by a command to love God with all your heart, soul, and might. Israel is to love God, walk in God's ways, and to hold fast to God. The verb *to hold fast* to God used in

Deuteronomy 11:22 is the same verb used in Genesis to describe the special connection between the man and his wife ("Therefore a man...clings to his wife," Gen 2:24).

Deuteronomy makes it clear that should the people turn from God and worship false idols, retaliation will be swift and merciless. "Take care, or you will be seduced into turning away, serving other gods and worshipping them, for then the anger of the LORD will be kindled against you and...then you will perish quickly off the good land that the LORD is giving you" (Deut 11:16–17).

God's Presence

Deuteronomy's deity is transcendent; since God is not physically on earth, his nearness to Israel is a spiritual connection. As explained in the chapter on Exodus, in the early years of Israel's existence as a nation, especially following the Exodus itself, the people needed a real, a concrete image, and a physical place where they believed God lived among them. It was strange and difficult enough to accept that God was invisible, that God was being itself ("I AM WHO I AM/I AM WHAT I AM/I WILL BE WHAT I WILL BE," Exod 3:14). In Exodus 25:8 God instructs Moses that the people are to make a sanctuary for the deity, "so that I may dwell among them." A few verses on, God says to Moses that an ark of the covenant is to be built. "There I will meet with you....I will deliver to you all my commands for the Israelites" (Exod 25:22).

In Deuteronomy the place for communication with God moves from the portable ark to a yet-to-be designated central locale. That place itself is not mentioned, but clearly it will be designated by God.[6] For example: "You are not permitted to offer the passover sacrifice within any of your towns that the LORD your God is giving you. But at the place that the LORD your God will choose as a dwelling for his name, only there shall you offer the passover sacrifice" (Deut 16:5–6; cf. 16:11, 15, 16).

God is associated with a certain place, chosen "as a dwelling for his name" (Deut 16:11). Yet, Deuteronomy's God lives in the heavens (Deut 26:15; 4:36). This connection with an earthly locale is very different from the here-and-now physical location of the ark. A generalized geographical spot is a far description from the mercy seat placed upon the ark where God met Moses, between the two cherubim, to deliver the commands for the Israelites (Exod 25:22).

The cherubim are conspicuously missing in Deuteronomy. In fact, the book plays down references to the ark. The consistent use of language such as *a place for God's name to dwell* "reflects a new theological conception of the Deity...by the author of Deuteronomy and his followers [and it] is intended to combat the ancient popular belief that the Deity actually dwelled within the Sanctuary."[7]

Mutual Expectations/B'rit/Covenant

In Deuteronomy, God and Israel have mutual expectations and obligations. This is represented by the covenant (in Hebrew, *b'rit* [*berit, b'rith*]) with God. It is summed up concisely in Deuteronomy 26:16–19. This passage, "which is rooted in the political and legal spheres, implies that the relationship between God and Israel is not a purely emotional or spiritual association, but one that also entails specific obligations that were mutually agreed upon and have consequences."[8]

Covenant is a term frequently employed in all five of the Torah's books, but it has special resonance in Deuteronomy, and it is used often. In addition, there are filial images suggested in the book. "Is not he [God] your father, who created you?"; "For you [are] to walk in his ways, to keep his statutes, his commandments..." (Deut 32:6; 26:17).

Israel's very existence depends on God. God "created her, redeemed her from Egypt, guided her safely through the wilderness, fights Israel's wars, and will give Israel her land."[9] Yet, this is not because of Israel's great merit, quite the contrary. Israel is repeatedly defiant and resistant. Deuteronomy 32:15–19 details in unflattering terms the rebellious nature of Israel. This behavior was all the more egregious because God sustained Israel in the desert, shielded him, cared for him, "guarded him as the apple of his eye. As an eagle...hovers over its young..." (Deut 32:10–11). God chose Israel because God loved Israel's ancestors, the patriarchs and the matriarchs.

The Promised Land

Israel is on a journey; its goal is the Promised Land, the area promised to Abraham, Isaac, and Jacob. On it the descendants of Israel will spread abroad to the west, to the east, and the north, and to the south (Gen 28:14). It is a countryside fertile and rich, described repeatedly as "flowing with milk and honey" (Deut 6:3; 11:9; 26:9, 15). It is a good land, with flowing streams, with springs, a land of wheat and barley, vines, fig trees and pomegranates, olive trees and honey. Filled with natural resources, it has stones and iron and copper (Deut 8:7ff.). This land is a wonderful gift from God, but Israel's possession of the land is conditional on her following God's commands. If she fails to do so, "you shall be plucked off the land....The LORD will scatter you...from one end of the earth to the other" (Deut 28:63–64).

Humanitarian Values

A society's values are shown not through material possessions nor intellectual accomplishments but rather through how that society treats the poor and disadvantaged, those who are powerless.

Though God dwells in the heavens, God is not indifferent to humans. God is just and caring (Deut 4:8). God is faithful (Deut 7:8–9). God is a righteous judge, who takes no bribes, who protects the orphan and widow, and loves the strangers. God provides them with food and clothing (Deut 10:17–18). What does God want, what does God require? "Only to fear the LORD your God, to walk in all his ways, to love him, to serve the LORD your God with all your heart and with all your soul, and to keep the commandments of the LORD your God" (Deut 10:12–13).

Deuteronomy 5 repeats the Ten Commandments, but with significant differences from the Decalogue first presented in Exodus. The Sabbath command in Deuteronomy focuses on humanity, not God. In Exodus, the Israelites are commanded to observe the Sabbath because God rested on the seventh day (Exod 20:11); in Deuteronomy, the reason given is God redeemed you from slavery in Egypt. You shall rest, as shall your children, slaves, animals, and resident aliens in your towns. Universal rest for all is the given purpose of Shabbat, not imitation of God's example of rest.[10]

Though the concept of caring for the stranger appears elsewhere in the books of the Torah (Exod 12:49; 22:21 [22:20 H]; 23:9; Lev 19:10, and so forth), it is in Deuteronomy that protection for the powerless has its strongest voice. Whole groups of people—debtors, escaped slaves, resident aliens, widows, orphans, animals, even convicted criminals—had legislation protecting them. Another group often not thought about as disadvantaged, the Levites, is also protected in Deuteronomy, because unlike the other tribes the Levites had neither land nor people who were designated as "fighting men," presumably trained in some kind of self-defense. The command to protect those who had none to protect them is grounded in the Israelites' own experience in Egypt (Deut 15:15, 24:22).

Legislation

God's laws, delineated in chapters 12–26, are legislation to rule society. It is a sacred responsibility to enforce this teaching. It is part of the special responsibility taken on by Israel. These are righteous laws, and Israel has accepted the obligations inherent in these laws. "To Deuteronomy, then, the laws require not only obedience, but also the proper attitude."[11] This legislation covers some areas, but many are left out. It is assumed that there will be law courts to work out the daily practical details of living in a civilized society.

Style

The writing in Deuteronomy is different from that in other books of the Bible. Each has its own characteristics, but this book more than any other is sermonic in style. Scholars have commented on its rhetorical and exhortatory nature.[12] This is a book of instruction. In Judaism, Moses lovingly is called *Moshe Rabbenu*, which even in its simple translations, "Moses our rabbi" or "Moses our teacher," conveys a sense of what this final segment of the Torah is about. Deuteronomy is cast as Moses' three final addresses to the people. This is Moses as *rabbenu*, as teacher and as rabbi. "The style is highly rhetorical, the speaker pleads and urges, threatens and comforts, exhorts and, at the last, invokes the very heavens to be his witnesses. The text has all the earmarks of preaching."[13]

2. THE DEUTERONOMISTS

Earlier in this book, reference was made to the mystery of Kadesh, and likewise to the mysterious deaths of Aaron's two eldest sons, Nadab and Abihu. Another set of biblical mysteries centers on Deuteronomy. Who wrote the book? Was it one person, or a group of editors? Was it the priests? The prophets? When did they live? How did they transmit this information? Some of these questions are answered in the next section, "Discovery of the Book of the Law." In the meantime, who was or were the Deuteronomists? To raise this question is to part ways from a traditional religious understanding of the book, which would say that the whole Torah, word for word, is the teaching of God to Moses on Mt. Sinai.

Following the theory that Deuteronomy was either composed or, at the least, set down in its present form around the eighth or seventh century BCE, what can one say about the editors? There are many competing theories for the Deuteronomists. Since there are different styles in the book, it is likely that this work is a fusion of different interests. Some scholars ascribe it to the priestly class that found it. Others see a strong prophetic hand in its composition. There are those who favor a combination of exiles from the northern kingdom and southern kingdom proponents of the Temple in Jerusalem. This theory suggests that when the Assyrians in 722 BCE had defeated the northern kingdom, at that time, or even before it, religious leaders fled to the south, bringing with them their viewpoint. Their ideas were initially accepted and incorporated into the reforms of King Hezekiah of Judah (reigned 715–687 BCE). Unfortunately Hezekiah's son and successor, Manasseh, ruled for fifty-five years, and he had no interest in such reforms. Consequently, the program of the Deuteronomists had no champion until the time of King Josiah, circa 622 BCE. For close to a century it remained either hidden or at least downplayed. Somewhere in that time, however, northern notions were fused with southern interests, such as the central sanctuary in Jerusalem, and the result was the core of Deuteronomy.[14]

Certainly the authors of Deuteronomy knew of the earlier codes, specifically the Covenant Code of Exodus (Exod 20–23) and the Holiness Code of Leviticus (17–26), for it repeats and supplements this earlier legislation.[15]

3. DISCOVERY OF THE BOOK OF THE LAW/TEACHING

About halfway through the reign of King Josiah of Jerusalem (640–609) a decision is made to do some repair work on the Temple. Then in 622 BCE, a book, or "the book of the law," or the book of the teaching, *Sefer haTorah,* is discovered in the Temple by Hilkiah the high priest (2 Kgs 22:8) and people working with him. It is brought to King Josiah, who seeks the advice of Huldah, a female prophet living in Jerusalem. This episode is recorded in 2 Kings 22–23 and paralleled in 2 Chronicles 34–35. This discovery inspires Josiah to make sweeping reforms. What exactly is found is not known. Most modern scholars agree that the center of that "book of the law" is at the core of what today is the Book of Deuteronomy.

Clearly, there are links between 'Deuteronomy's legislation and Josiah's reforms. Serving other gods and worshipping them, and specifically heavenly worship (sun, moon, and hosts of heaven), are prohibited (Deut 17:2–3). Josiah deposes idolatrous priests who made offerings to Baal, the sun, moon, constellations, and all the host of the heavens (2 Kgs 23:5). The observance of Passover, according to Deuteronomy, is to be solely at the centralized place that God will make known (Deut 16:1–8, and especially vss. 2, 6–7). Josiah orders that Passover is only to be celebrated in Jerusalem, a tradition that, according to the narrative in Kings and Chronicles, had not been observed in four hundred (!) years (2 Kgs 23:21–23; 2 Chr 35:18). As Deuteronomy calls for the demolition of the sacred places of worship where the previous inhabitants of the land had their shrines, so does Josiah actively destroy pagan shrines in Israel (2 Kgs 23:6ff., and especially vs. 15ff.).[16]

4. THE THREE ADDRESSES/DISCOURSES; CONCLUDING CHAPTERS

The First Discourse: Deuteronomy 1:1—4:43

Moses' first discourse covers chapters 1–4. The opening verses of chapter 1 set the time and place of his address. It takes place in the eleventh Hebrew month (which in the modern Western calendar is about January or February), in the fortieth, the final, year of the wilderness experience. It is spoken on the eastern side of the Jordan River, somewhere in the neighborhood of the Salt Sea. The rest of chapter 1 and then all of 2 and 3 is a historical review, a retrospective of the days in the desert.

In 1:6, Moses refers to Horeb, which is the name that the Book of Deuteronomy gives to Mt. Sinai.[17] Moses explains that God informs the people it is time to move on, that they are ready to conquer the land. Moses mentions in passing that he told the people that they had grown to such a size that he needed extra help. So in a combination of tribal choices and Mosaic appointments, a variety of leaders and judges are selected for the people. The people embark on their journey and travel as far as Kadesh-barnea (Deut 1:19).

Moses recounts that spies were chosen to scout out the land. They did so and brought back a report saying it is a good land. "But you were unwilling to go up. You rebelled…you grumbled in your tents" (vss. 26–27). God's reaction was swift and decisive. Not one person of the present generation shall enter the land, save Caleb and Joshua. God also was angry with me, Moses explains, and said I would not enter the land. As a result of your obstinacy and obstreperousness you were forced to stay at Kadesh for many days (Deut 1:46). Chapters 2–3 then recount the final year of the wilderness sojourn. Finally, the people are to realize their appointed destiny. They were given specific instructions, which route to take, which tribal units to avoid, and with which to engage. Deuteronomy 2:14 highlights the "Kadesh mystery," discussed in the chapter on Numbers.[18] Whatever is the answer to that puzzle, by their last year they had crossed the Wadi Zered and the Wadi Arnon, and had defeated King Sihon of Heshbon and King Og of Bashan. Then in that final year, Moses, one more time, had entreated God. Let me enter the Promised Land, he asked. The answer was not what Moses wanted to hear. "Enough from you! Never speak to me of this matter again!" Instead, God instructed Moses to go to the top of Pisgah and view the land, but he was not to enter. Rather, Moses was to charge Joshua and let him take the people on the next part of their journey (Deut 3:23–28).

Chapter 4 is very different from the preceding chapters. They dealt with history. Now Moses addresses the purpose of the people and their relationship to God in a wider sense. "Chapter 4 is the theological heart of Deuteronomy, explaining its most fundamental precepts, monotheism and the prohibition of idolatry."[19] Accept and observe God's teaching, explains Moses; do not add or subtract from it. Remember the Ten Commandments; do not serve idols or worship them. Chapter 4 features the rhetorical style mentioned earlier: Moses pleads and urges, threatens and comforts, exhorts and, at the last, calls the heavens to serve as witness.

Following the first speech, a few verses (4:41–43) make reference to the cities of refuge, and then the second discourse begins with verse 44.

The Second Discourse:
Deuteronomy 4:44—29:1 [28:69 H]

Moses' second discourse is his longest. It covers most of the book, from the end of chapter 4 through chapter 28. The first address began with a few verses setting the time and place. Here the locale is merely suggested in 4:44–49. It is east of the Jordan River, near Pisgah. Chapter 5 begins with a clear exhortation: Hear Israel! Pay attention to these laws, learn them, and observe them! Referring again to Horeb (instead of Sinai), Moses reminds the people that God's covenant was not only with the revered ancestors (Abraham, Isaac, and Jacob), but with us as well! Then comes the repetition of the Decalogue in Deuteronomy 5:6–21 (5:6–18 H).

The Decalogue (the Ten Commandments) in Deuteronomy differs in some ways from that found in Exodus. One major variance is the reasoning for the Sabbath law. As mentioned earlier, when it comes to the Sabbath command, the focus here is on humanity, not God. In Exodus, the reason for observing the Sabbath is that God rested on the seventh day (Exod 20:11). In Deuteronomy, the reason for the Sabbath rest is to achieve universal rest, something unknown in their experience in Egypt. Included in those who were to know the blessing of rest were the strangers. The Hebrew term *ger* ("stranger") refers to resident aliens. These were non-Israelites who, nonetheless, were part of Israelite society. Often they did not own land, and were poor, dependent upon others. The Torah regularly includes them as a protected minority, along with widows, orphans, and the poor.

Honoring parents was covered in the first Decalogue, but here there is an additional thought. Do this "that it may go well with you in the land that the LORD your God is giving you" (Deut 5:16).

The tenth commandment also differs in the versions in Exodus and Deuteronomy. In Deuteronomy, the language is more descriptive. Neither shall you covet, neither shall you desire…(so NRSV). The NJPS version has these words: You shall not covet, you shall not crave (Deut 5:21 [5:18H]). Tigay suggests that the commandment could be paraphrased with the words "do not scheme to acquire…do not long for."[20] In this set of the Ten Commandments, "the wife" is mentioned before "the neighbor's house." In Exodus, *house* meant "household"; here the word *house* means literally "house."

Chapter 6 contains words very familiar to Jews and Christians alike. As noted above, Deuteronomy 6:4 is the *Sh'ma*. It is the quintessential statement of God's unity. "Hear, O Israel! The LORD is our God, the LORD alone" (NJPS). Alternate versions of this statement are The LORD our God is one LORD; The Lord our God, the Lord is one; or The LORD is our God, the LORD is one. Jews know these words because they are recited twice every day, as part of the evening and morning prayers. Many Jews recite those words before retiring at night. Christians know the quotation from Deuteronomy 6:4 because Jesus declares this as the Great Commandment (Mark 12:29–30).

The statement that God is God "alone" is followed by a paragraph known in Hebrew as the *Ve-ahavta*. This, too, is very familiar to Jews and Christians. It begins, "You shall love the LORD your God with all your heart, and with all your soul, and with all your might." (See "Deuteronomy in the Christian Scriptures" below.) The full paragraph in the Hebrew, which ends with the words "write them on the doorposts of your house and on your gates," is also part of the daily liturgy in Judaism.

Chapter 6 then continues with admonitions to be faithful to God, especially when you enter the new land. Deuteronomy's continuing theme of instruction is underscored in this chapter. Verse 7 reads, "Recite [these words] to your children and talk about them when you are at home and when you are away," and verses 20–21 explain: "When your children ask you in time to come…then you shall say.…"

Chapters 7 and 8 exhort the people to destroy utterly the seven nations of the land into which they are going. Do not show mercy to them, do not intermarry with them, and absolutely break down, burn, and smash their shrines and places of worship. They are large and strong, but you will prevail. Remember, it was not because you were more numerous than other nations, indeed you were the fewest, but God loves you and set an oath with you (Deut 7:7–8). Follow God's laws and you will prosper; turn from God and you will suffer. Do not be afraid; God will be with you. The conquest will be slow, but it will happen (Deut 7:22ff.).

God is protecting you, as God protected you in the wilderness. This is a splendid land to which you are going: rich in material resources and abundant in food products (Deut 8:7–10). When you get there and prosper, do not forget God. Do not think this came about because of your own power and strength (Deut 8:17).

With our modern sensibilities, how are we to understand the proscription against the Canaanites? The Torah text is clear: utterly obliterate the local population. Ours is an age that has seen massive attacks on innocent people, the worst example being the Holocaust. Yet, subsequent to that there have been other atrocities—among the Ibo, the Tutsi, and the Hutu in Africa; the "killing fields" in Cambodia; the "ethnic cleansing" in the former Yugoslavia.

Traditional Jewish commentators throughout the ages were appalled at the call for such violence. They sought ways to suggest that this really did not happen.[21] Modern scholars take a different tack. Some suggest that these lines are hyperbole; others suggest that they mean what they say, but that they never were instituted in practice. Von Rad writes of the "theoretical nature of Deuteronomy which is easily inclined to be doctrinaire."[22] Tigay points out that modern scholarship considers that the law meant what it said, but that it was "purely theoretical and was never put into effect."[23] These laws were religious in motivation, to prevent the Israelites from joining with or being influenced by their potential neighbors who practiced abhorrent religious acts such as child sacrifice and necromancy (cf. Deut 12:31). It is vital to note that these prohibitions were *not* based on ethnicity; they were aimed at anyone who engaged in such practices. Israelites who practiced these rituals were likewise to be put to death (Deut 13:12–18 [13:13–19 H]).

Chapters 9 and 10 continue a familiar theme: your success is not a sign of your special qualities. Rather it is because of the utter wickedness of the current inhabitants, and because God promised this land to Abraham, Isaac, and Jacob (Deut 9:3ff.). Moses blasts Israel for its past provocation, reminding the people of the depths of their destructive behavior, their apostasy with the golden calf. He reminds Israel that God wanted to wipe them out and start anew, and, but for Moses' intervention with God, they would not be alive. He reminds them that he placed the second set of the Ten Commandments in the ark (the first having been smashed [Exod 32:19]).

Deuteronomy 10:12–13 states that God demands that people are to walk in God's ways, love God, and serve God with their heart and soul, for their own good.[24]

Chapter 11 continues with a historical lesson, noting the rebellion of Datan and Abiram (though no mention is made of Korah [Num 16]).

The verses of Deuteronomy 11:13–21 are incorporated into the daily liturgy of Judaism. Like the verses from chapter 6, they follow the *Sh'ma* ("Hear, O Israel…") This paragraph explains that *if* Israel follows God's commands, *then* God will provide rain in its proper season. This reflects an underlying mentality in Deuteronomy: God controls all nature, and provides or withholds in proportion to the obedience of the people.

These same verses also make mention of something that would in time be called *phylacteries* (*tefillin* in Hebrew). At this point it merely says take these words and "bind them as a sign on your hand, and fix them as an emblem [or frontlet, symbol, or headband] on your forehead" (Deut 11:18). Similar legislation is found in Deuteronomy 6:8. See Text Study at the end of the chapter, "God's Unity; Love God."

Chapters 12–26 form the Law Code in Deuteronomy. A variety of areas are covered.

Chapter 12 begins with admonitions to destroy the local pagan shrines in the Promised Land, and then goes on to reiterate that God will choose a special place to be associated with the divine name. There also are statements about proper and improper animals that may (or may not) be eaten for food, along with a repetition about not eating blood (Deut 12:23ff.). The closing verses warn against the detestable practice of child sacrifice, practiced by the local inhabitants. Finally, the chapter ends with a frequent admonition in this book: do not make changes in the legislation (12:32 [13:1 H]; cf. 4:2; 5:32 [5:29 H]).

Chapter 13 is concerned with prophets or diviners of dreams who would seduce the people, leading them to other gods. Even if their prediction comes true, do not follow them. This is merely a test. Do not be fooled. In fact, you are to put these people to death. If near kin or close friends would secretly entice you to worship other gods, neither yield to them nor show them compassion. Execute them; they are a danger in your midst (Deut 13:9 [13:10 H]). If a whole town goes astray, annihilate it.

Chapter 14 turns initially to mourning practices, then to ritual food taboos, and tithes. A whole variety of animals are specifically mentioned. As in Leviticus 11, to be considered proper, animals need to have a cleft hoof and chew the cud; water dwelling animals need to have fins and scales; fowl need to be clean birds, essentially domestic fowl. Refrain from eating something that has died by itself; and likewise, do not boil a kid in its mother's milk (Deut 14:21).

Chapter 15 deals with debts and various measures to offer protection for the poor. Do not be hard-hearted toward the poor; rather be generous with them. Give liberally (Deut 15:7–11). The chapter concludes with legislation dealing with the sacrifice of first-born cattle (vss. 19–23).

Parts of Deuteronomy clearly are linked to the Covenant Code of Exodus 20–23. For example, Exodus 21:1–11 is paralleled in Deuteronomy 15:12–18; Exodus 21:12–14 parallels Deuteronomy 19:1–13; Exodus 22:29f. is connected to Deuteronomy 15:19–23.[25]

Chapter 16 concentrates on the celebration of the holy days of Passover/*Pesach*—the feast of Unleavened Bread; Weeks/*Shavuot* (also known as Pentecost), the early summer harvest; and the festival of Booths/*Succot,* the late summer/early autumn harvest. These festivals are also mentioned in Leviticus 23 and Numbers 9, as well as in Exodus. It is significant that the other festivals, such as the Day of Atonement, are not included here. The command to observe the festivals at the place that God shall designate is repeated several times (Deut 16:2, 6, 7, etc.)[26] This chapter closes with the call to appoint judges who will render just decisions. "Justice, and only justice, you shall pursue, so that you may live and occupy the land that the LORD your God is giving you" (vs. 20).

Chapter 17 continues with judicial matters, including instruction for a thorough investigation of someone accused of astral worship. If someone is accused of a capital crime, two witnesses are necessary, and these witnesses have to participate in the execution. If the judicial decision is too difficult, the people are instructed to "go up to the place that the LORD your God will choose, where you shall consult with the levitical priests and the judge who is in office in those days" (Deut 17:8–9).

In this chapter, for the first time there comes legislation dealing with someone who will serve as an earthly ruler: a king over Israel (vss. 14–20). What is very significant is that there are limited laws here, and the ruler is more an administrator than a powerful temporal monarch.

Chapter 18 commences with legislation that addresses the special place of the Levites. What is different here from laws that were promulgated in Exodus through Numbers is that now the subject is the "whole tribe of Levi" (vs. 1). In the prior books, there was a marked difference between the descendants of Aaron and the rest of the tribe of Levi. Aaron and his direct family were the priests. They alone were in charge of the sacrifices, and the rest of the

Levites supported them. In Numbers 16 Moses had criticized the rebel Korah and his levitical followers with this statement: "Hear now, you Levites! Is it too little for you that the God of Israel has separated you from the congregation of Israel, to allow you to approach him in order to perform the duties of the LORD's tabernacle, and to stand before the congregation and serve them...yet you seek the priesthood as well!" (Num 16:8–10). Here in Deuteronomy, in contrast to the earlier books, the levitical priesthood is not limited to one family (cf. Lev 7:28–36; Num 18:8–9).

In Deuteronomy 18:9ff. the laws momentarily return to material spoken about previously: the abhorrent practices of the nations now living in Canaan (cf. Deut 12:29–31). The main focus of this section is to consider the role of the prophet in Israel. Prophets were an integral part of the leadership of ancient Israel. For the writers of Deuteronomy, the prophet is an extremely important and authoritative leader. While Deuteronomy consciously seeks to limit the power of the monarch, it strengthens the role of the prophet.[27] Of course, there were other leaders as well: priests, the elders, and the monarch with his attendant staff. The prophet, however, is described as the successor of Moses. "The LORD your God will raise up for you a prophet like me from among your own people; you shall heed such a prophet" (Deut 18:15). Moses goes on to say that this is God's plan and that God will put words in the prophet's mouth. Further, if anyone fails to heed the prophet, God will call that person into account. Then, Moses anticipates the obvious question from the people, how will we know if this is a real prophet? He delivers this caveat: you will know that the prophet is a true prophet because what he says will come about (vss. 21–22). For a discussion of how Christianity linked Moses to Jesus, see below, "Deuteronomy in the Christian Scriptures."

Chapters 19, 20, and the first part of 21 address the asylum cities, and then various judicial and military matters. First three and then an additional three cities shall be set aside for those who kill unintentionally. The people are to make sure that these cities are readily accessible. Intentional murder, however, is not covered by this legislation. As in 17:6, one needs two witnesses to a crime, though here (Deut 19:15) it is not necessarily a capital matter. In verse 21, the law of talion is repeated (see the section "The Laws of Retaliation/*Lex Talionis*" [Lev 24]).

Chapter 20 addresses the reasons for deferments from battle, including the case of someone who is recently betrothed. Then comes legislation that covers certain rules for warfare and the treatment of defeated populations. In what is an extraordinary law for its time and place, Israel is ordered not to destroy the fruit trees of a besieged city (Deut 20:19).

The first nine verses of chapter 21 explain what happens when a murdered corpse is found in the open countryside. When the guilty party cannot be found, the whole community is held responsible, and expiation needs to be done.

The next chapters, the rest of chapter 21 through the end of chapter 25, are a miscellany of various laws, largely dealing with domestic matters. What are the rules for marrying a woman captured in war, what rights does she have? If you have two wives, what are the rules for inheritance? If your child is willfully disloyal, what recourse do you have? Do you have to show proper respect to an executed criminal? All these questions are covered in Deuteronomy 21:10–23.

Returning lost property, cross dressing, sparing a mother bird with her young, building regulations—these subjects are covered in the opening verses of chapter 22. Then come laws that were first broached in Leviticus 19:19, regarding seeds, animals, and mixing textiles. Deuteronomy 22:12 connects to Numbers 15:37–41, the wearing of fringes on one's garments.

Laws concerning virginity, false accusations, adultery, and rape round out chapter 22.

In chapters 22–25 there are a number of laws dealing specifically with women. Among the subjects covered there are matters of fathers controlling daughters and wives (Deut 22:13–30), the slandered bride (Deut 22:13–21), the betrothed woman (Deut 22:23–27), the nonbetrothed virgin (Deut 22:28f.), the *qedesha/ kedesha* (female priest?) and the *zonah* (prostitute) (Deut 23:17–18 [23:18–19 H]), the newly married woman (Deut 24:5), levirate marriage (Deut 25:5–10), and the woman who grabs a man's genitals (Deut 25:11f.).[28]

Though chapter 23 begins with a law dealing with a forbidden marriage, it moves to certain groups who are to be excluded from the congregation of Israel, such as Ammonites and Moabites. Yet the offspring of Egyptians and Edomites are acceptable. The reason for excluding the Ammonites and Moabites presents a difficulty. Here (Deut 23:3–4 [23:4–5 H]) these groups stand accused of not providing food and water when Israel journeyed in their territory. These sentences contradict Deuteronomy 2:28–29, where the Moabites did provide food; and according to Deuteronomy 2:37, the Israelites did not come into contact with the Ammonites. That these laws were not always accepted at their face value is underscored by the fact that Ruth, a citizen of Moab, is the great grandmother of King David (cf. Ruth 4:22).

Deuteronomy 23:9–14 (23:10–15 H) deals with public health issues that all military camps face: what to do with human excrement. This section also deals with nocturnal emissions, which were considered a matter of ritual pollution (cf. Lev 15:16).

The rights of escaped slaves, the prohibition of prostitution, various laws of interest for lending, laws dealing with vows, and taking food that technically belongs to your neighbor completes the legislation of chapter 23.

Chapter 24 continues with the same mixture of laws. The first verses deal with prohibitions against remarriage to the same woman; then, in an apparent extension of the legislation in Deuteronomy 20:5ff., follows a law that a newlywed is to be excused from service in the army for a year.

Reflecting how people lived such a subsistent existence at that time, Deuteronomy explains that it is forbidden to take a handmill or an upper millstone as a way to compel someone to repay a loan (vs. 6). Presumably the person owned this handmill or millstone and literally ground out his living through his work. To deprive him of his livelihood was unacceptable. Protection for the underprivileged, whether poor and needy or widows or resident aliens, is underscored in verses 10–15, 17–22. These are some of the most striking humanitarian laws in the Bible (see Text Study at the end of the chapter, "Protecting Dignity"). Deuteronomy 24:16 states that people are responsible for their own crimes; parents are not liable for children or children for parents.

Chapter 25 begins with the penalty for crimes, and while the person is to be punished publicly, he is not to be degraded. Human dignity, even of the guilty, needs to be respected. Verse 4 addresses an ox that is threshing. Do not muzzle the ox; let it eat. Then follow the laws of levirate marriage (vss. 5–10), which provide that, if a married man dies childless, his property will remain within the family clan. The word *levirate* comes from the Latin *levir,* "husband's brother." This is a central issue in the Book of Ruth and was also at the center of the controversy in Genesis 38, the narrative of Tamar and Judah.

Deuteronomy 25:11–12 deal with the punishment to be exacted when a woman intervenes improperly in a fight between her husband and another man. It is similar to the legislation found in Exodus 21:18–19, 22–25. The next verses deal with honest weights and measures, similar to Leviticus 19:35–36. The closing verses of chapter 25 recall the Amalekite atrocities first mentioned in Exodus 17:8–16. Here, however, the crimes of the Amalekites are spelled out in greater detail: how they pitilessly attacked the stragglers, the faint, and weary. The voice of Deuteronomy is clear: you shall exact retribution; "do not forget" (vs. 19).

Chapter 26. Whereas many of the immediately preceding chapters were a miscellany of messages, beginning with chapter 26, legislation containing similar matters is once again the norm. The opening eleven verses deal with what farmers are to declare when they bring their first fruits. As we would expect, their first fruits are to be brought to "the place that the LORD your God will choose as a dwelling for his name" (Deut 26:2; cf. chapters 12 and 16 above). Then come some tithe declarations, verses 12–15. The chapter concludes with an exhortation that the people are to honor and keep all these statutes and ordinances, and to obey God. God has obtained your consent, and God has declared you "his treasured people" (vs. 18; cf. Exod 19:5).

Chapter 27 generally is included in the second great address of Moses, but it has a very different sense to it. It really is an independent unit. Notably Moses is spoken about rather than the one speaking. It is a descriptive passage. Consider the wording in verses 1, 9, and 11: "Then Moses...charged all the people; Then Moses...spoke to all Israel; The same day Moses charged the people...." The directions given in chapter 27 are for a future time, when the Israelites will actually enter the land. When they get to

Mount Ebal, which overlooks the area of Shechem, they are to erect steles (stone pillars) and coat them with plaster. Then they are to "write on them all the words of this law [teaching]" (vs. 3). Exactly what those words are to be is not specified. It may be part or all of chapters 12–26; it may be less than that or possibly more. It may be the statement of God's unity (Deut 6:4) or the Ten Commandments (Deut 5). The people are also to build an altar and sacrifice burnt offerings on it. Then, after all the people have crossed the Jordan, representatives of each of the twelve tribes shall stand on two mountains opposite each other, Mount Gerizim and Mount Ebal (vss. 12–13). The Levites shall then pronounce both blessings and curses. The curses are listed here (vss. 15–26) and the blessings, presumably, would be the antidotes to the curses (i.e., Blessed are those who refrain from making idols, and so on). This section is a very old part of the history of Israel. Both Levi and Joseph are listed as tribes, that is, the Levites are not yet a group by themselves, and Joseph has not been subdivided into the tribes of Ephraim and Manasseh (cf. Gen 48:5; Num 1:10). On Mount Gerizim are the tribes who are descendants of Jacob through his primary wives, Leah and Rachel (Simeon, Levi, Judah, Issachar, Joseph, and Benjamin). On Mount Ebal are the descendants through the concubines, Bilhah and Zilpah, plus Leah's sons Reuben, who had been disenfranchised [cf. Gen 49:3–4], and Zebulun, who was the youngest of Leah's children. On Mount Ebal, then, are Reuben, Gad, Asher, Zebulun, Dan, and Naphtali (Deut 27:13).

Chapter 28 describes in striking detail the consequences that will accrue to Israel should they follow God's teaching, and likewise the "awesome array of curses that dwarf the catalogue of blessings preceding them."[29] The curses outweigh the blessings by about 3:1. The blessings promise abundance and fruitful harvests—human, animal, and from the soil. You will be blessed wherever you go, and your enemies will flee from before you. You shall be the top, and never the bottom. So it goes for the first fourteen verses. Then the tables turn, and for every blessing there is a matching curse, and worse, much worse. Disobedience brings disaster; curses and threats thunder down in a hailstorm of destruction. The people will suffer intolerably; they will know deprivation, depression, and disease. The enemy shall be the head, and Israel the tail. "In the morning you shall say, 'If only it were evening!' and at evening you shall say, 'If only it were morning!'—because of the dread that your heart shall feel and the sights that your eyes shall see" (Deut 28:67).

Moses' second discourse ends on a note that these are the terms that God commanded Moses to conclude with the Israelites in the land of Moab, in addition to the covenant concluded at Horeb (Deut 29:1 [28:69 H]).[30]

The Third Discourse: Deuteronomy 29:2 [29:1 H]—30:20

Moses' third address commences with a statement that, though the people had seen all the miracles and wonders, they did not really comprehend the magnitude of those events until this very moment. This meaning is reinforced by the comments in Deuteronomy 29:7–9 [29:6–8 H] which congratulate Israel for the defeat of their enemies and exhorts them to observe the words of the covenant. In NRSV and NJPS, verse 4 [3 H] suggests that Israel does not yet understand. Yet, this cannot be the meaning of verse 4 [3 H], for then the whole discourse would have been for naught.[31]

Beginning with verse 10 [9 H] Moses delivers a powerful rhetorical address. You are assembled here this day; you are standing here as tribal leaders, elders, officials, men, children, women, aliens, even those of lowly status (those who cut wood and draw water) to enter into the covenant with God. This is the covenant long promised to Abraham, Isaac, and Jacob. God is not establishing this covenant with you alone. "I am making this covenant, sworn by an oath, not only with you who stand here with us today before the LORD our God, but also with those who are not here with us today" (Deut 29:14–15 [29:13–14 H]). This covenant is not bound by time; it is an eternal document. It is concluded with those who are actually present and with all their descendants, whether physical or spiritual descendants.[32]

This covenant, however, is only for those who are sincere. If there is among the people some who think they can go their own way, God will utterly reject them (vs. 18–21 [17–20 H]).

189

The rest of the verses of this chapter explain, in a similar manner to the curses above, what will happen to those people who do not follow God's covenant.

The last verse in the chapter is most intriguing. "The secret things belong to the LORD our God, but the revealed things belong to us and to our children forever, to observe all the words of this law" (Deut 29:29 [29:28H]). In its context it may mean that there still are matters that God has not revealed (or possibly, not yet revealed) but that there are many things that we do know and are to follow. It may be that while nothing is hidden from God, nonetheless, we humans have plenty of knowledge and need to act on it. Perhaps it is a statement that God knows the future, and we do not. Akin to this is the observation that this is a wisdom maxim, "which affirms the limits of human wisdom apart from the law which God has revealed (cf. also 4:6ff.)."[33] These words in Deuteronomy resonate with the teaching of the wisdom tradition in the Bible, such as Proverbs 8.

Chapter 30 continues Moses' discourse. On a positive note, Moses says that even though you will have turned away, you will repent, and God will accept you (Deut 30:2–3). God will bring you back to the land. God will punish your enemies and will reward you with goodness. God will delight in your well-being. In the first ten verses the verb *return/repent* (Hebrew root, *shuv*) is repeated several times, referring both to God and to humans.

With 30:11–20, Moses' rhetoric again reaches wonderful heights. In these ten verses, there is powerful imagery. These are the closing words of his third and final discourse. He points to the heavens and the far distant horizon. "Surely, this commandment…is not too hard for you, nor is it too far away." It is not in heaven that you would require someone to go there to get it for you. Nor is it beyond the sea that you would require a great hero to go there. This learning, this teaching, is right here. "No, the word is very near to you; it is in your mouth and in your heart for you to observe" (vs. 14).

Life and death, blessings and curses are set before the people. Moses appeals to "heaven and earth" to serve as witnesses: "I have set before you life and death, blessings and curses. Choose life so that you and your descendants may live" (vs. 19). Moses' reference to "blessings and curses" in this verse echoes the similar images he used earlier, in 11:26–28.

Moses completes this third and final address with reference again to the proverbial ancestors, Abraham, Isaac, and Jacob.

Concluding Chapters: Deuteronomy 31–34

As chapter 31 begins, the book turns from oration to narration, for this is not only the closing period of Moses' life but also the closing out of the Torah, and, at the same time, preparation for the days ahead. Details need to be arranged. In the opening verses, Moses reiterates that Joshua will succeed him. This had been stated before (Num 27:18ff.). The transition takes place publicly. He tells Joshua, "Be strong and bold" (vs. 7). Have no fear or dread.

Then, in an aside (vss. 9–13) Moses writes down the laws and hands them over to the priests, explaining that they are to read them publicly every seven years on the festival of Booths (Tabernacles/*Succot*). This will take place at a location that God will choose! Men, women, and children are to be there to hear the reading of the law, and resident aliens as well. This repeats a familiar theme in Deuteronomy. Rehearse and repeat the tradition so the next generation will know it (cf. Deut 6:7; 11:19).

As chapter 31 continues, it seems to repeat itself. God now calls for a private session with Moses and Joshua at the tent of meeting. Moses is informed again that his death is imminent and that the people will rebel after his death. He is to write down a song/poem (the Hebrew word *shir* can mean either) and teach it to the people (vs. 19). When disaster comes, these words will testify against them. Then God speaks to Joshua, son of Nun, the words that Moses had said to him earlier, "Be strong and bold" (vs. 23). Moses then writes down the words of this law/teaching (book of the law [teaching]/*Sefer haTorah*). He has the Levites who carry the ark put the book of the law beside the ark of the covenant so it will remain as a visible witness against the people. The chapter concludes on a note of predicted pessimism: once Moses dies the people will rebel.

Chapter 32 is often titled the "Song of Moses." This is not the first example of an extended song/poem associated with Moses, for

191

during the early part of the Egyptian Exodus there also is another Song of Moses, or as it is alternately called, the Song of the Sea (Exod 15:1–18).

Once again, this is powerful rhetoric. The author of the song commences with a call, using the images of the natural world: heaven and earth, rain, dew, showers, new grass, and tender plants. God's teaching, he suggests, will be torrential; other parts will be as soft as the moisture of dew. These immediate images are agrarian and pastoral. In a climate that values moisture and does not take it for granted, the images indicate how precious and rare is abundant precipitation. These metaphors would not be utilized where rainfall is plentiful, such as in the rain forest or the equatorial jungle. The Song of Moses presents powerful pictures. God is described as the Rock, with the solidity of a mountain cliff, dependable and unmoving. The term rock is used several times (vss. 4, 15, 18, 30, 31). God is an eagle with outspread wings. God is a warrior with arrows (vss. 23, 42), with blade and sword (vss. 41, 42).

At the end of the chapter, following the recital of the song/poem, God instructs Moses to ascend Mt. Nebo. He will view the land from a distance, but he will not enter it. Moses is soon to die, but he still has something to share with the people.

Chapter 33 is termed the Blessing of Moses. As Jacob had blessed his children before his death (Gen 49) so here does Moses pray for his "children," his charges, his people. Each tribe gets a special blessing. The blessings vary in length. Of special interest is the blessing for Levi (note again that there is a blessing for Levi; there is also one for the tribe of Joseph, which in fact mentions Ephraim and Manasseh in verse 17). After each of the tribes is acknowledged, there is a kind of coda, which blesses Israel (vss. 26–29).

Chapter 34 closes out Deuteronomy. There, aged Moses, one hundred twenty years old, still full of vigor, beholds the Promised Land from afar. Chapter 34 serves as an epilogue to Deuteronomy. A mere twelve lines, it notes that Moses died "at the LORD's command." It insinuates that God buried Moses in a place unknown to humans. The narrative also stresses that the leadership will continue, for Joshua is there to carry on the divine plan. The final words in the book praise Moses and say that he was unique among Israel's leaders. "Never since has there arisen a prophet in Israel like Moses, whom the LORD knew face to face." Indeed, Moses was simply unequaled.

5. DEUTERONOMY IN THE CHRISTIAN SCRIPTURES

The most famous line in the Book of Deuteronomy is the affirmation of the unity of God: Deuteronomy 6:4, the *Sh'ma* ("Hear, O Israel: The LORD is our God, the LORD alone." [Alternatively: "Hear, O Israel: The LORD is our God, the LORD is one."]). This is followed by the affirmation of commitment to God: "You shall love the LORD your God with all your heart, and with all your soul, and with all your might" (Deut 6:5). In Mark's Gospel a scribe comes to Jesus and asks, "Which commandment is the first of all?" Jesus replies, "The first is, 'Hear, O Israel: the Lord our God, the Lord is one; you shall love the Lord your God with all your heart, and with all your soul, and with all your mind, and with all your strength'" (Mark 12:28–30). It is interesting that Jesus quotes Deuteronomy 6:4 correctly but then adds a few words to Deuteronomy 6:5. The parallel passages in Matthew (Matt 22:37) and Luke (Luke 10:27) refer to loving God but do not quote the words of the *Sh'ma*.

1 Timothy 6:15 and Revelation 17:14, 19:16 echo the words of Deuteronomy 10:17, "God of gods and Lord of lords."

Deuteronomy 12:32 [13:1 H] urges that all God's teaching be observed, "do not add to it or take anything from it," a sentiment also expressed earlier in the book (4:2; 5:32 [5:29 H]). The author of Revelation feels similarly about his work, for he offers a clear warning to those who would tamper with his words. "I warn everyone who hears the words of the prophecy of this book: if anyone adds to them, God will add to that person the plagues described in this book; if anyone takes away from the words of the book of this prophecy, God will take away that person's share in the tree of life and in the holy city, which are described in this book" (Rev 22:18–19).

The concern of false prophets, raised in Deuteronomy (Deut 13:1ff. [13:2ff. H]), is also found in the Gospels. When sitting at the Mount of Olives, Jesus' disciples approach him and ask about the sign of his coming and the end of the age. He describes a difficult and tumultuous time and then warns them of false prophets and false messiahs (Matt 24:23ff.; Mark 13:21ff.).

A question related to the identification of the false prophet is identification of the true prophet. Moses had said that, at a future time, God would provide just such a person. "I will raise up for them a prophet like you from among their own people" (Deut 18:18). In the Gospels, a highly charged narrative portrays Jesus, accompanied by Peter, James, and his brother, John. They are on a "high mountain, by themselves." There, Jesus is transfigured before them. Suddenly Moses and Elijah are also there, talking with Jesus (Matt 17:1ff.; Mark 9:2ff.; Luke 9:28ff.). About a week before this, in Luke's Gospel, Jesus had asked his disciples, "Who do the crowds say that I am?" They answer that there is a difference of opinion, for some claim Jesus is John the Baptist (who recently had been killed); others suggest Elijah. Still others say that "one of the ancient prophets has arisen" (Luke 9:18–19; cf. Matt 16:13ff.; Mark 8:27ff.).[34]

That Jesus is "transfigured...his face shone like the sun, and his clothes became dazzling white" (Matt 17:2; cf. Mark 9:3; Luke 9:29) is purposely described. As Craig S. Keener explains, "a variety of allusions combine to point especially to Moses in the Old Testament. After Moses beheld God's glory, his own face shone with that glory (Ex 34:29–35...); most scholars regard this account about Moses as the primary background for the revelation of Matthew 17."[35]

Moses' powerful rhetoric had a great appeal to Paul. Moses said that God's teaching is not in the heaven or beyond the sea. It is there with them. There is no need to say, "'Who will go up to heaven for us...' Neither is it beyond the sea, that you should say, 'Who will cross to the other side of the sea for us....' No, the word is very near to you; it is in your mouth and in your heart for you to observe" (Deut 30:12–14). In Romans 10:6–8 Paul explains that the righteous do not say "'Who will ascend into the heaven?' (that is, to bring Christ down)..."; rather they understand that the "word is near to you, on your lips and in your heart."

6. DEUTERONOMY IN RABBINIC LITERATURE

T wo of the most accessible midrashic collections on Deuteronomy in English are *Midrash Deuteronomy Rabbah,* and *Sifre: A Tannaitic Commentary on the Book of Deuteronomy.*

Prayer: The Service of the Heart

As has been discussed several times earlier in this book, when the Romans destroyed the Temple in Jerusalem in 70 CE, the whole sacrificial system came to an abrupt halt. Fortunately, Synagogue Judaism was well in place, able to replace the priestly rites of the central sanctuary. The notion that acts of kindness could serve as a substitute for the daily sacrifices was addressed by the great Pharisaic leader of the first century, Rabbi Yohanan ben Zaccai.[36]

In Deuteronomy 11:13 Moses explains that if the people heed God's commandments, "loving the LORD your God, and serving him with all your heart and with all your soul," they will know great bounty from the land. The rabbis pondered, what is this "service of the heart," and their answer was prayer. "Scripture says, *With all your heart and with all your soul* (11:13)—is there such a thing as (Temple) service in one's heart? Therefore what does the verse mean by *and to serve Him?* It refers to prayer…just as the service of the altar is called 'service' [Hebrew, *avodah*], so is prayer called 'service' [Hebrew, *avodah*]."[37]

God's Domain and Ours: It Is Not in Heaven

The intriguing words that God's teaching is "not in heaven" but rather in the mouths and hearts of the people (Deut 30:12) serve as a daring scriptural proof text in the Talmud. The famous episode is known as "Aknai's oven." Several rabbis were debating about the actual physical structure of a particular kind of oven. Was it technically of one piece or made of multiple sections? The majority of the sages voted one way, but Rabbi Eliezer stubbornly continued to argue his position. "If the proper interpretation follows my reasoning," he said, "this carob tree will prove it!" The tree moved several hundred feet and resettled itself. The sages said, "Proof cannot be brought from a carob tree." Rabbi Eliezer persisted. "If I am right, let the water in this ditch attest for me." The water began to flow backward. The sages retorted, "No proof comes from a stream of water." "If my interpretation is correct," said Rabbi Eliezer, "let these walls prove it." The walls began to close in on the rabbis. One of the sages, Rabbi Joshua, got up and addressed the walls. "When the rabbis are debating important matters of tradition, what business is it of yours?" Out of respect for Rabbi Joshua the walls did not fall, but out of respect for Rabbi Eliezer they did not return to their original position. In anger and desperation, Rabbi Eliezer said, "If my interpretation is correct, let heaven back me up!" Suddenly a divine voice was heard, "Why do you dispute with Rabbi Eliezer, his is the correct interpretation." Rabbi Joshua arose and quoted the line from Deuteronomy "It is not in heaven." His colleague Rabbi Jeremiah explained, "The Torah was given at Mt. Sinai. We do not listen to heavenly voices, because you long ago said in the Torah, 'You shall follow the majority.'"[38] Framing the matter somewhat differently, the rabbis teach, Do not think that another Moses is going to come along and teach us a new Torah. It states clearly, "It is not in heaven." This means that "no part of it has remained in heaven."[39]

Repentance Is Always Possible

Based on the line "The LORD our God is whenever we call to him" (Deut 4:7), the rabbis explain, "the gates of prayer are sometimes open and sometimes closed, but the gates of repentance always remain open."[40]

Justice in All Matters

The Talmud comments on the fact that the word "justice" is repeated. "Justice, and only justice, you shall pursue, so that you may live and occupy the land that the LORD your God is giving you" (Deut 16:20). This means that there has to be justice in both a judgment and in a compromise.[41]

Begin with Simple Matters

Building on the verse "This commandment…is not too hard for you" (Deut 30:11), the rabbis explain that people should not be put off by the vast amount of Jewish teaching. Begin with simple matters, and then expand your knowledge.[42]

Studying, Retaining, Performing

"If you will diligently observe this entire commandment…" (Deut 11:22). "If people merely learn the Torah, they have fulfilled one commandment; if they learn and keep what they have learned, they have fulfilled two commandments; if they learn, keep, and perform, there are none more meritorious."[43]

A Time to Turn Over Leadership

When it came time for Moses to die, he offers God an alternative idea. I, Moses, will live longer and simply let Joshua assume the leadership. God, though skeptical, agreed. Initially, Moses deferred to Joshua. Then they went to the tent of meeting, and God's cloud came down, separating the two men. When the cloud lifted, Moses asked Joshua, "What did God say?" Joshua replied, "When you were the leader, did you share information?" At that moment Moses realized the error of his ways and said it is better to die than to be envious, and so he resigned himself to his death.[44]

The Futility of Planning Ahead

"Your time to die is near" (Deut 31:14) inspired the following story. Rabbi Simeon ben Halafta was walking home one dark evening and chanced to meet the Angel of Death. The angel was looking strange, and the rabbi asked him, "Who are you?" "I am God's messenger," the angel replied. "So why are you looking so perplexed?" The Angel of Death replied, "On account of the talk of human beings who say, 'I am going to do such and such' but none of them know when they are going to die."

The story continues. Rabbi Simeon is curious about the time of his own death and asks, "When will I die?" "I cannot tell you," said the Angel of Death, "I have no control over the likes of you. Often God finds delight in your deeds and grants you extra time."[45]

Moses' Reluctance to Die

The same verse, "Your time to die is near" (Deut 31:14), is the basis of a very different midrashic teaching. Here Moses again is very reluctant to die. He offers argument after argument why he should not die. He drew a circle and stepped in it, refusing to move until God rescinded the decree. The very foundations of the earth shook. Finally, God had enough and sent one of the angels to take Moses' life. Moses refuses to go with the angel. God then enlists the angel Gabriel to go to fetch Moses' soul. Gabriel—if this can be believed—politely refuses. Moses is such a tremendous person, with such wonderful qualities, how can I do so? God then asks Michael, who also begs to be excused. Michael explains, "Moses and I studied together, how can I take his life?" Finally, God sends Sammael, the Angel of Death, who is all too willing to accomplish this task. When Sammael meets Moses, Moses takes his famous staff and starts to chase Sammael away. Only when God specifically tells Moses that the deity in person will come to fetch Moses' soul does the great leader acquiesce. Moses, finally, agrees to die.[46]

In Many Languages

The section "Exodus in Rabbinic Literature" explains that the rabbis said God's words were heard in seventy voices, seventy languages, so that all the nations of the world would understand.[47] That idea is made even more specific, naming Latin and Arabic as two of the languages. This is amazing, because Latin was associated with the Romans, who had exiled the Jews from Jerusalem and destroyed the Temple. Later Latin was associated with Christianity. Arabic, certainly after the seventh century CE, was associated with Islam. Yet, here is what the rabbis said

> When God revealed [the divine presence] to give the Torah to Israel, [God] spoke to them not in one language but in four languages. As it is said [Deut 33:2] "The Lord came from Sinai—this refers to the Hebrew language; and rose from Seir

unto them—this refers to the Roman [Latin] language. [God] shined forth from Mount Paran—this refers to the Arabic language; and [God] came from the Myriads of Kodesh [understanding the words *Riberboth-kodesh*/Myriads of holy ones as a proper name]—this refers to the Aramaic language."[48]

7. TEXT STUDY

A. 2 Kings 22:1—23:30 (cf. 2 Chr 34–35). The Discovery of the Book

This is the famous "discovery" of the "book of the law/teaching," which was suddenly found when young King Josiah authorized repairs to be made on the Temple. See above, the section "Discovery of the Book of the Law/Teaching." Of particular note is that when the king wants to know what to do ("Go, inquire of the LORD for me...concerning the words of this book" [2 Kgs 22:13]) the scroll is brought to Huldah, a female prophet. Huldah then makes several prophecies.

Lawrence Boadt suggests that Josiah's "law book" was some form of the Book of Deuteronomy. The "king's reforms were a serious attempt to return to a faithful understanding of the covenant of Moses as it was described by the authors of Deuteronomy." He then lists ten changes that Josiah instituted, changes that are arguably based on the laws of Deuteronomy.[49] Among these reforms:

Removes all foreign idols	Deut 12:1–32 [12:1—13:1 H]	2 Kgs 23:13
Ends cult of the stars/host of heaven	Deut 17:3	2 Kgs 23:4–5
Ends worship of sun and moon	Deut 17:3	2 Kgs 23:5, 11
Forbids cult of the dead	Deut 18:11	2 Kgs 23:24

B. Deuteronomy 4:1–40.
Observe God's Laws!

This is the conclusion of Moses' first address/discourse. Having set the historical stage, now Moses explains what God expects of the people. You are about to enter the land. Take seriously this legislation. Do not add or subtract from it. To your regret you have seen what happens when you commit apostasy (vs. 1–4). When you observe God's laws faithfully, you will show your wisdom, and the nations all about will admire you for your discernment (vss. 5–8).

The next unit (vss. 9–31) centers on the prohibition of idolatry. Remember, says Moses, you were there at the mountain. You stood before God at Horeb (Sinai). Remember what you saw with your own eyes, and teach these things to your children and your children's children. Of course, this is a kind of rhetorical flourish, for technically the generation who were adults at Sinai died out over the forty years. Nonetheless, in a sense all these people were at Sinai, and they are the link between the generation of the desert experience and those entering the Promised Land. "The LORD spoke to you out of the fire. You heard the sound of words but saw no form; there was only a voice" (vs. 12). God gave me the Ten Commandments for you, written on two stone tablets. You understand that God is formless, so therefore do not succumb to the temptation to make idols depicting God. God allows the nations all about to have idols, yet you must not be lured into following them (vs. 19). In the next two verses Moses remarks, as a kind of aside, that because of the people's apostasy, God punished him: he will be unable to cross the Jordan to the Promised Land. Again, he warns, do not make any form of idols, for God is a devouring fire. God is "an impassioned God" (NJPS, vs. 24).

When you enter the land, should you become complacent and build idols, Moses says, "I call heaven and earth to witness against you." You will be punished; God will scatter you; only a few of you will be left on the land. You will end up in other lands, and then you will repent, and "return to the LORD your God" (vs. 30). Since God is merciful, God will neither abandon nor destroy you, but remember the ancient covenant.

200

In the final verses of this section (Deut 4:32–40) Moses appeals to the people's sense of history. Has any people *ever* experienced what you have? Ask from one end of heaven to the other, is yours not a unique experience? "Has any people ever heard the voice of a god speaking out of a fire, as you have heard, and lived?" (vs. 33). Then, recalling the miracles and mighty acts in Egypt, Moses alludes to the "mighty hand and outstretched arm" wherein God redeemed the Israelites from their captivity. Not only that, but God has brought you to a new land, which you are about to inherit. In the closing words, Moses underscores familiar ideas: "take to heart" that God is the one deity of the world; "there is no other"; consequently, keep God's commands that "you may long remain in the land that the LORD your God is giving you for all time" (vss. 39–40).

C. Deuteronomy 6:4–9. God's Unity; Love God

This section is familiar to both Christians and Jews for different reasons. It is familiar to Christians because it is found in the Synoptic Gospels; it is part of what Jesus refers to as the Great Commandment (discussed above). It is the centerpiece of Jewish worship, featured both in the evening and morning prayer service. The initial word, *Sh'ma,* has a number of possible translations, depending on its context. It can mean "hear" or "listen" or "understand."[50] "You shall love the LORD your God," with your heart and soul. The heart is considered to be the center of thought or intention, and the soul is the center of emotions or passions. In the rabbinic mind, one was to love God with both the Good Inclination (*Yetzer Tov*) and the Evil Inclination (*Yetzer haRa.*)[51]

Love God exceedingly, with all your might. Be loyal to God. Teach Torah to your children; repeat the lessons, and recite them at all times. The phrase "when you lie down and when you rise up" was taken to mean at the evening and morning liturgy.

Bind them as a sign on your hand, as an emblem on your forehead. In time these phrases were understood to refer to phylacteries (Hebrew, *tefillin*). By the rabbinical period these were hollow leather boxes, about 1.5 inches square, with straps to affix the boxes to one's head and arm during morning prayers. In each box is a parchment that contains four sets of verses, all of which make reference to wearing the phylacteries (Deut 6:4–9; 11:13–21; Exod 13:1–10, 11–16). Many Jews continue to put on *tefillin* as part of their weekday morning ritual. The *tefillin*/phylacteries are mentioned in a negative context in Matthew 23:5.

Write them on the doorposts of your house; on your gates. This commandment continues to be followed in Judaism by placing a mezuzah on the right doorpost of entrances to one's home. The mezuzah is a rectangular hollow box that contains two scriptural verses (Deut 6:4–9; 11:13–21). The mezuzah on a doorpost indicates that this is a dwelling where a Jewish family is living. "And on your gates." Houses have doorposts; they rarely have gates. The gates here refer to the gates of the city. The city gate, or the gate that led to the city plaza, was the center of public activity. People often passed through the city gates, and inscribing God's teaching on the walls of the gates was an effective way of ensuring wide visibility.[52] That is why, in Genesis, one of the promises to Abraham includes this statement: "Your offspring shall possess the gate of their enemies" (Gen 22:17). Later in Genesis, Abraham goes to the city gate to negotiate a burial site (Gen 23:10), and in Ruth, when Boaz wants to make a public statement, he goes to the city gate (Ruth 4:1).

D. Deuteronomy 24:10–22.
Protecting Dignity

When one reads these verses their intent becomes clear: protect the dignity of the poor and the needy. Verses 10–11: The loaner is not allowed to enter the house of the person who is the borrower. This would humiliate the borrower, who also is a child of God. You have to remain outside of the house and wait until the pledge is brought to you. Verses 12–13: If the person is so "dirt poor" that he or she needs their garment to keep warm at night, then this is an impoverished society. Likewise, in verses 14–15, one is not to take advantage of someone who is needy, whether an Israelite or an alien. The owner or master is to pay the person before the sun sets; the poor person may be in desperate straits. Verse 17 protects the widow, the alien, and the fatherless—all people without someone to stand up for them. Verses 19–22 hearken back to similar legislation in Leviticus 19:9–10 and 19:33. It also recalls the story of Ruth (Ruth 2:2–7).

E. Deuteronomy 24:16. Guilt: Parents and Children

The "modern" notion that individual people are responsible for their own wrongdoing has its antecedents in this biblical law. In the ancient Near East, families were considered an extension of the person. This is the first biblical prohibition protecting family members. Very similar teachings are found in Jeremiah 31:29–30 and Ezekiel 18.[53]

Notes

1. Moshe Weinfeld points out that "it is true that Deuteronomy constitutes a second covenant beside the Sinaitic one (cf. 28:69 [29:1 NRSV and most other Christian Bibles]) and thus may have been rightly considered to be secondary. In fact, according to Deuteronomy 5:28 [5:31 NRSV and most other Christian Bibles], though all of the laws were delivered to Moses at Sinai, the people received them only at the plains of Moab, and a covenant was established there in addition to the covenant concluded at Sinai (28:69 [29:1])" (*Deuteronomy 1–11*, Anchor Bible [New York: Doubleday, 1991], 1).

Certainly it is correct to argue that the covenant at Sinai was *only* the Ten Commandments (cf. Deut 4:13) and that the additional teaching mentioned in Deuteronomy 5:31 (5:28 H) is revealed only at Moses' second discourse at Moab. Deuteronomy 29:1 (28:69 H) states clearly that "These are the words of the covenant that the Lord commanded Moses to make with the Israelites in the land of Moab, *in addition* to the covenant he made with them at "Horeb."

2. When the word *Torah* was translated as *nomos* (law), a serious injustice was done. The Torah, of course, includes laws, but it is far broader than the term *nomos* implies. Torah includes history, religious concepts, ethical teachings, and so much more. By defining it as law, the critics of Torah hoped to narrow the Torah's scope, to depict it merely as a system of ritualistic laws, numerous and cumbersome. By limiting the Torah to law, they could more easily contrast their own emphasis on faith and spirit. They conveniently ignored the elements of faith and spirit in the Torah itself.

Therefore, the popular translation of Torah as law, *nomos, ley, loi,* etc., is erroneous....Since the translation is fundamentally wrong, it should be dropped" (Marc Angel, "Law, Halakha," in *A Dictionary of the Jewish-Christian Dialogue, Expanded Edition,* ed. Leon Klenicki and Geoffrey Wigoder, Stimulus Book [Mahwah, NJ: Paulist, 1995], 117).

As part of the introductory notes to the NRSV, the editors explain that clearly "the Torah includes many legal matters; for instance, the book of Leviticus is exclusively 'law.' The translation is too restrictive, however, to do full justice to the meaning of the Hebrew word. In its larger sense the Hebrew word *torah* refers to the 'teaching' or even the 'revelation' that God gives the people" ("The Pentateuch," in *New Oxford Annotated Bible with the Apocrypha,* ed. Bruce M. Metzger and Roland E. Murphy [New York: Oxford University Press, 1991], xxxv). See Lawrence Boadt, *Reading the Old Testament: An Introduction* (Mahwah, NJ: Paulist, 1984), 184.

3. Everett Fox, *The Schocken Bible, Volume I, The Five Books of Moses,* trans. Everett Fox (New York: Schocken), 1995, I, 841.

4. There is broad agreement that the first discourse begins in chapter 1 and continues through most of chapter 4. NRSV explains that the three addresses are Deuteronomy 1:6—4:40; 5:1—28:68; and 29:1 [28:69 H])—30:20). Jeffrey H. Tigay follows a very similar division, Deuteronomy 1:6—4:43; 4:44—28:69; 29—30 (*The JPS Torah Commentary: Deuteronomy* [Philadelphia and Jerusalem: Jewish Publication Society, 1996], xii). Plaut's reading of the second discourse covers Deuteronomy 4:44—11:25, and the third is Deuteronomy 11:26—28:69 (W. Gunther Plaut, *The Torah: A Modern Commentary,* ed. W. Gunther Plaut [New York: Union of American Hebrew Congregations, 1981], 1289).

5. In his introduction to Deuteronomy, Jeffrey H. Tigay offers over a dozen major themes that are unique to this book or which receive special emphasis (*JPS: Deuteronomy,* xii–xix). For an outline of the total contents of Deuteronomy, see Weinfeld, *Deuteronomy 1–11,* 2–4; Boadt, *Reading the Old Testament,* 349; A. D. H. Mayes, *Deuteronomy. The New Century Bible Commentary* (Grand Rapids, MI: Eerdmans; London: Marshall, Morgan & Scott, 1979), 108–10.

6. See Boadt, *Reading the Old Testament,* 352f.

7. Weinfeld, *Deuteronomy 1–11,* 37.

8. Tigay, *JPS: Deuteronomy,* xiv.

9. Ibid., xv.

10. Ibid., xiii.

11. Ibid., xvi.

12. Boadt, *Reading the Old Testament,* 347f.; Samuel Sandmel, *The Hebrew Scriptures: An Introduction to Their Literature and Religious Ideas*

(New York: Knopf, 1963), 413, 416; Gerhard von Rad, *Deuteronomy: A Commentary* (Philadelphia: Westminster, 1966), 19f.

13. Dudley Weinberg and W. Gunther Plaut, "Introducing Deuteronomy," in *The Torah: A Modern Commentary*, ed. Plaut, 1295.

14. Cf. Boadt, *Reading the Old Testament*, 354ff., James King West, *Introduction to the Old Testament*, 2nd ed. (New York: Macmillan, 1981)185f.

15. Weinfeld, *Deuteronomy 1–11*, 19–37.

16. For a detailed analysis of the reforms by Josiah, see Weinfeld, *Deuteronomy 1–11*, 65–84.

17. The word *Sinai* appears but once in Deuteronomy (Deut 33:2). This Sinai/Horeb tradition, coincidentally, is also reflected in the narrative about Elijah, who has an encounter with God at Mt. Horeb (1 Kgs 19; see Zucker, *Israel's Prophets*, 41ff.).

18. Weinfeld, *Deuteronomy 1–11*, 165–67.

19. Tigay, *JPS: Deuteronomy*, 41.

20. Ibid., 72.

21. Cf. Plaut, *The Torah*, 1381; Babylonian Talmud *Avodah Zarah* 20a.

22. Von Rad, *Deuteronomy*, 133.

23. Tigay, *JPS: Deuteronomy*, 471.

24. These words echo Micah's statement in the prophets (Mic 6:8).

25. Numerous other works have delineated these connections and the interested reader is directed to consult with these sources (Boadt, *Reading the Old Testament*, 350; Moshe Weinfeld, "Deuteronomy," in *Encyclopedia Judaic* [Jerusalem: Keter, 1970], 5:1579; von Rad, *Deuteronomy*, 13).

26. See comments by von Rad, *Deuteronomy*, 111ff.

27. Tigay, *JPS: Deuteronomy*, 172.

28. For a discussion about these points, see Tikva Frymer-Kensky, "Deuteronomy," in *The Women's Bible Commentary*, ed. Carol A. Newsom and Sharon H. Ringe (London: SPCK; Louisville, KY: Westminster John Knox, 1992), 56–61. Frymer-Kensky writes that the term *temple prostitute* used in NRSV Deuteronomy 23:17 is incorrect and should be *female priest* (p. 59).

29. Plaut, *The Torah*, 1520.

30. Tigay understands Deuteronomy 29:1 (28:69 H) to refer to the second discourse but acknowledges that some scholars would regard this verse as the introduction to the third discourse (*JPS: Deuteronomy*, 274). See also von Rad, *Deuteronomy*, 178.

31. Cf. Tigay, *JPS: Deuteronomy*, 275, comment on vs. 3.

32. See *Midrash Exodus Rabbah* 28.6.

33. Mayes, *Deuteronomy*, 368.

34. See also David J. Zucker, "Jesus and Jeremiah in the Matthean Tradition," in *Journal of Ecumenical Studies* 27, no. 2 (1990).

35. Craig S. Keener, *A Commentary on the Gospel of Matthew* (Grand Rapids, MI: Eerdmans, 1999), 437.

36. *Avot de Rabbi Natan: The Fathers according to Rabbi Nathan,* chapter 4. As explained in a previous chapter, a similar concept is also found in the Christian scriptures. A scribe says to Jesus that affirming God's unity, love of God, and love of one's neighbor are "much more important than all whole burnt offerings and sacrifices" (Mark 12:32–33).

37. *Sifre: A Tannaitic Commentary on the Book of Deuteronomy* (trans Reuven Hammer, New Haven and London: Yale University, 1986), *Piska* 41, cf. Babylonian Talmud *Ta'anit* 2a.

38. Babylonian Talmud *Baba Metzia* 59b. In this anecdote Rabbi Jeremiah infers his answer by reinterpreting the words from Exodus 23:2 where it says, "You shall not follow a majority in wrongdoing." As you do not follow the majority in wrongdoing, so you *do* follow the majority when they are correct.

39. *Midrash Deuteronomy Rabbah* 8.6.

40. Ibid., 2.12.

41. Babylonian Talmud *Sanhedrin* 32b.

42. *Midrash Deuteronomy Rabbah* 8.3.

43. *Sifre: A Tannaitic Commentary on the Book of Deuteronomy,* *Piska* 48.

44. *Midrash Deuteronomy Rabbah* 9.9.

45. Ibid., 9.1.

46. Ibid., 11.10.

47. *Midrash Exodus Rabbah* 5.9; cf. 28.6.

48. *Sifre: A Tannaitic Commentary on the Book of Deuteronomy,* *Piska* 343.

49. Boadt, *Reading the Old Testament,* 344. For a full list see this reference.

50. Grateful thanks to Rabbi Bonita E. Taylor for this insight.

51. *Sifre: A Tannaitic Commentary on the Book of Deuteronomy,* *Piska* 32.

52. Tigay, *JPS: Deuteronomy,* 79.

53. See Zucker, *Israel's Prophets: An Introduction for Christians and Jews* (Mahwah, NJ: Paulist, 1994), 90, 100ff.

Bibliography

Abrahams, Israel. "Numbers, Typical and Important." In *Encyclopedia Judaica*, vol. 12. Jerusalem: Keter, 1972.

Anderson, Bernhard W. "The Pentateuch." In *The New Oxford Annotated Bible with the Apocryphal/Deuterocanonical Books: New Revised Standard Version,* edited by Bruce M. Metzger and Roland E. Murphy, xxxv–xxxvi. New York: Oxford University, 1991.

Angel, Marc. "Covenant." In *A Dictionary of the Jewish-Christian Dialogue, Expanded Edition,* edited by Leon Klenicki and Geoffrey Wigoder, 33–37. Mahwah, NJ: Paulist Press, 1995.

———. "Law, Halakha." In *A Dictionary of the Jewish-Christian Dialogue, Expanded Edition,* edited by Leon Klenicki and Geoffrey Wigoder, 117–19. Mahwah, NJ: Paulist Press, 1995.

Avot de Rabbi Natan: The Fathers According to Rabbi Nathan. Translated by Judah Goldin. New York: Schocken, 1974.

Babylonian Talmud (various volumes, *Sanhedrin, Yoma, Megillah*). London: Soncino, 1938.

Boadt, Lawrence. *Reading the Old Testament: An Introduction.* New York and Mahwah, NJ: Paulist Press, 1984.

Bright, John. *A History of Israel.* Philadelphia: Westminster, 1959.

Cassuto, Umberto. *A Commentary on the Book of Exodus.* Jerusalem: Magnes, Hebrew University, 1983.

———. *A Commentary on the Book of Genesis, Part One.* Jerusalem: Magnes, 1978.

Childs, Brevard S. *The Book of Exodus: A Critical, Theological Commentary.* Philadelphia: Westminster, 1974.

———. *Introduction to the Old Testament as Scripture.* Philadelphia: Fortress, 1979.

Cohen, A. *Everyman's Talmud.* London: Dent; New York: Dutton, 1949.

Cohen, Norman J. *The Way into Torah*. Woodstock, VT: Jewish Lights, 2000.

Deutsch, Celia. "Salvation." In *A Dictionary of the Jewish-Christian Dialogue, Expanded Edition,* edited by Leon Klenicki and Geoffrey Wigoder, 183–86. Mahwah, NJ: Paulist Press, 1995.

Etz Hayim: Torah and Commentary, edited by David L. Lieber. New York: The Rabbinical Assembly, the United Synagogue of Conservative Judaism, 2001.

Finkelstein, Israel, and Neil Asher Silberman. *The Bible Unearthed*. New York: Free Press, 2001.

Fox, Everett. "The Bible and Its World." In *The Schocken Guide to Jewish Books*, edited by Barry W. Holtz, 28–46. New York: Schocken, 1992.

Frymer-Kensky, Tikva. "Deuteronomy." In *The Women's Bible Commentary*, edited by Carol A. Newsom and Sharon H. Ringe, 52–62. London: SPCK; Louisville, KY: Westminster John Knox, 1992.

Gaster, Theodor H. *Festivals of the Jewish Year*. New York: William Sloane, 1953.

———. *Myth, Legend, and Custom in the Old Testament*. Gloucester, MA: Peter Smith, 1981.

Greenberg, Moshe. "Exodus, Book of." In *Encyclopedia Judaica*, vol. 6. Jerusalem: Keter, 1972.

Hallo, William W. "Exodus and Ancient Near Eastern Literature." In *The Torah: A Modern Commentary*, edited by W. Gunther Plaut, 367–77. New York: Union of American Hebrew Congregations, 1981.

———. "Leviticus and Ancient Near Eastern Literature." In *The Torah: A Modern Commentary*, edited by W. Gunther Plaut, 740–48. New York: Union of American Hebrew Congregations, 1981.

Heinemann, Joseph. "The Nature of the Aggadah." In *Midrash and Literature,* edited by Geoffrey H. Hartman and Sanford Budick, 41–55. New Haven and London: Yale University, 1986.

Hyatt, J. Philip. *Exodus: The New Century Bible Commentary*. Grand Rapids, MI: Eerdmans; London: Marshall, Morgan & Scott, 1971.

Bibliography

Keener, Craig S. *A Commentary on the Gospel of Matthew*. Grand Rapids, MI, and Cambridge, UK: Eerdmans, 1999.

Kepnes, Steven. "'Turn Us to You and We Shall Return': Original Sin, Atonement, and Redemption in Jewish Terms." In *Christianity in Jewish Terms*, edited by Tikva Frymer-Kensky, David Novak, et al., 293–304. Boulder, CO: Westview, 2000.

Lacocque, André. "Revelation." In *A Dictionary of the Jewish-Christian Dialogue, Expanded Edition,* edited by Leon Klenicki and Geoffrey Wigoder, 168–69. Mahwah, NJ: Paulist Press, 1995.

Laytner, Anson. *Arguing with God: A Jewish Tradition*. Northvale, NJ, and London: Aronson, 1990.

Leibowitz, Nehama. *Studies in Shemot: The Book of Exodus*. Translated by Aryeh Newman. Jerusalem: World Zionist Organization, 1976.

Levine, Baruch A. *The JPS Torah Commentary: Leviticus*. Philadelphia: Jewish Publication Society, 1989.

Mayes, A. D. H. *Deuteronomy: The New Century Bible Commentary*. Grand Rapids, MI: Eerdmans; London: Marshall, Morgan & Scott, 1979.

Mekilta de-Rabbi Ishmael. Translation by Jacob Z. Lauterbach. Philadelphia: Jewish Publication Society, 1949.

Meyers, Carol L. "Everyday Life—Women in the Period of the Hebrew Bible." In *The Women's Bible Commentary*, edited by Carol A. Newsom and Sharon H. Ringe, 244–51. London: SPCK; Louisville, KY: Westminster John Knox, 1992.

The Midrash on Proverbs, translated by Burton L. Visotzky. New Haven and London: Yale University, 1992.

The Midrash on Psalms (Midrash Tehillim), translated by William G. Braude. New Haven and London: Yale University, 1987.

Midrash Rabbah (Genesis, Exodus, Leviticus, Numbers, Deuteronomy). London: Soncino, 1939.

Midrash Tanhuma: Exodus and Leviticus, vol. 2. S. Buber Recension. Translated by John T. Townsend. Hoboken, NJ: Ktav, 1997.

Midrash Tanhuma: Genesis, vol. 1. S. Buber Recension. Translated by John T. Townsend. Hoboken, NJ: Ktav, 1989.

Milgrom, Jacob. "Book of Leviticus." In *Encyclopedia Judaica*, vol. 11. Jerusalem: Keter, 1972.

———. *The JPS Torah Commentary: Numbers*. Philadelphia: Jewish Publication Society, 1990.

Mishnayot: The Mishnah, edited by Phillip Blackman. New York: Judaica, 1965.

New American Bible. Cleveland, OH: Collins World, 1970.

New Oxford Annotated Bible with the Apocryphal/Deuterocanonical Books (NRSV), edited by Bruce M. Metzger and Roland E. Murphy. New York: Oxford University, 1991.

Niditch, Susan. "Genesis." In *The Women's Bible Commentary*, edited by Carol A. Newsom and Sharon H. Ringe, 10–25. London: SPCK; Louisville, KY: Westminster John Knox, 1992.

Noth, Martin. *Numbers: A Commentary*. Philadelphia: Westminster, 1968.

The Pentateuch and Haftorahs, second edition, edited by Joseph H. Hertz. London: Soncino, 1962.

Pesikta de-Rab Kahana: Rabbi Kahana's Compilation of Discourses for Sabbaths and Festal Days. Translated by William G. Braude and Israel J. Kapstein. Philadelphia: Jewish Publication Society, 1975.

Pesikta Rabbati: Discourses for Feasts, Fasts and Special Sabbaths. Translated by William G. Braude. New Haven and London: Yale University Press, 1968.

Pirke de Rabbi Eliezer. Translated by Gerald Friedlander. New York: Sepher-Hermon, 1981.

Porton, Gary G. "Midrash: The Palestinian Jews and the Hebrew Bible in the Greco-Roman Period." In *Aufstieg und Niedergang der romischen Welt*, edited by Hildegard Temporini and Wolfgang Haase, II 19.2, 104. Berlin and New York: de Gruyter, 1979. (Quoted in Jacob Neusner, *The Way of Torah: An Introduction to Judaism*, 5th edition [Belmont, CA: Wadsworth, 1993].)

Rabinowitz, Louis Isaac. "Synagogue Origins and History." In *Encyclopedia Judaica*, vol. 15. Jerusalem: Keter, 1972.

Ramsey, A. M. "The Authority of the Bible." In *Peake's Commentary on the Bible*, edited by Matthew Black, 1–7. London: Nelson, 1962.

Sakenfeld, Katherine Doob. "Numbers." In *The Women's Bible Commentary*, edited by Carol A. Newsom and Sharon H. Ringe, 45–51. London: SPCK; Louisville, KY: Westminster John Knox, 1992.

Sanders, E. P. *The Historical Figure of Jesus*. London and New York: Allen Lane/Penguin, 1993.

Sandmel, Samuel. *The Hebrew Scriptures: An Introduction to Their Literature and Religious Ideas*. New York: Knopf, 1963.

Sarna, Nahum M. *Exploring Exodus*. New York: Schocken, 1986.

―――. "Genesis, Book of." In *Encyclopedia Judaica*, vol. 7. Jerusalem: Keter, 1972.

―――. *The JPS Torah Commentary: Exodus*. Philadelphia: Jewish Publication Society, 1991.

―――. *The JPS Torah Commentary: Genesis*. Philadelphia: Jewish Publication Society, 1989.

―――. *Understanding Genesis*. New York: Schocken, 1970.

The Schocken Bible, Volume I. The Five Books of Moses. Translation by Everett Fox. New York: Schocken, 1995.

Setel, Drorah O'Donnell. "Exodus." In *The Women's Bible Commentary*, edited by Carol A. Newsom and Sharon H. Ringe, 26–35. London: SPCK; Louisville, KY: Westminster John Knox, 1992.

Sifra: An Analytical Translation [*Sifra* to Leviticus], edited by Jacob Neusner and William Scott Green. Atlanta: Scholars Press, 1988.

Sifre: A Tannaitic Commentary on the Book of Deuteronomy. Translated by Reuven Hammer. New Haven and London: Yale University Press, 1986.

Sifré to Numbers: An American Translation and Explanation, vol. 2, edited by Jacob Neusner. Brown Judaica Series. Atlanta: Scholars Press, 1986.

Stott, John R. W. *The Cross of Christ*. Downer's Grove, IL: InterVarsity, 1986.

TANAKH: The Holy Scriptures. Philadelphia: Jewish Publication Society, 1985.

The Tanach: The Stone Edition, edited by Nosson Scherman. New York: ArtScroll, Mesorah Publications, 1996.

Tanna Debe Eliyyahu: The Lore of the School of Elijah. Translated by William G. Braude and Israel J. Kapstein. Philadelphia: Jewish Publication Society, 1981.

Teubal, Savina J. *Sarah the Priestess: The First Matriarch of Genesis.* Athens: Swallow/Ohio University, 1984.

Tigay, Jeffrey H. *The JPS Torah Commentary: Deuteronomy.* Philadelphia and Jerusalem: Jewish Publication Society, 1996.

The Torah: A Modern Commentary, edited by W. Gunther Plaut. New York: Union of American Hebrew Congregations, 1981.

Trible, Phyllis. "Depatriarchalizing in Biblical Interpretation." *Journal of the American Academy of Religion* 41 (1973): 30–48.

Views of the Biblical World, vol. 1, edited by Benjamin Mazar, Michael Avi-Yonah et al. Chicago and New York: Jordan, 1959.

Von Rad, Gerhard. *Deuteronomy: A Commentary.* Philadelphia: Westminster, 1966.

———. *Genesis: A Commentary.* Revised Edition. Philadelphia: Westminster, 1972.

Wegner, Judith Romney. "Leviticus." In *The Women's Bible Commentary,* edited by Carol A. Newsom and Sharon H. Ringe, 36–44. London: SPCK; Louisville, KY: Westminster John Knox, 1992.

Weinberg, Dudley, and W. Gunther Plaut, "Introducing Deuteronomy." In *The Torah: A Modern Commentary,* edited by W. Gunther Plaut, 1289–96. New York: Union of American Hebrew Congregations, 1981.

Weinfeld, Moshe. "Deuteronomy." In *Encyclopedia Judaica.* Jerusalem: Keter, 1970.

———. *Deuteronomy 1–11.* Anchor Bible. New York: Doubleday, 1991.

West, James King. *Introduction to the Old Testament,* second edition. New York: Macmillan, 1981.

Wilson, Marvin R. *Our Father Abraham: Jewish Roots of the Christian Faith.* Grand Rapids, MI: Eerdmans; Dayton, OH: Center for Judaic-Christian Studies, 1989.

Yancey, Philip. *The Bible Jesus Read.* Grand Rapids, MI: Zondervan, 1999.

Zucker, David J. "Betrayal (and Growth) in Genesis 22." *CCAR Journal* 46, no. 2 (1999): 60–72.

———. "Conflicting Conclusions: The Hatred of Isaac and Ishmael." *Judaism* 39, no.1 (1990): 37–46.

———. *Israel's Prophets: An Introduction for Christians and Jews.* Mahwah, NJ: Paulist, 1994.

———. "Jacob in Darkness (and Light): A Study in Contrasts" *Judaism* 35, no. 4 (1986): 402–13.

———. "Jesus and Jeremiah in the Matthean Tradition." *Journal of Ecumenical Studies* 27, no. 2 (1990): 288–305.

———. *The Prophets: An Introduction for Christians and Jews.* New York and Mahwah, NJ: Paulist Press, 1994.

———. "Rescuing Rebecca's Reputation: A Midrash on Genesis 27." *CCAR Journal* 48, no. 1 (2001): 80–87.

———. "A Still Stranger Stratagem: Revisiting Genesis 27." *Conservative Judaism* 56, no. 2 (2004): 21–31.

Glossary

BCE, CE Before the Common Era, Common Era. The same time as the religiously exclusive terms Before Christ (BC) and *Anno Domini* (AD).

Bemidbar Hebrew title for the Book of Numbers; literally, "...in the wilderness [of Sinai]."

Bereshit Hebrew title for the Book of Genesis; literally, "When [God] began to [create]"/"In the beginning."

Bible The Hebrew scriptures; the Jewish scriptures; the Hebrew Bible; the Jewish Bible; the holy scriptures of Judaism; comprised of three sections, *Torah*/Teaching; *Neviim*/Prophets; and *Ketuvim*/Writings. The newest standard Jewish translation of the Bible is *TANAKH: The Holy Scriptures* (Philadelphia: Jewish Publication Society, 1985). Note that Christians will refer to the Bible as comprised of two sacred documents, the Old Testament and the New Testament. While Jews recognize that the Christian scriptures are sacred to Christians, only those books that Christians term the Old Testament, that is, the Hebrew or Jewish scriptures/Bible, are sacred for Jews.

Canaan	The Promised Land; a similar locale to the modern state of Israel.
CE	See BCE, CE.
Christian scriptures	The holy scriptures of Christianity; those books produced by the early Christian church; the New Testament; see Bible.
Devarim	Hebrew title for the Book of Deuteronomy; literally, "[These are] the words."
Gemara	Major commentary on the Mishnah, providing the "completion" of the Talmud, compiled c. 500 CE.
Gospels	The first four books of the Christian scriptures, Matthew, Mark, Luke, John.
Halakhah	Literally, the "way," normative traditional Jewish law/teaching.
Hebrew	Ancient (and modern) Semitic language; the language of the Jewish Bible.
Hebrew Bible, Hebrew scriptures	The holy scriptures of Judaism; see Bible.
Humash	Another name for the Pentateuch, the Torah. *Humash* is derived from the Hebrew word *hamesh*, "five," that is, the first five books of the Bible.
Israelites	The twelve tribes of Israel; the children of Israel; *B'nai Israel.*
Jewish Bible, Jewish scriptures	The holy scriptures of Judaism; see Bible.
Judaism	The religion and culture of the Jewish people.

Ketuvim	The Writings, the third section of the *TaNaK*, the Hebrew Bible, comprising Psalms, Proverbs, Job, the Song of Songs, Ruth, Lamentations, Ecclesiastes, Esther, Daniel, Ezra, Nehemiah, and Chronicles.
Lectionary	The tradition of reading set biblical selections at the regular worship service.
Menorah	The seven-branched lampstand.
Midrash	A collection of rabbinic sermons and interpretations that supplement the Bible, involving many genres: tales and allegories, ethical reflections, epigrams and legends; compiled c. 400–1550 CE.
Midrashim	Plural of midrash.
Mishnah	Initial section of the Talmud, six volumes, compiled 200 CE.
Neviim	The Prophets, the second section of the *TaNaK*, the Hebrew Bible; comprising Joshua, Judges, Samuel, Kings, and the fifteen literary prophets: Isaiah, Jeremiah, Ezekiel, and the Twelve (Hosea, Joel, Amos . . . Malachi).
New Testament	See Christian scriptures.
NJPS	New Jewish Publication Society translation of the Hebrew scriptures.
NRSV	The New Revised Standard Version.
Old Testament	See Hebrew scriptures; Bible.
Pentateuch	The first five books of the Bible, the Torah: Genesis, Exodus, Leviticus, Numbers, Deuteronomy.

Glossary

Pesach	Passover, the early springtime festival of freedom, commemorating the Exodus from Egypt.
Pharaoh	In the Bible, the anonymous ruler(s) of Egypt.
Preexilic	Time prior to the Babylonian Exile (c. 586–538 BCE).
Purim	The festival derived from the Book of Esther.
Reed Sea	The sea the Israelites passed through (see Exod 14); mistakenly called the Red Sea.
Rosh Hashanah	The Jewish New Year, one of the two High Holy Days.
Septuagint	The Greek translation of the Torah, completed c. 250 BCE.
Shabbat	The Sabbath.
Shavuot	Weeks, the early summer harvest festival; Pentecost.
Sheol	The underground place where the dead go for a short period of time before they cease to exist.
Sh'ma (Shema)	"Hear," first word of the Bible's statement, "Hear, Israel, the LORD is your God, the LORD alone" (Deut 6:4).
Sh'mot	Hebrew title for the Book of Exodus; literally, "[These are] the names."
Succot	Booths, the late summer/early autumn harvest festival.
Synoptic Gospels	The Gospels of Matthew, Mark, and Luke.

Tabernacle	Various items first mentioned in the Book of Exodus, including the ark, the tent of meeting, the lampstand, the table, and the altar of burnt offering.
Talmud	The vast compendium of Jewish thought developed in the postbiblical world between c. 200 BCE and 500 CE. There are two Talmuds, the Babylonian Talmud, which is the more authoritative, and the Jerusalem Talmud.
TaNaK, Tanakh, Tanak	An acronym for the titles of the three divisions of the Hebrew scriptures: **T**orah/Teaching; **N**eviim/Prophets; **K**etuvim/Writings.
Torah	"The Teaching," the first section of the *TaNaK*, the Hebrew Bible; comprising Genesis, Exodus, Leviticus, Numbers, Deuteronomy; "a Jewish teaching"; or by extension, Jewish learning in general.
Vayikra	Hebrew title for the Book of Leviticus; literally, "And he [The LORD] called."
Yom Kippur	The Day of Atonement, one of the two High Holy Days.

Abbreviations

The following abbreviations are used in this work.

JEWISH SCRIPTURES, HEBREW BIBLE

Gen	Genesis
Exod	Exodus
Lev	Leviticus
Num	Numbers
Deut	Deuteronomy
Josh	Joshua
Judg	Judges
Sam	Samuel
Kgs	Kings
Isa	Isaiah
Jer	Jeremiah
Ezek	Ezekiel
Joel	Joel
Mic	Micah
Zech	Zechariah
Mal	Malachi
Ps (Pss)	Psalms
Prov	Proverbs
Ruth	Ruth
Eccl	Ecclesiastes
Neh	Nehemiah
Chr	Chronicles

CHRISTIAN SCRIPTURES, CHRISTIAN BIBLE

Matt	Matthew
Mark	Mark
Luke	Luke
John	John
Acts	Acts of the Apostles
Rom	Romans
1, 2 Cor	1, 2 Corinthians
Gal	Galatians
Eph	Ephesians
1, 2 Tim	1, 2 Timothy
Heb	Hebrews
Jas	James
1, 2, 3 John	1, 2, 3 John
1, 2 Pet	1, 2 Peter
Jude	Jude
Rev	Revelation

OTHER ABBREVIATIONS

BCE	Before the Common Era
CE	Common Era
c.	circa (about)
cf.	*confer* (compare)
H	Hebrew
NJPS	New Jewish Publications Society (TANAKH)
NAB	New American Bible
NEB	New English Bible
NIV	New International Version
NRSV	New Revised Standard Version
R	Rabbi
RSV	Revised Standard Version

Abbreviations

TaNaK   Torah-Neviim-Ketuvim (the New
        Jewish Publication Society
        translation of the Jewish
        Scriptures)

Questions for Study

CHAPTER ONE:
INTRODUCING THE TORAH

1. Briefly describe the various meanings of the Hebrew word **torah**.
2. What do the following abbreviations signify: **BCE, CE, BC,** and **AD**?
3. What is **midrash** and its importance?
4. How did the synagogue and prayer in Judaism develop historically?
5. How is the term **Old Testament** understood?
6. What is the significance of the acronym **Tanakh** or **TaNaK**?
7. Explain the differences in the enumeration of the books of the Bible.
8. What are the five sections into which biblical history may be divided?
9. What role do women play in the Bible?
10. Describe the five various sources of the **Torah**.
11. What is meant by the term **rabbi**?
12. What role does the Bible play in Jewish life?
13. How do Christians view the books of the Jewish Bible?
14. Explain the meaning of this paradoxical statement: "The Bible is at the same time timeless and time-centered."

CHAPTER TWO: GENESIS

1. How is the first book of the Bible, **Genesis,** understood?
2. How is the number **seven** a **Genesis** number?

3. What are the seven major themes in **Genesis**?
4. What are the clear patterns of storytelling in the **Book of Genesis**?
5. What biblical stories comprise the primeval history?
6. What are some of the key elements in the **Abraham Cycle**?
7. What are some of the key elements in the **Isaac/Jacob Cycle**?
8. What are some of the key elements in the **Joseph Cycle**?
9. How do the Christian scriptures understand and interpret **Genesis**?
10. How does the rabbinic literature make use of **Genesis**?
11. How is the name of the man, **Adam,** in the second creation account a pun?
12. What is the significance of Abraham's being incredulous?
13. How does the **midrash** interpret the son of Hagar playing with the son of Sarah in terms of family tension?
14. What are the various interpretations of the **Blessing of Jacob**?

CHAPTER THREE: EXODUS

1. Why is the **Exodus from Egypt** the most crucial event in the Bible?
2. Briefly summarize the three major themes in **Exodus: biography, history, legislation**.
3. What are God's three roles in the **Book of Exodus**?
4. What is meant by this following statement referring to the Exodus event: "The absence of proof does not mean the proof of absence."
5. How many Israelites left Egypt?
6. How is Moses depicted in **Exodus**?
7. If "God hardens Pharoah's heart," what difficulties does this concept raise?
8. What is the significance of **Passover**?
9. Why is Miriam important in **Exodus**?
10. What are the key elements of the **Covenant Code**?
11. What is the significance of the **tabernacle** and the **priesthood**?
12. How is **Exodus** depicted and understood in the Christian scriptures?

13. How are the themes of Passover—*sacrifice, freedom/redemption,* and *renewal*—paralleled in Easter?
14. How does the rabbinic literature understand and interpret *Exodus*?
15. What is the importance of the *Sabbath day*?
16. Why is the *tabernacle* and the aspects associated with it important: the *ark,* the *sanctuary,* and *ritual*?

CHAPTER FOUR: LEVITICUS

1. How are the major themes of *religious practices, law, priesthood, relationship to God,* and *ritual purity* depicted in *Leviticus*?
2. What are the five principal forms of sacrifice?
3. How are the laws of *kashrut,* or *kosher,* understood?
4. Briefly describe *Leviticus's* concept of *purity* and *impurity*.
5. What is the significance of *Yom Kippur* and the *Scapegoat ritual*?
6. What are the major themes of the *Holiness Code*?
7. How does *Leviticus* depict *lex talionis*?
8. How do the Christian scriptures understand and interpret *Leviticus*?
9. How is *Leviticus* described in rabbinic literature?
10. How is *Leviticus* part of ongoing Jewish tradition?
11. What are some explanations and interpretations of the death of the sons of the high priest Aaron, Nadab and Abihu?
12. What are some of the social justice concerns raised in *Leviticus*?

CHAPTER FIVE: NUMBERS

1. What is the derivation of the name *Numbers*?
2. How does the *Book of Numbers* calculate the forty-year journey?
3. Briefly describe the major themes of *Numbers*.
4. What is the *Priestly Blessing* in Numbers 6:24–26?

5. What are some problems with the census?
6. What is the significance of the number **seventy**?
7. What are some of the difficulties and problems that arise among the Israelites during the journey in the wilderness?
8. Who are Caleb and Korah?
9. What is the **Kadesh mystery**?
10. Briefly describe some of the events that took place as the Israelites journey toward the Promised Land.
11. Who are Balaam, King Balak, and Baal?
12. How do the Christian scriptures understand and interpret **Numbers**?
13. How is **Numbers** described in the rabbinic literature?
14. What important role does Miriam play in **Numbers**?
15. What are **cherubim**?

CHAPTER SIX: DEUTERONOMY

1. What is the meaning of the word **Deuteronomy**?
2. What are some of the major themes in **Deuteronomy**?
3. Who were the **Deuteronomists**?
4. What is the significance of the discovery of the **Book of the Law** or the **Book of the Teaching**?
5. What are some of the key elements found in the **first discourse** in Deuteronomy?
6. How is the **Decalogue** in **Deuteronomy** different from that found in **Exodus**?
7. Briefly describe some of the major themes of the **second discourse**.
8. What are the three seasonal **holy days** described in **Deuteronomy 16**?
9. How is **law** and its various forms portrayed in **Deuteronomy**?
10. How does the **third discourse** differ from the previous two?
11. How do the concluding chapters 31–34 in **Deuteronomy** differ from the previous chapters?
12. What is the **Song of Moses**?
13. How do the Christian scriptures understand and interpret **Deuteronomy**?

14. How does the rabbinic literature view and portray **Deuteronomy**?
15. What is the practice of **tefillin** and **mezuza**?

Name Index

Subject Index